COME FOLLOW ME

To Father Stanley Rother

Whose witness of Martyrdom

Has been a source of personal inspiration

and an enduring lesson of discipleship

COME FOLLOW ME

DISCIPLESHIP REFLECTIONS ON THE SUNDAY GOSPEL READINGS FOR LITURGICAL YEAR C

DANIEL H. MUEGGENBORG

GRACEWING

First published in England in 2015

by

Gracewing
2 Southern Avenue
Leominster
Herefordshire HR6 0QF
United Kingdom

www.gracewing.co.uk

ISBN 978 085244 876 2

Typeset by Gracewing

Cover design by Bernardita Peña Hurtado,
incorporating *The Sermon on the Mount*
by Carl Heinrich Bloch (1834–1890)

CONTENTS

INTRODUCTION

In the summer of 2011, I returned to parish ministry having completed a six-year assignment to the Pontifical North American College in Rome where I had served as Director of Admissions and Vice Rector. The experience of seminary formation had awakened within me a desire to introduce quality faith enrichment and discipleship ministries into a parish environment.

Shortly after arriving at the Parish of Christ the King, I was contacted by John O'Connor who encouraged me to meet regularly with a group of men to study the scriptures so as to grow in discipleship. We began our early morning *Prayer Breakfast* meetings in January 2012 and these men have become brothers in Christ over the years since we started. They are as follows: Brad Fussell, Jonnie Gendron, Ted Hinson, Stephen King, David Littlefield, Mark Maguire, Kevin Murray, John O'Connor, David Phillips, Steve Poleman, David Reinecke, Tom Ritchie, Bill Senger, Jeff Smith, and Kevin Veit.

The experience of these meetings changed my life as a priest. It has been an honor and privilege to see the movement of God and the work of the Holy Spirit active in the lives so many parishioners. Their discussions and questions have challenged me to speak openly and honestly about my own discipleship and faith.

In the three years after the establishment of this initial group, several more *Prayer Breakfast* groups have developed. The success of this ministry and the effect it has had in the lives of so many men and women is evidence of both the hunger people have for the Word of God in Scripture and for the power of the Word to evoke faith in those who study it.

This writing is a series of exegetical, in-depth, reflections based on the assigned Gospel reading for the Sundays of a given liturgical year. Each reflection contains a few insights that are explained and then applied to the lived experience of a Christian disciple.

I also wish to acknowledge the various excellent biblical commentaries from which the vast majority of insights were drawn that are presented in these reflections. I strongly encourage anyone who wants to become a student of scripture to consult these commentaries directly. In no way do I claim these biblical insights to be my own. I am utterly dependent upon the research of generations of scholars. These reflections do not so much represent an original work on my part as they do a composition of insights gained from studying three essential biblical commentary series and some online homily resources from a noted theologian.

The following biblical commentary series were used extensively and repeatedly in the compilation of these reflections. Each of these series has a separate volume for specific Gospels and other biblical writings. The reader is encouraged to consult these commentary series:

- *The Anchor Bible* (New York, Doubleday)
- *The New Interpreters Bible* (Nashville, Abingdon Press)
- *Sacra Pagina* ("A Michael Glazier Book." Collegeville: The Liturgical Press)

In addition to these three essential commentaries, I also gained insights from the homilies given by the Most Rev. Robert Barron from the Word on Fire website. Bishop Barron is one of the most talented theologians and communicators in the Catholic Church today. He is also a man of great humility, authenticity, and fidelity. His homilies are an invaluable resource for all disciples and are readily available as part of the "Resources" section of the Word on Fire website (www.wordonfire.org). I researched the fifteen-year collection of his homilies in preparation for each of the weekly reflections contained in this book and used those insights, which especially pertained to the biblical text. The reader is encouraged to consult the Word on Fire website for further study of these resources and for the other excellent evangelization resources available from that ministry.

The primary purpose of this writing is to promote a personal discipleship-focused study of the Gospels and to facilitate small group discussions. It is hoped that this book can be of benefit to parishioners, homilists, and parish ministry staff.

As you read through these reflections in preparation for the Sunday Mass, it will be important to use a Bible so as to consult the many scriptural references. The New American Bible Revised Edition is referenced throughout the reflections. The abbreviation "cf." is used to indicate such opportunities to confer or compare other relevant biblical texts. The abbreviation "v." is used to identify corresponding scriptural quotes and/or passages.

There is no substitute for the Word of God in Scripture. These reflections may shed light on the biblical texts but should never replace those sacred texts in personal prayer and study.

When using these reflections for small group discussion, the following recommended process is simple and effective:

1. Start with an opening Prayer.
2. Read the relevant Biblical text.
3. Review one reflection at a time and focus the discussion on the application questions.
4. Then proceed to review the next reflection and focus on those questions.
5. Continue this process until all the reflections for a given Gospel passage have been reviewed.
6. Conclude by praying for the members of the group and interceding for particular needs.

Acknowledgements

This book relies heavily on the scholarship and research of the essential sources that are listed in the bibliography. It also represents the cumulative effort of many people who assisted in the editing and composition process. Most of all, it would not have been possible without the guidance, support, and encouragement of some parishioners who are authentic disciples of Jesus Christ.

Most of all, I wish to acknowledge the following people who were involved in this publication:

Rev. Jose Elkin Gonzalez, STD, who assisted in editing each reflection and provided references from the rich spiritual tradition of the Church to enhance and focus various topics.

A. J. Tierney for her work in formatting and reviewing the text to ensure consistency and conformity.

Henry Harder for his assistance and expertise in proofreading the text.

John O'Connor for his mentoring and encouragement that led to the development of these discipleship reflections.

First Sunday of Advent

Our scripture passage for this Sunday comes from the Gospel of Luke 21:25–28, 34–36. In this passage, Jesus speaks about the great and fearful day of the coming of the Son of Man at the end of time. Then He says to His disciples: "stand erect and raise your heads." That is a way of saying that for disciples, the coming of the Son of Man at the end of time will be a cause for joy, courage, and hope. This passage provides excellent insights for our lives as disciples.

Jesus tells us that the principal reason for our joy when the Lord comes is that our "redemption is at hand." The term "redemption" means that we will be freed or released from the forces that oppose and oppress us as faithful Christians: human weakness, sin, and political and cultural forces that are contrary to the Gospel. For Christians the "End" which Jesus describes is really the "Beginning" of true freedom! That is why the Lord's coming may cause anxiety, confusion, fear, and dread in the lives of non-believers, but Christians will find that moment to be a source of joyful fulfillment of their hope. This teaching presumes that Christians are, in fact, living "for the Lord." It is easy, however, to become spiritually distracted and find ourselves pursuing values other than those of Jesus and the Gospel.

> *How is the Christian faith today opposed or oppressed by the cultural or political forces of our world?*
> *What would be your response if the Lord were to come for you today?*
> *How would you prepare to meet the Lord?*
> *What keeps you from living your faith life fully and freely?*

Next, Jesus tells His disciples to "Beware that your hearts do not become drowsy," meaning that we should watch carefully so our lives do not go astray while preparing for judgment. Dissipation (drinking bouts) and the distractions of daily life (identified as something that chokes the Word of God in Lk 8:14) are specifically mentioned as common temptations that cause disciples to lose sight of their focus on the Lord. The temptations of dissipation and daily distractions represent the temporary concerns and consolations that often dominate our attention. When we are having a bad or stressful day, it is easy to seek comfort in simple pleasures rather than in the security of God's friendship and love. When we are immersed in the successes and failures of daily life, it is easy to lose sight of the eternal relationship to which God calls us. These temptations can ultimately lead us to place our security, hope, sense of worth, and identity in something other than God. Although these false sources may be more tangible in the moment, they are only temporary and eventually pass away. Only our relationship with God endures forever. If we live for the Lord, then our lives will manifest that relationship through moral integrity and uprightness. It is that moral response of Christians that most prepares us to meet the Lord. Jesus did not tell His disciples that they should hide in seclusion when the Son of Man comes. Nor did Jesus tell His disciples that they should only prepare themselves by prayer. Rather, the best way to prepare ourselves to meet the Lord is by our conversion and holiness of life. This is not a self-centered focus that is only concerned for one's self. Rather, it is the realization that both our actions and our prayer need to be conformed and focused on what is eternal rather than on what is only temporary.

> *How easy is it for you to lose sight of God in the course of your day?*
> *What are the typical temporary pleasures of life people pursue instead of finding comfort in God's friendship?*
> *What are the distractions of daily life that claim so much of our attention, energy, and resource but end up giving us a false sense of security, worth, identity, or hope?*
> *Who do you know who has experienced a practical moral change in their life because they came close to meeting the Lord?*

As we begin a new year in the life of the Church, it is always a good opportunity to stop and take inventory of our growth in faith and consider what has taken place in the past year as well as what we want to take place in the next year. In short, it's time to make a "New Year's Resolution" for discipleship.

What would you like to be different in your faith life one year from now?
What steps will you take to make it happen?
What have been milestones of your growth in discipleship this past year?

Finally, it is worth paying particular attention to the opening and closing prayers of Mass for this Sunday. Each of these prayers speaks profoundly about the teachings we have just studied from Luke's Gospel.

As you reflect on these prayers, which line of the text has particular meaning for you?
During this season of Advent, what is one resolution you could make that would help you focus more on the things of eternal life rather than the daily distractions of this life?

Grant your faithful, we pray, almighty God,
The resolve to run forth to meet your Christ
With righteous deeds at his coming,
So that, gathered at his right hand,
They may be worthy to possess the heavenly Kingdom.
Through our Lord Jesus Christ, your Son,
Who lives and reigns with you
In the unity of the Holy Spirit,
One God for ever and ever.

May these mysteries, O Lord,
In which we have participated,
Profit us, we pray,
For even now, as we walk amid passing things,
You teach us by them
To love the things of heaven
And hold fast to what endures.
Through Christ our Lord.

SECOND SUNDAY OF ADVENT

Our scripture passage for this Sunday comes from the Gospel of Luke 3:1–6. In this passage, we read about John the Baptist who is sent to "prepare" for the way of Jesus. He accomplishes this preparation through his message of repentance that levels "mountains" and fills "valleys." In short, he is preparing a smooth road so God can enter people's hearts and minds. That work of preparation is something we all experience and something we are all called to do for ourselves and for others.

The first aspect to note about this passage is the very solemn introduction. This opening verse provides the context in which the Word of God comes to John the Baptist. Beyond its dramatic nature, this introduction is a statement that the preaching of John in the remote Judean wilderness will have a ripple effect that will reach every part of the world. Indeed, the message of Jesus will rattle the powers of Imperial Rome (see the reference to Tiberius Caesar in Lk 3:1). Likewise the ministry of Jesus will challenge the religious, cultural, and political influences of Judaism and Jerusalem (see the references to Herod, Pilate, and the High Priests in Lk 3:1-2). All of these references are telling us that the obscure ministry of John the Baptist is initiating a revolution the likes of which the world has never seen! Indeed, the Kingdom of God may have small beginnings (v. the parable of the Mustard Seed in Lk 13:18–19) but its power cannot be constrained or destroyed. The message of the Gospel will not only affect people's hearts, it will also affect their worship, their politics, their market, their cultural practices, and so forth. From these small beginnings of John's ministry will come the Church—the greatest transforming movement in world history.

How do people try to "constrain" the message of the Gospel today?

What influences in our society would be especially challenged by the message of the Gospel and how can we be the instruments of that challenge?

*The Word of God is powerful and effective today even as it
was in the life and ministry of John the Baptist; when has
a message of faith transformed your life in a revolutionary
way?*

*What part of your life is waiting to be transformed by the
Gospel and conformed to Jesus and how can you open yourself to the Lord's grace during this time of Advent?*

In announcing the need for preparation, John draws upon the
imagery of Isaiah 40:3–5 in which instructions are given to road
workers to prepare a "Royal Way" for the Lord. Such preparation
of travel routes was common in the ancient world and a way in
which visiting kings were made to feel welcome. The people would
also beautify their homes and public buildings to make their city
pleasing to the king hoping that the king, in turn, might honor the
citizens of that place.

*What parts of your life do you think God considers most
beautiful?*

What parts would God want you to clean up?

As we grow up, our families teach us how to be receptive and open
to the experience of faith. Sometimes we meet people who inspire
us and make us want to imitate their good example and their relationship with God. Sometimes, too, we are blessed to have people
thrown in our lives who "take off our rough edges" by leveling our
personal "mountains" and who build us up by filling our "valleys."
They are the people who love us enough to help us become the best
person we can be. Of interesting note, Luke is the only one of the
four Gospels that includes this description of John's ministry which
is taken from the Prophet Isaiah 40:3–5. The work of reversing a
disordered world is an important way in which Luke understands
and presents the ministry of Jesus (v. divine reversal in Lk 1:51–53,
13:30, 16:25, and 18:14).

*If Jesus stepped into our world today, what disordered part
of our culture would He reverse?*

*Who has most helped to shape you into a Christian man/
woman?*

*What are some of the misplaced priorities (mountains) in
your own life that need to be re-ordered so as to conform
to the Gospel?*

*What are some of the weaknesses (valleys) that need to be
strengthened so you can be a better disciple?*

Who needs you to assist them in becoming a better disciple?

John carried out his ministry of preaching and baptizing in the
desert. There is an important reason for that choice of location.
The desert is the place where God first formed His people as they
followed Moses for forty years. Now John goes there to prepare a
new people for Jesus. This preparation happens through baptism,
repentance, and the forgiveness of sins. In baptism, John is leading
the people through the waters of the Jordan in a definitive act by
which they leave behind their former lives and begin a new life as
members of God's people. In repentance, John is teaching them
to re-think their lives and to see things from God's perspective. In
the forgiveness of sins, John is setting the people free from their
past failures and absolving their guilt so they can move forward to
carry on with their lives by a new beginning.

*Which of these three aspects of John's ministry appeals to
you the most?*

*What can you do this Advent season to experience more
deeply these graces?*

Third Sunday of Advent

Our scripture passage for this Sunday comes from the Gospel of Luke 3:10–18. In this passage, we see three groups approaching John the Baptist with the same question: "What should we do?" This is an important question for Luke—indeed, it is the fundamental question of real discipleship. We will see this question emerge at other places in the Gospel of Luke and in the Acts of the Apostles as well (cf. the lawyer who questions Jesus in Lk 10:25, the rich man with the abundant harvest in Lk 12:17, the dishonest manager in Lk 16:3, the ruler in Lk 18:18, the crowds to Peter at Pentecost in Acts 2:37, and the guard in Acts 16:30).

Luke repeats this question through the Gospel and the Acts of the Apostles because he wants to stress that faith is not just a matter of how we pray or of how we feel. Rather, faith is lived out in what we do. Thus, the crowds ask verbs of action, not of sentiment or intellectual assent. Likewise, the answers are personal and appropriate to each person and represent moral actions that correspond to conversion and repentance.

To the crowds in general, John commands generosity to those in need through the right use of material resources. Such a radical sharing of goods implies more than just casual charity; it is really a sharing of life appropriate for brothers and sisters. For this reason, John calls us to be committed to one another in a new relationship of love and responsibility and to manifest that relationship through the common sharing of our resources.

Who inspires you as being an example of sacrificial Christian generosity?

What is the abundance of resource you can share with someone in need during this Advent time?

What are the thoughts, fears, or false beliefs that prevent people from responding generously when faced with other's need?

*How can we as a parish community foster a greater sense
of Christian charity among parishioners?*

To the tax collectors, John doesn't tell them to leave their jobs but
to bring integrity into their professions by being people of honesty
and justice. It is important to remember that being a tax collector
in Jesus' time was considered an inherently "sinful" job because tax
collectors collaborated with the Romans and because they were
notorious for charging more than was required. This instruction
of John is a call to overcome self-centeredness and greed so as to
act with honesty and justice. Thus, we are challenged to dignify
our professional roles and positions by bringing Christian integrity
and virtue into everything we do as well.

*What are some of the inherent misconceptions people tend
to have about your profession?*
*What are the common temptations to abuse power that
prevail in your profession?*
*What can you do to restore dignity and integrity as a Chris-
tian disciple in your profession?*

To the soldiers, John tells them to be grateful even when they suffer
hardship. Being a soldier was not a very fun experience for those
serving in a remote Roman province like Palestine. It was all too
easy for soldiers to use force and intimidation to make others suffer (bullying) or extort comfort for themselves at others' expense
(extortion). John instructs the soldiers to stop the cycle of suffering
by choosing to be content with their pay, meager as it may be. They
are not to make others suffer just because they themselves have to
endure a hardship.

*How do you see the cycle of hurt being passed on from one
person to the next in situations you face?*
*When have you chosen to stop the cycle of hurt or anger
and how did you do that?*
*How does the temptation to use violence as a solution to
problems manifest itself today?*
*Jesus will teach a non-violent yet active resistance to evil.
What does this Gospel message of non-violence mean to
you?*

The central question for us on the Third Sunday of Advent is this: What would John say to you if you asked him "What must I do"? That is always a good question for prayer and reflection as we prepare ourselves to meet the Lord. However, it certainly would have been easier for the crowds to ask, "How must I pray?" or "How should I feel?" but they didn't. They asked the real question of discipleship and the real expression of repentance: "What must I do?" In addition to asking the questions, the crowds also listened to John's response and conformed their lives in practical ways to the demands of the Gospel and so should we.

Which response of John to the three groups has the most meaning or presents the greatest challenge for your life as a disciple?

Fourth Sunday of Advent

Our scripture passage for this Sunday comes from the Gospel of Luke 1:39–45. It is the story of Mary going in haste to visit her cousin Elizabeth. When she arrived, Elizabeth recognized something extraordinary about Mary's visit as John leaped in her womb. Elizabeth immediately cried out: "Most blessed are you among women, and blessed is the fruit of your womb. And how does this happen to me, that the Mother of my Lord should come to me?"

That cry is the recognition of a sacred moment—a moment of encountering God and knowing that something incredible has just taken place. It calls forth humility, gratitude, reverence, and praise. What a great moment! The prophets spoke about how God would one day "visit" His people. Now Elizabeth is "visited" by God present in Jesus in the womb of Mary, and Elizabeth recognizes that this encounter with her cousin is nothing ordinary at all; rather, it is a sacred moment. We all have sacred moments when we realize that God has touched our lives in extraordinary ways through ordinary people. These are moments that evoke within us that same sense of humility, gratitude, reverence, and praise: moments when we realize and understand that God is in control of our lives and always has been and always will be; moments when we know we are loved, forgiven, and not alone. We don't live every day caught up in those "moments" but God does provide them for us every now and then to sustain our faith and invite us to trust the Lord during the difficult times as well.

What have been some of the moments in your life when you have experienced the presence of God in an unexpected way through another person?
Think back on those feelings of humility, gratitude, reverence, and praise—what experience has evoked those responses from you?

When have you influenced another person's life with a godly visit?

Mary is declared "Blessed" by Elizabeth because she trusted that the Lord's word to her would be fulfilled. Mary's discipleship, then, is defined by her confident trust in God's promises. It is easy for us to trust in the Lord's promises when we are experiencing success and the praise of others. It can be difficult to trust in God's promises when we are asked to embrace sacrifice, disappointment, conflict, and rejection. The enduring quality of Mary's discipleship is that she trusted the Lord even when it meant accepting such difficulties. Later in the Gospel, Jesus will identify the distinctive quality of Mary's great faith when He says, "Blessed are those who hear the word of God and do it" (Lk 11:28).

> *What are some of the Lord's promises that you trust in and upon which you base your life?*
> *What are some of the Lord's promises in which you have difficulty placing your trust?*
> *To be a disciple is to first and foremost trust the Lord—in what part of your life do you have the most difficulty trusting God?*
> *When have you felt that the Lord has let you down because of a particular trial you have had to face?*
> *How does Mary's discipleship inspire you to trust more deeply in God's promises?*

Mary's first action as a disciple is to bring the "Good News" of Jesus to others (namely, her cousin Elizabeth). This action teaches us that disciples are not people who keep the Good News of the Gospel to themselves. Rather, an essential part of discipleship is to bring the message of Christ to others. In this passage, Mary is a good disciple who has become a good missionary. God's revelation is always personal but never private. Rather, God reveals Himself for the good of all people. Jesus is the ultimate revelation of the Father and Mary carried that revelation to others. How easy it would have been for the Blessed Mother to stay at home and wait for others to come to her! Sometimes that is how we approach ministry in our church communities. This Gospel passage challenges us to be active witnesses of faith who show initiative and reach out to others.

Who has brought the message of the Gospel to life for you?
Who needs to experience the presence of Jesus through you
today?
When was the last time that you were so excited about
something new (the latest cell phone, a new car, or movie
or television program) in your life that you wanted to tell
someone else?
Have you ever been motivated enough about a message of
faith to communicate it to someone else?
As you look back on the things you have told others about
in the past week, whose missionary have you been (con-
sumerism or Christianity)?
How can our churches be more determined in our efforts to
bring Jesus to others in our community rather than waiting
for people to come to us?

One last thing to note about this passage is the very important title Elizabeth gives Mary when she calls her the "Mother of my Lord". In early Christianity there were some movements in the Church that were hesitant to attribute such titles to the Blessed Mother because of perceived parallels in pagan mythology. For those movements, Mary could only be referred to as the "Mother of Jesus" but not the "Mother of God" or the "Mother of the Lord." These disagreements culminated and were finally resolved at the Council of Ephesus (AD 431) and Chalcedon (AD 451). The positive result of these councils was that the divinity of Jesus was professed even in the womb of Mary as well as our Lord's humanity. Mary is the source of Jesus' human nature, and God the Father is the source of Jesus' divine nature and personhood. Although these issues are not often discussed in Christianity today, the role of Mary is sometimes a source of controversy and division. For Catholics, it is always important to remember that Mary receives her identity and honor in relationship to Jesus—as do we. The reality is that God gave Mary a place of honor in the divine plan of salvation and as disciples we are called to respect and revere her divine instrumentality. Like Mary who received her title out of her relationship to Jesus, we receive our great title of "Christian" from our Baptism in which we are called to bear Christ to others.

How do you show honor and respect for the Blessed Mother in your life as a disciple?

What is the danger of honoring Mary apart from her relationship with Jesus?

Catholics are sometimes misperceived as people who "worship" Mary. How does this passage of scripture help you to appropriately respond to such misperceptions?

FEAST OF THE HOLY FAMILY

Our scripture passage for this Sunday comes from the Gospel of Luke 2:41–52. In this passage we read about the finding of the child Jesus in the Temple. The celebration of this feast invites us to look at the Holy Family of Jesus, Mary, and Joseph so as to better understand who we are called to be both as individual Christian families and the Family of God in the Church. This passage offers several points for our reflection.

The first part of this passage informs us that the holy family went to Jerusalem for Passover because it was their "custom". Thus, this is was not a one-time trip but something they did every year and for other feasts as well. Practicing their faith was a regular part of life. Therefore, there is nothing unusual about them going to the Temple; rather, it was an ordinary part of life. This is the first point for our reflection. In order for families to find their children in God's House, that is the Church, they actually have to bring their children to God's House on a regular basis. It must be a normal part of family life to come regularly to church. Certainly that was true of the Holy Family of Nazareth as this passage indicates. Families today face many challenges in attending church on the Lord's Day as a regular part of their "usual" family practice. For some it is the soccer schedule, for others it is the unwillingness to give up what they perceive to be their "personal" time on the weekend. Whatever it is, the passage from the Gospel of Luke reminds us that we are called to follow the example of the Holy Family of Nazareth and make our pilgrimage as a family to the House of the Lord with regularity.

What does your usual Sunday look like?
What are the distractions that tempt people away from attending church as a usual part of the Lord's Day?
What religious customs did you practice in your family that have stayed with you throughout your life?

*Parents are the first teachers of children in the ways of faith;
what did your parents teach you?
What do you most want to teach your children about faith
and how will you do it?*

Next, the passage informs us that Jesus was twelve years old when they went to the Temple. That is the age at which a child was to begin observing the religious rules. Thus, the Holy Family of Nazareth is preparing Jesus to live His faith with responsibility, accountability, and maturity. To the extent that children are capable of learning and living their faith, they should be encouraged to do so. Sometimes children know all the verses to a pop song but cannot memorize the Creed. Something is wrong when we encourage children to grow in other areas of their lives but not in their faith lives. This passage teaches us that the Holy Family of Nazareth took seriously the expectation that Jesus would live out His faith as He grew older. It is a good example for us to follow.

*What tasks are children given today that can demonstrate
responsibility, accountability, and maturity?
How can children be challenged to better demonstrate these
qualities when it comes to their faith life?*

When Jesus is left behind in Jerusalem, He goes to the Temple. That is because He identified the Temple as His "home" as the Father's house. Our local church community should feel like home for us as well. Jesus obviously went to the Temple because He felt welcomed there. Sometimes our children don't feel welcomed at church services. Sometimes parents with small children don't feel welcomed either—especially when those children become irritated. As a community, we need to remember that Jesus was a child who was made to feel "at home" in the Temple and we have a responsibility as a community to create that same environment of hospitality and welcome for our children and young families as well.

*What kinds of things make children or families feel unwel-
comed today?
What might we do as a community to make them feel more
welcomed and "at home"?*

Finally, the Holy Family is reunited as Jesus speaks His first words in the Gospel of Luke. He says: "Did you not know that I must be in my Father's house?" This is an important statement. It is a challenge to Mary and Joseph to realize that Jesus must first and foremost fulfill the Father's plan. (Note that the word used in Greek does not mean "house" but refers to "things" or "affairs" of the Father.) That is a reminder to Christian parents that the ultimate challenge they face is not to get their children to do what the parents want but to encourage their children to say "yes" to what God wants. Parents have the awesome task of introducing their children into a relationship with God as "Father" just as Jesus was able to refer to the Father. Finally, the challenge of Christian parenthood is to accept the will of God for their children even if they do not understand it or would not choose it themselves. Jesus has finally reached the point where He can pursue the Father's will. Mary and Joseph were challenged to rejoice in Jesus' action rather than reprimand Him for it. If parents truly raise their children to seek the will of God and to do it, then they should not be surprised when those actions actually take place.

> *How can parents seek greater openness and understanding of the will of God for their children?*
> *How can parents better help their children to know God's will in their own lives and to do it?*
> *If your child behaved like Jesus in today's passage, what would your response be to His statement, "Did you not know I had to be about my Father's affairs?"*
> *What are some of the things children do today in fulfillment of God's will that parents are sometimes not happy about?*

Solemnity of the Epiphany

Our scripture passage for this Sunday comes from the Gospel of Matthew 2:1–12. In this passage, we read the well-known story of the Magi who visit the child Jesus in Bethlehem and bring gifts of gold, frankincense, and myrrh. This passage offers some good points for our reflection and prayer.

One of the first things to note is that this passage contains the first words actually spoken by any person in Matthew's Gospel. The Gospel writers were careful to use the first words as a kind of theme for their writing. Thus, the first spoken question "Where is the newborn King of the Jews?" is a theme that will resonate throughout Matthew's Gospel. To be King in the Jewish world was not just a position of political power. The Jewish people believed that God alone was their King and that any human regent had the responsibility to represent God. Some kings did a better job of being a representative of the Divine than others! The people looked to the King to manifest God's justice, mercy, wisdom, and protection. The Magi are seeking to see the face of God in human representation, and they don't find it in Herod. Herod represented ruthless power and political cunning (he even executed three of his own sons). Throughout the Gospel of Matthew, Jesus will show us the face of the Father and in doing so will authentically serve as God's perfect representative to the people. For that authentic and complete representation, Jesus will properly be hailed as "King of the Jews" when He dies on Calvary. Herod caused others to suffer through his self-centered and untamed ambitious pursuit of power. Jesus suffered for others and opened the doors of God's mercy and forgiveness through His death and resurrection. Each of us in our baptism has received the commission to carry on the kingly ministry of Jesus. That means we are to be God's representative to the people with whom we interact.

Do people see Herod or Jesus in us?
Who represents the face of God, the heart of God, to you?

Who looks to you to be a minister of God's justice, mercy,
truth, wisdom, or protection?
In what settings are you a good representative of God?
In what settings do you find it most difficult to live out the
Kingly mission of your baptism?
If someone approached you and asked: "Where can I find
the King of the Jews?", what would you say to them?

The gifts the Magi bring are all statements of who Jesus is. Gold is
the gift proper for a King. Frankincense was offered by the High
Priest to God in the Temple. Myrrh was used as a perfume in the
burial preparation of a body. Thus, the identity of Jesus is manifested in these three gifts: He is King, God, (and/or High Priest)
and Man that is someone who would die.

Who is Jesus to you?
How does your faith in Jesus manifest through the gifts you
offer him?
What are the gifts you offer to the Lord?

The star has historically been interpreted as a symbol for the light
of faith leading people to Christ. For each person the path is unique
and personal yet there are some common elements. For example,
some people are led to seek God through the wonder of nature
(the natural sciences). Others are led to seek God through events
of salvation in their lives. Still others are led to seek God because
of the influence of another person of faith. God reveals Himself to
us in a variety of ways but there comes a point where we need to
consult the scriptures to really learn who God is through the person
of Jesus. Regardless of what began our journey of faith, scripture
completes the truth of who God is. That is why the Magi could
not complete their journey until the scriptures were consulted.
The Word of God in scripture does shed light on our experience
of faith and more clearly reveal to us the reality of God working in
our lives. When we read the scriptures, we grow in understanding
and our eyes are opened.

How has the study of scripture opened your heart and mind
in new ways?

What have you learned about God through your reflection
on the Word that you did not previously understand?
What was the "light" that led you to desire to meet Jesus in
a deeper and more personal way?
Who is someone you know that is searching in the darkness
and how can you be a light to them?
What can you do to foster your love for the Word of God in
scripture and share that love with your family and friends?

Lastly, one cannot help but think about the contrast between the Magi and Herod. Herod had all the knowledge of scripture but did not seek Jesus. The Magi were gentiles who searched in the darkness without the knowledge of scripture but were willing to travel far distances to meet this newborn king of whom they only had vague knowledge. Herod saw Jesus as a threat to his way of life. The Magi saw Jesus as the source of new and deeper life. Herod lived comfortably in his palace in Jerusalem. The Magi wandered through cold nights and long days to fulfill their journey of faith. Herod had so much but gave nothing. The Magi had only what they could carry but they gave everything they had. When it comes to our life of faith, Herod represents that attitude that tries to put God in the passenger seat! As the saying goes, "If God is your co-pilot then it's time to trade places!" Herod had no interest in trading places. The Magi, on the other hand, could not wait to pay homage to the true Lord and King of their lives. Herod was unchanged by the birth of Jesus. The Magi were transformed by their encounter with Jesus and even returned home "different" from the way they came.

When does the message of the Gospel become uncomfort-
able or challenging for you?
When have you gone outside of your "comfort zone" to serve
the Lord?
What do you admire most about the Magi and their jour-
ney of faith?
What aspect of Herod do you find most troubling?
What experience of God in your life has most changed you,
such that you became a different person because of that
experience?

*Jesus offers Himself to us in every Eucharist we celebrate.
How can the attitude of Herod creep into our thoughts and
prayers at Mass?*

It's interesting that one of the most common images of early Christian art in the catacombs of Rome is that of the three Magi worshiping Jesus.

*Why do you think the early Christians of Rome identified
with the Magi so strongly during the times of persecution?*

Feast of the Baptism of the Lord

Our scripture passage for this Sunday comes from the Gospel of Luke 3:15–16, 21–22. In it, we read the well-known account of Jesus' baptism and the Father's words revealing Jesus as His "Son in whom he is well pleased." This passage offers several points for our reflection as disciples.

For three Sundays in a row, we read various Gospel passages that show how Jesus is "revealed". Last week, He was revealed by the visit of three Magi coming from the east. This week, He is revealed by a divine proclamation and the voice from heaven. Next week, He will be revealed as the one who steps in to solve an impossible crisis (the Wedding at Cana turning water into wine). Each of these three weeks shows us that the presence and action of Jesus is revealed in a variety of ways—from total strangers, to moments of heavenly inspiration, to near miraculous occurrences.

How have you come to recognize the presence of Jesus active and present in your life?
Which of those above scenarios describes a situation in your life when Christ has been active and "revealed" Himself?

Notice in this passage that Jesus is at prayer and it is in response to his prayer that the heavens opened, the dove descended, and the Father spoke. That's pretty powerful prayer! Luke shows Jesus praying more than any other Gospel and always during an important event.

What's your prayer like?
How do you pray?
What are obstacles you have experienced in your prayers?
What are resources that have helped you grow in your prayers?
What has happened in the context of your prayer?

As we celebrate the Baptism of the Lord, it is a good time to recall our own baptism. The baptism of John was simple; it just washed away sin. Baptism in the name of Jesus is much more powerful. It makes us members of the Body of Christ, members of the Church, a Temple of the Holy Spirit, adopted children in the family of God, and people who now carry on the mission of Jesus in the world. There's an important analogy: Baptism is to the Christian Life what a wedding is to a marriage. Baptism is a sacrament that fundamentally changes our life purpose, mission, identity, and destiny. Every day from the moment of our baptism we choose to either live out that mission or to deny it.

> *When do you find it "easy" to live your baptism?*
> *When do you find it most difficult to live your baptism?*

In today's passage, we hear the Father speak the words every son desires to hear: "You are my beloved Son, in you I am well pleased." That's a way of saying "I'm proud of you."

> *What was your father or mother most proud of about you?*
> *Did your father or mother ever speak those words to you?*
> *What do you think God is most proud of in your life?*
> *What are you most proud of in the life of your son/daughter/friend? Have you told them that?*

Finally, there is a reason why the Baptism of the Lord brings to fulfillment the Christmas season and it is this: In Christmas we celebrate the gift of God's salvation to the world in the birth of Jesus while in Baptism we celebrate our ability to share in that gift. It's one thing for God to give so great a gift to the world, but it's another thing for us to be able to receive that gift. "For God so loved the world that he gave his only Son, so that everyone who believes in him might not perish but might have eternal life" (Jn 3:16). In Baptism, we have access to the gift of eternal life in Jesus. Thus, the gift of God comes to fulfillment in our reception of that gift. Hence, the baptism of Jesus makes holy the waters in which we are baptized and opens to us the possibility of eternal life. One of our challenges as adults is to consciously accept the grace of our baptism so that we can fully realize our identity in Christ. Our baptism has given us grace upon grace but we cannot realize the tremendous blessings we have received until we say "yes" to the divine life of God becoming manifest in our very being. Sometimes people have an understanding of baptism that is almost magical—like a religious act that we do in order to "check the box" for being a good parent. However, we need to realize that Baptism is to the Christian life what a wedding is to a marriage. It begins a lifelong journey that is intended to bring us into the very presence of God for eternity and it fundamentally changes our identity. It's one thing to celebrate the gift; it's another thing to make the gift our own.

> *As you reflect on the Feast of the Baptism of the Lord, how can you learn more about the meaning of your own baptism?*
>
> *How does the analogy between baptism and a wedding change your understanding of what it means to be a Christian disciple?*
>
> *What are practical ways in which you "open the gift" of life in Christ you received in your Baptism?*

FIRST SUNDAY OF LENT

Our scripture passage for this Sunday comes from the Gospel of Luke 4:1–13. In this text we hear of the temptation of Jesus by Satan while in the desert for forty days. The temptations are three-fold and have important applications for our lives. Traditionally, these temptations have been understood as overcoming the three desires for Pleasure, Power, and Prestige. While that is a valid application of the passage, the temptations can also mean much more than that.

The first temptation is for Jesus to turn stones into bread. When you think about it, what would have been the "sin" if Jesus had done it? This temptation was about more than just food; it was the temptation for Jesus to discard the limits of His humanity and to exercise His power as God. Literally, it was the temptation for Jesus to break the bounds of human limitations and to be "like God". That was what Adam did when he chose to eat of the Tree of Knowledge (so he could be "like God"). Jesus overcomes this temptation by choosing to live with his hunger rather than feed it in a way that violated the limits of humanity.

> *When can we be tempted to want to be "like God" in setting our own rules for right and wrong?*
> *How can we try to be "like God" in treating others as less than ourselves?*
> *Do we try to be "like God" in thinking it's OK to satisfy our every want in any way we can?*
> *This temptation is also the tendency to think that our life comes from something other than God—our work, our riches, our relationships, and so forth. How are we tempted to find our life fulfilled in ways other than what God intends?*

The second temptation is for Jesus to be "successful" at the cost of being "faithful". Jesus came as the Messiah and people had certain expectations for how the Messiah should act. While Jesus did fulfill some of the messianic expectations, He did not fulfill all of them. It is tempting to please people by meeting their expectations but sometimes those expectations can go against who we are as disciples. In those moments, we are called to be faithful rather than successful in the eyes of others. Some people in Jesus' time expected the messiah to be a political ruler—someone who would set Judea free from Roman occupation. Here, Satan tempts Jesus to accomplish His goal at the cost of losing His soul. That is the temptation to put something else in the center of our Lord's life and service rather than keeping it focused on God and the Father's will. It is also the temptation to give in to others' expectations of us and to become the person others want us to be rather than the person God wants us to be.

> *When are you tempted to cut moral or ethical corners for the sake of ever-greater success?*
> *When are you tempted to do what others want even it means violating your conscience or your faith?*
> *When are you tempted to become someone just to make others happy rather than becoming the person God intended you to be?*

The third temptation is for Jesus to throw Himself off the temple so as to "test" God's presence and protective action. It is the temptation to doubt that God is with us in moments of crisis. Think of how easy it is to experience a tragedy and to doubt that God was present all along. Think also of how many people "lose faith" because of a devastating event in their lives. Jesus overcame the temptation to make the Father prove His love and His presence. Our Lord would not put the Father to the test. He remained faithful and trusting in the Father's love even as He died on the cross. Jesus' last words in Luke's Gospel are an act of trust and confidence in the Father's care ("Father, into your hands I commit my spirit"—the very words used to close the day at evening prayer in the temple before people went to sleep each night Lk 23:46). Jesus had no need to test the Father's presence because Jesus did not doubt the Father's presence. He didn't need proof; He had faith.

> *When do we find ourselves doubting God's presence in our lives?*

What are ways in which we can try to make God prove His presence in our lives?

Jesus overcame these three temptations as He began His ministry and we will have to overcome them as well if we will follow faithfully where He leads us. Each of these temptations surfaced in the Exodus as the Hebrew people wandered for forty years in the desert. They, too, tried to rely on their own ability to sustain and protect their livelihood and gave in to the temptation to hoard manna and to think that God would not care for them. They, too, were tempted to set up idols so they could attempt to successfully control God's presence and action rather than faithfully surrender to the Lord's will. They were also tempted to believe that God had abandoned them in the midst of their trials and that they were being punished because of the difficulties they faced as they wandered. Jesus overcame the temptations by which the people of Israel failed in their faith. Our Lord has shown us what a disciple's life looks like when we, too, overcome those same perennial temptations in our lives.

Which of these temptations most affects you?
What can you do during the Lenten Time to grow stronger and more confident in your trust in God?

SECOND SUNDAY OF LENT

Our scripture passage for this Sunday comes from the Gospel of Luke 9:28b–36. It is the account of the Transfiguration of Jesus. In this story, we hear of how Jesus converses with Moses and Elijah about the "Exodus" He is to accomplish in Jerusalem. After their discussion, Peter wakes up and sees only the glory of the moment. Here are some points for our reflection as disciples who are called to follow the Lord wherever He leads us.

Peter could not be happier. In Luke 9:18–20 Jesus posed this question to His disciples: "Who do the crowds say that I am?" Although Peter responded to that question by saying, "The Messiah of God," his answer failed to capture the full reality of Jesus' identity. Just a few verses before the scene in today's Gospel passage, we see Jesus teaching His disciples that He must suffer and die before rising from the dead (v. Lk 9:21–22). Of course, where Jesus leads the disciples must follow (v. Lk 23–27). The disciples didn't like the message that Jesus would lead them to suffering and death. They wanted to follow a messiah who would lead them to victory and glory instead. That's why Peter is so overjoyed to now see this moment of the transfiguration. Finally Peter sees the reason for which he himself was following the Lord: glory. Peter didn't hear the entire conversation that took place between Jesus, Moses and Elijah about the "Exodus"—a reference to Jesus' suffering, death and resurrection. Peter only sees a glorious moment and so Peter only understands half the message of this experience. Peter wants to freeze the moment and capture the presence of Jesus where it is comfortable, rewarding, and glorious. Peter does not want to leave that mountain and follow Jesus to Jerusalem! It's almost as if Peter is saying, "Let's stop here, Lord, we've gone far enough." For Peter, he thought he had reached the destination of his discipleship—a place of glory. However, the faith to which Jesus calls us is lived in daily discipleship as we progress step by step on our journey to Jerusalem with the Lord. It is a discipleship that does not stop at a place that is comfortable but one that faithfully follows wherever Jesus leads.

> *What tempts us to stop short and settle for "good enough" when it comes to our lives of discipleship?*
> *What do we seek in our prayer and life of faith—moments of glory or the ability to faithfully follow the Lord each day?*
> *How can we become complacent in our faith and want to stop deepening our discipleship?*
> *How can people today be tempted to seek only glorious moments rather than sacrificial moments in their faith?*

The disciples will need to remember the Glory of the Transfiguration especially when they face difficult moments like Jesus' persecution and crucifixion. The Transfiguration is a moment that will sustain them and give them hope in the midst of trial. In all of our lives God gives us certain moments when He reveals His love and His presence to us. These moments are meant to sustain us when we feel burdened or abandoned as well. They give us hope in the midst of trial. It might be easy to recognize the divinity of Jesus as He stands in conversation with Moses and Elijah but it will be difficult for the disciples to see that same divine presence on the cross of Calvary. We have moments in our lives when we can find it difficult to recognize the presence of God as well. That is why the Lord blesses us with other moments that reassure us of His grace and love.

> *What are some of your moments or experiences of God's love and mercy that sustain you in difficult times?*
> *In what experiences or situations do you find it difficult to recognize the presence of God?*
> *Moses and Elijah were speaking to Jesus about His Exodus (death, resurrection and ascension), which was intended to prepare the Lord for His impending trial. How does God prepare you for the trials you face?*

The voice of the Father corrects Peter's misunderstanding by announcing, "This is my Son, my Chosen One. Listen to him." Peter had recognized Jesus only as "Master" but not as God incarnate. The Father announces Jesus as His own divine son and He instructs the disciples that the proper response is to listen to Him. That is, don't just hear Him, but actually listen to Him. To "listen" to the Son of God means paying attention to the teachings of Jesus with openness, receptivity, and a desire to respond. It means being attentive to the message of the Gospel and seeking ways to apply it to our daily lives. It also means that when we have lots of other influences attempting to tell us what to do (culture, friends, business world, media, greed) that we choose to not listen to those influences but instead listen to the voice of Jesus. It means that when we make a decision, we choose to follow the guidance of Jesus and not the other forces at work in our lives.

> *How do you seek out the guidance of Jesus in your life?*
> *When have you consciously rejected the influence of other factors and chosen to do what is "right" in the eyes of God?*
> *In what part of your life do you need to listen more to the voice of Jesus guiding you?*
> *What are some of the other voices that try to influence you each day?*

Our need to refine our spiritual listening is stressed by the Church when we are invited on the Second Sunday of Lent to pray with these words: "O God, who have commanded us to listen to your beloved Son, be pleased, we pray, to nourish us inwardly by your word, that, with spiritual sight made pure, we may rejoice to behold your glory, through Christ our Lord."[1]

---

1.   See Collect, Daytime Prayer, Second Sunday of Lent.

THIRD SUNDAY OF LENT

Our scripture passage for this Sunday comes from the Gospel of Luke 13:1–9. In this passage, Jesus teaches His disciples about the need to read the "signs of the times" and to have a personal change of heart in light of the events taking place around them. This message is important for us as well especially during this Lenten time when we pray for the grace of repentance.

Jesus begins His teaching by responding to the crowd's question about a tragedy that occurred through human malice—namely, Pilate had killed some Galileans. The historical facts surrounding this tragedy are not known but the religious presumption of Jesus' time was that disaster is punishment for sin (cf. Jb 4:7, Ex 20:5, and Jn 9:2–3). This belief (principle of direct retribution) was based on a misunderstanding of God's justice by which the good are rewarded in this life and the bad (sinners) are punished in this life. Thus, if bad things happen to people then the presumption was that they were sinners. Jesus teaches the crowd that their understanding is mistaken. Sometimes bad things happen because of human free will and the evil actions of individuals (Pilate). Jesus then provides another example of tragedy that is the result of natural disaster rather than human malice: the collapse of the Tower of Siloam.

In this second example the people suffered from an accidental event. Again, Jesus points out that such things are not an indication of the victim's sinfulness but a reality of life. The greater tragedy occurs when people fail to make good use of the gift of time and opportunities for repentance prior to such a tragedy. Finally, Jesus gives the parable of a fig tree that does not bear fruit and of how it, too, will be destroyed. In this final example, however, the destruction will be the specific result of not bearing fruit. Jesus goes on to describe how the tree will be given time and encouragement to bear that fruit. In this final example, Jesus is teaching us that the greatest tragedy is that which we bring on ourselves by our failure to repent and change our lives—especially when we are given time and encouragement to do so. This is a powerful lesson for us as disciples. When we see tragedies occurring around us then it should motivate us to evaluate our own lives and encourage us to make the needed changes so that we can be in right relationship with God and others.

> *When do people today try to interpret tragedy as a sign of God's punishment for sin?*
> *How can your awareness of other people's tragedies cause you to examine your own life and reconsider your actions and priorities so as to change your behavior?*
> *Every historical event can be a teaching moment. What are some of the recent historical events in our world that you believe God has allowed for the purpose of such a teaching moment?*
> *What does the statement, "the greatest tragedy is that which we bring on ourselves by our failure to repent and change our lives" mean to you?*

Jesus then goes on to describe the various efforts that will be undertaken in order to motivate a fig tree to bear fruit. The image of a fig tree is well developed in the Old Testament and was used as a symbol for Judah or Israel (v. Hos 9:10, Mi 7:1, Jer 8:13, 24:1–10). Thus, we should not understand this parable as some generic teaching about a plant but as the specific will of God for His people. When we hear the words "repentance" and "fruit" used together in this passage then we should remember the first time these terms were associated in the Gospel of Luke when John the Baptist preached to the crowds in Luke 3:8–14. In that passage, John instructed the crowds that it was necessary to bear the "fruits of repentance" and he then gave concrete examples. Those examples included generosity for those in need, integrity in one's professional life, and justice in the face of hardship. Repentance, then, is not an interior feeling or religious sentiment of compunction but is a real "change of mind" that brings about a corresponding "change of life" in every day actions. Repentance means to take on the mind of Christ and to act according to the values of the Gospel. The salvation of the fig tree depends upon its ability to actually bear such fruit. This parable is telling us that in God's mercy the Lord gives us both time and encouragement to experience that repentance which bears fruit as well. Thus, God's patience allows us the gift of time so that we cooperate with the Lord's grace (v. 2 Pt 3:15). The problem is that we oftentimes fail to make good use of the time and opportunities we have for repentance. Perhaps it is a habit of procrastination that leads us to postpone the uneasy confrontation of our shortcomings and our decision for deeper discipleship. As it was previously stated, sometimes tomorrow never comes whether it is a matter of another person's ill will (Pilate) or accidental disaster (Tower of Siloam); it can even be our own failure to respond to God's grace that brings about our spiritual and even physical destruction.

> *How does the above understanding of repentance, that is thinking again or taking on the mind of Christ, change the way you desire to "repent" in your life?*
> *What other reasons do you think people can have for not repenting when they have the time and encouragement to do so?*
> *What is the "fruit," the realized concrete actions of daily life, which God wants to bring about in your life?*

In an effort to stimulate the tree to produce fruit, Jesus tells us that the gardener puts manure around it and tills the soil. That's a very important image and the term "manure" is a significant one. We should not whitewash it by calling it "fertilizer"! Manure has a purpose—to stimulate growth so as to produce the good fruit of repentance. Sometimes God has to put manure in our lives to wake us up to our need to repent as well. The reality is that "manure happens". It's not a sign of God's punishment but of God's mercy calling us to greater repentance. It is meant to be a fertilizer for our faith. When things go well, we rarely feel our need to turn toward God. More often than not, it's when tragedy strikes in our lives or in the lives of others that we turn to the Lord. We see an example of this faithful search in the midst of tragedy happening when the crowd poses the question to Jesus about the death of Galileans by Pilate. So often when we find ourselves dealing with difficult or painful situations, we experience self-pity and say, "Why me?" However, with an attitude of right faith, we can also find ourselves in prayer asking that same question "Why me?" not out of self-pity but out of a sincere desire to know how our lives are meant to be changed for the better and our spiritual growth stimulated by that manure (fertilizer for faith). Lent is a good time to look at some of the manure that is been dumped around each of our lives and to bring it before God so the Lord can toil the soil of our hearts and allow it to give growth to deeper faith rather than remain on the surface and cause self-pity.

> *What does this reflection mean to you?*
> *When have you asked the question "Why me?" out of self-pity?*
> *When have you taken on the attitude of faith that asks that question "Why me?" for the purpose of seeking growth?*
> *When have you seen difficult moments become the catalyst for others to grow deeper in their faith?*
> *What manure is sitting on the surface of your life that you need to allow God to till into your life and heart as to become a positive motivation for spiritual growth (repentance)?*
> *What have been some of the more significant moments of spiritual growth in your own life that have been the result of difficulty, tragedy, or trial?*

Lent is a time of repentance in which we are called to turn away from sin and grow closer to the Lord in all areas of our lives. The parable of the fig tree is given to us in the middle of our Lenten Time to motivate us to use wisely the remaining weeks and not to miss opportunities for additional growth in faith. Jesus said that the fig tree would have three years to produce fruit. That time corresponds to the three years of our Lord's public ministry. The good news is that we do have time to repent; the challenge of this gift is that we are responsible for using it wisely and productively so as to bear the fruit God wants from each of us.

> *How does this passage motivate you to renew your resolve during this Lenten Time?*
> *The timing of God's judgment may be uncertain but the fact of God's judgment is certain; how can these remaining days of Lent provide additional opportunities for you to prepare for God's judgment?*

What Lenten practices help you to cultivate the soil of your heart so as to be more sensitive and receptive to God's encouragement?

FOURTH SUNDAY OF LENT

Our scripture passage for this Sunday comes from the Gospel of Luke 15:1–3, 11b–32. This text contains the famous parable of the Prodigal Son. As you read this parable, you will note that there are three primary persons who are the protagonists at different points of the story—the younger son, the father, and the older son. This parable is the literally the heart of Luke's Gospel. It surfaces in the middle of Jesus' journey to Jerusalem and is the culmination of three parables of divine mercy. This important placement of the parable warrants our consideration of how it speaks to our lives. At various moments we may have been each of these three types of people.

The first person in this parable is the younger son. He receives so much but also ignores so much as well. He was rich in the love of others, a secure position, a family, and a father who loved him. He chooses to break those family ties and abandons both location and relationship as he travels to a foreign land far away from those who love him. Eventually he squanders his inheritance on his self-centeredness and foolish pursuits. Finally, after he hits "rock bottom" and is lower than the pigs, that is he longs to eat the food that fills their stomachs, he decides it's time to come home and not for the purest of reasons. He's still thinking of himself because he's more motivated by hunger rather than by a desire for reconciliation and relationship with his father. When we are told that he "comes to his senses", that is a way of saying that he began to regain his identity. In his prepared speech, however, he expresses his desire to be treated as a servant rather than a son. Maybe he's embarrassed to come back as a son because he knows that he doesn't deserve that honor. Maybe he's trapped in his guilt and now believes himself only worthy of being a servant. He did "come to himself" (literal meaning of "coming to his senses") so he does remember his former life and wants to return to it. It may be an impure motivation, but it's a start! In fact, it's enough to change his course and start the process of conversion. Repentance for the younger son means learning to say "Father" again. In using the word "Father", the younger son shows that he does, in fact, desire reconciliation more than recompense.

The example of the younger son has much to say to us as disciples. Sometimes we can find ourselves losing our identity because we have gradually drifted away from a loving relationship with the Father. Or perhaps we feel that we are alienated and in a foreign land where no one cares for our needs. For each of us, there is a point of awakening when we realize our need to return and restore the relationship we have lost. The emptiness and hunger of the stomach is nothing compared to the emptiness and hunger for love, acceptance, and forgiveness experienced by the human heart in such moments. Sometimes we don't know how to find our way home to the Father. It is in those moments especially that the example of the Prodigal Son inspires us: We have only to show up and ask to be a member of the Father's family once again. Our words don't have to be perfect; God will work with our imperfect and even impure motivations because the Father desires to restore relationship with us more than we could ever imagine.

> *What positive growth has taken place in your life because of some difficult struggle or painful situation you faced?*
> *Who were the many people who helped you along the way to recover your sense of self and restore your dignity?*
> *By asking his share of the property and then selling it while his father was still living, the younger son was basically saying to the father that he was already "dead" to him. How do people today treat others as though they are already dead?*
> *What emptiness or hunger leads people to seek God?*
> *What can cause people to think they are unworthy of relationship with God?*

The second person in this parable is the Father. He is someone who is described as "moved with compassion". Note how active his love is as he "sees", "feels", "runs", "embraces," and "kisses" the younger son. The father's compassion reaches out to welcome his son home and he goes to meet him half way on his journey. One particular note of interest is how he sees the younger son from afar and "runs" to greet him. To run in the cultural world of Jesus was considered foolish and something shameful; thus, the Father is even willing to be seen as "foolish" by others when it comes to loving his son. When the younger son starts his rehearsed speech, the Father stops him after he says what is true but before he can say what is self-serving. The father doesn't want a servant; he always valued the relationship with his son and that's what he wants back. He is not embarrassed to love his son. In fact, he throws a public feast to announce to the whole town that he has his child back! It's also important to note that the father's mercy extends to both sons and not just one. We see the father go out to the older son just has he had done for the younger son. The father reaches out to all his lost and wayward children to bring them back regardless of the reason for their alienation. The example of the father's mercy and active love has much to say to us as disciples who are called to express that same mercy toward others in our life. Many scholars call this the parable of the "Merciful Father" rather than the "Prodigal Son" for this reason.

> *Who has played the role of the "Merciful Father" in your life by calling you back to your authentic self?*
> *When have you helped restore someone's dignity by your love and forgiveness?*
> *How can people be considered "foolish" because of their active loving desire to reconcile with someone who has strayed?*
> *Sometimes it can be easy for us to wait until others come to us before we are willing to reconcile with them. The father in this parable met his repentant son half way. What can you do to meet someone half way in his or her journey of repentance?*

The third person in this parable is the older brother who will not join the celebration with the father and will not even come into the same room as his younger brother. In fact, he will not use the terms "Brother" or "Father" in his discourse. The older brother is judgmental, angry, and condemnatory in stark contrast to the father who is loving, merciful, and forgiving. In the older brother we see that both sons were alienated from the father: one relationally (older brother) and the other physically (younger brother). The older brother reveals the source of his judgmental attitude when he describes his role as that of a slave who is only concerned about reward from, not relationship with, his father. When he says that he has never violated the father's commandments, he is expressing the attitude of the Pharisees in Luke 15:1–2 who do not believe they need to repent. Because of that attitude of self-righteousness, he wants to make others earn mercy, and he seeks retribution for other's mistakes, wrongdoings, and failures. The older brother also reveals an interesting characteristic when he comments about how the father never gave him so much as a kid goat to celebrate with his friends. Note that his desire was not to celebrate with the father but with his friends. Thus, the older son was more concerned with reward (kid goat) than he was with relationship with his father. His refusal to join in the banquet didn't stop the celebration; rather the older son's refusal just prevented him from sharing the joy of the father. He is like the Pharisees who stand outside condemning Jesus for eating and drinking with "tax collectors and sinners." The older brother is not interested in conversion, reconciliation, relationship, or forgiveness. For him, life is about following the rules, getting what you deserve, and finding fault with others. Not only does the older son not want the father's love, the older son is actually angry at the father's mercy. Repentance for the older son will mean learning to say "Brother" again. This example of the older brother has much to say to us as well. Sometimes we can find ourselves demonstrating a self-righteous attitude like that of the older brother. In those moments, we need to remember that Jesus calls us to be people who help reconcile with Him and not people who make it more difficult for others to change their lives.

> *Sometimes people who have been away from the church for a long time can be hesitant to return because they feel like others would not welcome them back. What can we do as a parish community to manifest the Father's Mercy more readily and visibly in our community—especially toward those who desire to turn their lives around?*
> *How can people be resentful of God's mercy today?*
> *How can people today pursue a life of faith based on a desire for reward rather than relationship?*
> *How does resentment cause people to miss out on the joy of God's mercy?*

For whom do you need to learn to say "Brother" or "Sister" again?
How can people make it difficult for others to repent and change their lives?

FIFTH SUNDAY OF LENT

Our scripture passage for this Sunday comes from the Gospel of John 8:1–11. This is the passage in which Jesus meets the woman caught in adultery who is about to be stoned to death by the scribes and Pharisees. There are several interesting dynamics that occur in this passage and offer points for our reflection.

The first point to note is the attitude of the Pharisees and scribes who are trying to entrap Jesus. They have cleverly devised a plan to put Jesus in an awkward position by which they think he will end up either condemning the woman to death or contradicting the Mosaic Law. In order to carry out this plan of entrapment, they set up a situation in which they report that a woman has been caught in the very "act" of adultery. Thus, she was entrapped as well—but note that there is no mention of the man. Thus, a double standard is revealed in their plan. Throughout the conversation with Jesus, the Pharisees and scribes treat the woman as an object and instrument of their ultimate goal, which is to discredit the Lord. She is not a person to them but only an unfortunate bystander in their plot to seek Jesus' demise. In the face of such callous malice, Jesus first responds by ignoring their challenge by writing on the ground. When they press the issue with Him a second time, our Lord responds by discrediting them when He says, "Let he who has no sin cast the first stone." Suddenly they walk away as they realize the injustice of trying to apply a standard to others that they are not willing to apply to themselves. With their hypocrisy exposed, they no longer condemn the woman nor ask Jesus to do so. In this interaction, Jesus is challenging all of us to examine the injustice we practice in our relationships as well.

Who tries to entrap religious leaders today so as to discredit their message?
How are people used as pawns today for the personal pursuits of others?

When do you see a double standard used in our society by which some are held accountable for their actions and others are not?

It is sometimes said that we are most critical of others about those things we most dislike in ourselves; what does this saying mean to you in light of this story?

How does this encounter with Jesus challenge you to reconsider the standard you are using for others?

The second point is the development of the relationship between Jesus and the woman. She is just an instrument for the scribes and Pharisees. They are using her—probably by entrapment—to set the stage for their testing of Jesus. She is nothing but an object to them. However, in the course of the scene Jesus engages the woman in a personal conversation. He addresses her as "you"—a word that is used only for familiar people and never for strangers. Thus, Jesus is establishing relationship with the woman by his conversation. He is also breaking many social barriers by talking with a woman in public, which was something that was forbidden in the cultural world of Jesus. In all of this, Jesus is caring for her as a person and showing great respect for her—even in her sinfulness. She, in turn, accepts the relationship and calls Him "Lord" —a sign that she is acknowledging that she stands before mercy incarnate. It is only when the relationship is established that Jesus releases her and challenges her to sin no more. This is an important dynamic because Jesus first invites us into relationship with Him and then challenges us into discipleship. Sometimes we think that we have to get our act together before we can approach the Lord. The reality is that we can only have our act together because we have met the Lord!

How has the Lord challenged you to deeper discipleship that is to "sin no more" as a result of your developing relationship with him?

How has your involvement in scripture study challenged you to deeper discipleship?

When have you seen someone being treated in an inhumane way by others and what was your response?

When have you brought dignity to another person's life by your decision to establish a relationship with them?

The third interesting dynamic is in the contrast between the woman and the scribes and Pharisees. She is someone who was "bound" to her sin in a very public way. She came to know all too painfully the consequences of her actions and she had no choice but to face them. What a humiliating moment. But when the crowd left, she chose to stay. She stood before Jesus a sinner acknowledging her sin. In that moment, Jesus set her free and changed her life. That moment of forgiveness and freedom was only possible because she chose to stand before Jesus acknowledging her sin. That's what it means to "bind" and "loose" people from their sins. We can't be forgiven for something that we don't acknowledge as being our sin. In a real sense, the first step in forgiveness is to be "bound". The second step in forgiveness is to stand before Jesus asking to be set free. With that humility and trust in the mercy of God, the Lord challenges us to change our lives and go forth. However, the scribes and Pharisees had a very different experience. They, too, were bound to their sin as they examined their consciences and realized their own need for forgiveness. However, they walked away when they realized their sinfulness and chose to go home still bound to their sin rather than to approach Jesus seeking forgiveness and mercy. As a result, nothing changed in their lives. This passage speaks about the dynamic of the Sacrament of Reconciliation in which we freely acknowledge our sin and come to the Lord seeking a new beginning. In this sacrament of healing the Church reminds us that "Penance requires … the sinner to endure all things willingly, be contrite of heart, confess with the lips, and practice complete humility and fruitful satisfaction."[2] Penance is a loving confrontation in which the mercy of God awaits us as well.

> *What has been your experience of the Sacrament of Reconciliation?*
> *How has it been "life changing" and "freeing" for you?*
> *Whom do you more easily identify with —the woman who stands before Jesus in public shame or the Pharisees who keep their sin to themselves and walk away quietly?*

---

2. See CCC 1450.

Lastly, Jesus gives the woman not only a second chance at physical life ("Has no one condemned you?") but He also gives her an invitation to eternal life by remaining free of sin and in relationship with him ("Sin no more"). This final point is a significant aspect of this passage and worthy of more reflection because it speaks directly to us as disciples. In short, Jesus helps the woman move beyond a discipleship that is based on observing rules due to fear of punishment to a discipleship that is based on a loving relationship with God. It would have been an act of mercy had Jesus only let the woman go. That action would have meant giving her back her life. Her motivation for avoiding sin in the future would have been for the sake of not putting herself at risk again that is being stoned. Such an act of mercy in itself would have been notable, but Jesus goes much further than just giving her life back; he invites her to avoid sin not only for the sake of reducing her risk but also because of a loving relationship with Him. Her motivation to do the right thing should be governed more by love than by fear. The same is true for us. Sometimes when we are held accountable for our sin we just pray to be delivered from the moment but God wants more from us than our avoidance of punishment; God wants us to enter into a deep and life-changing communion of love with Him and to let our decisions and actions be guided by that love. Such a life will not only lead us to avoid sin but actually inspire us to please God by our pro-active actions of love and mercy for others. That is the disciple Jesus wants us to be!

> *When do you feel like you are motivated in your Christian life by fear of punishment?*
> *When do you feel you are primarily motivated by love for God?*
> *How can we as a faith community help people move beyond a discipleship based on fear of punishment to a discipleship based on love for God?*

In her diary St. Faustina wrote a prayer that can inspire us to receive and live in God's mercy:

> O Lord. I want to be completely transformed into Your mercy and to be Your living reflection. May the greatest of all divine attributes, that of Your unfathomable mercy, pass through my

heart and soul to my neighbor. Help me, O Lord, that my eyes may be merciful, so that I may never suspect or judge from appearances, but look for what is beautiful in my neighbors' souls and come to their rescue. Help me, O Lord, that my ears may be merciful, so that I may give heed to my neighbors' needs and not be indifferent to their pains and moanings. Help me, O Lord, that my tongue may be merciful, so that I should never speak negatively of my neighbor, but have a word of comfort and forgiveness for all. Help me, O Lord, that my hands may be merciful and filled with good deeds, so that I may do only good to my neighbors and take upon myself the more difficult and toilsome tasks. Help me, O Lord, that my feet may be merciful, so that I may hurry to assist my neighbor, overcoming my own fatigue and weariness (...) Help me, O Lord, that my heart may be merciful so that I myself may feel all the sufferings of my neighbor. (...) May Your mercy, O Lord, rest upon me.[3]

3. M. Kowalska, *Diary of Saint Maria Faustina Kowalska: Divine Mercy in My Soul* (Stockbridge: Marian Press, 2005), p. 163.

PALM SUNDAY

Our scripture passage for this Sunday comes from the Gospel of Luke 22:1–23:56. In this reading, we hear of Jesus' Last Supper, betrayal by Judas, trial both before the Sanhedrin and Pilate, suffering, crucifixion, death, and burial. Various details are immersed in this account of our Lord's final hours of earthly ministry. Our reflection this week will focus on only a few of these details and how they affect our lives as disciples.

Note how Jesus takes time to accomplish some of His most outstanding ministry during His passion and crucifixion. Our Lord is continuing His incredible works of mercy while He is suffering. Some points, which illustrate this particular care, include the following:

- At the Last Supper, Peter professes his loyalty to Jesus. Jesus, for His part, knows that Peter and the others will all abandon and betray Him. Yet He still shares the Eucharist with them (his very life) and prays for them. He even prays for Peter by name so that when Peter "turns," that is repents and converts from his sinful denial, that Peter would become a source of strength for the other disciples. It would certainly be difficult for us to do that for our friends if we knew they were about to betray, abandon, or deny us. Jesus loved His disciples to the end despite their sin and failure (v. Lk 22:31–32).

- When the guards come to arrest him, one of Jesus' disciples cuts off the ear of one of the slaves of the high priest. Jesus takes time to heal the injury of those who were about to arrest him. He cared for their suffering even as they were about to begin His trial and prosecution (v. Lk 22:51).

- Notice, too, how Pilate sends Jesus to Herod for questioning. The scene ends with Luke telling us that, "Herod and Pilate became friends with each other that very day, for before this they had been at enmity with each other." It is no accident that this reconciliation occurred with Jesus in the middle. He healed a broken friendship between Pilate and Herod even as they were shuffling the Lord back and forth from one to the other as part of a sham trial. He reconciled those who had been at enmity with one another (v. Lk 23:12).

• When Jesus is carrying His cross and meets the women weeping, He takes time to comfort them. Even while He is heavily burdened with the weight of the cross our Lord is not so burdened that He cannot offer a consoling word to others (v. Lk 23:27–29).

• As He is on the cross, Jesus prays for forgiveness of His persecutors. He had taught His disciples to "pray for your enemies" and "do good to those who hurt you" in the Sermon on the Plain. Now, He is showing us what love of one's enemy looks like in practice as He absolves His very executioners (v. Lk 23:34).

• While He is on the cross, He consoles the Good Thief who asks, "Jesus, remember me when you come into your kingdom." Jesus responds with the same generous mercy He lived each day of His life. What He gave the Good Thief went far beyond what was asked. He said: "Today you will be with me in Paradise." Even as he died, Jesus was reconciling a sinner to God and giving salvation to one who sought it (v. Lk 23:39–43).

All of these above moments are particular to Luke's Gospel. Luke relates them to us because he wants us to see that Jesus practiced His own teaching to the very end.

> *How do you treat others when you are having a bad day?*
> *What helps you to rise above your own concerns to address the needs of others?*
> *Which of the above interventions of Jesus struck you as particularly meaningful and why?*
> *Who is willing to die for you?*
> *And for whom are you willing to die?*
> *As you go through this Holy Week, how can you make time to bring your needs to the Lord and receive His ministry?*

A second distinctive element of the Passion Narrative in Luke's Gospel is how the Evangelist phrases the three-fold challenges to Jesus on the cross by the people, the soldiers, and the criminal (v. Lk 23:35–39). These three groups not only mock Jesus but also actually tempt Him to prove His identity. This temptation is more than human malice. Luke's Gospel is very clear that when Satan tempted Jesus in the desert at the beginning of our Lord's ministry (v. Lk 4:1–12), the Evil One did not give up. Rather, Satan is said to have departed from Jesus "until an opportune time" (v. Lk 4:13). Throughout Luke's Gospel, Satan has been lying in wait for the opportune time to once again tempt Jesus. Now that the Passion of Jesus begins, Luke tells us in 22:3 that "Satan entered into Judas, the one surnamed Iscariot." The opportune time has arrived and Satan is ready to renew his effort to thwart our Lord's mission. It is in this light that we must understand the taunts of the three groups in Luke 23:35–39 as Jesus dies on the cross. Luke has carefully presented their taunts with language that parallels the temptations in the desert so that Jesus is challenged to prove His identity as the Christ, the Chosen One, the King of the Jews. This last experience of temptation for Jesus is to save Himself from suffering and death.

The irony of these temptations lies in the fact that Jesus brings salvation not by avoiding suffering and death but by faithfully accepting it in fulfillment of the Father's will. Still, the temptation to prove His identity by doing what the crowds expect was subtle and powerful. This is an important teaching for us as disciples. Satan waits for opportune times to tempt us to prove our identity as Christians. Just like Jesus, Satan waits for moments that are particularly important in our faith life and discipleship to try and thwart us from being faithful to the Father's will and to claim for ourselves what we want for ourselves based on our disordered passions rather than obediently living according to God's commands. Christians throughout the centuries have noted that spiritual attacks are intensified especially during opportunities for great spiritual growth. We should not be surprised by that reality as we see it happening to Jesus on the cross of Calvary.

What are the "opportune times" and circumstances for Evil to tempt you?

What would have been the "sin" if Jesus had chosen to come down from the Cross and save Himself?

When are you most tempted to give in to other people's expectations of how you should act even when you know that those expectations go against your values as a disciple?

In 1 Peter 5:8 we are warned to stay "alert and sober" because Satan is prowling like a roaring lion looking for someone to devour. When have you felt that Satan has attacked you during a time that was meant to be an opportunity of increased grace?

What do you think allowed Jesus to recognize and dismiss the temptations He faced on the cross?

As Jesus died on the cross He offered His final words as a witness to His faith so as to instruct us in our faith. He said, "Father, into your hands I commend my spirit." Those are the words of Psalm 31:5 that were often used in Jewish night prayer as preparation for sleep. By saying these words, Jesus was bearing witness to the confidence and faith He had in the Father's power to raise Him up. He approached His death with the same confidence that one approaches their nightly sleep. Jesus was teaching us to trust God and not be concerned about those who can kill the body (v. Lk 12:5). In His final prayer on the cross our Lord shows us what that faithful trust looks like. As you read the entirety of Psalm 31, various other insights emerge that help understand why Jesus chose this Psalm as His final prayer. It speaks of God's help in time of need, of faithful resolve and not giving into temptation, and of ultimate deliverance from the forces of evil.

What prayer do you pray before you go to sleep each night? How does the text of Psalm 31 help you better understand the interior faith and spirituality of Jesus on the Cross? How can you use this Psalm throughout Holy Week to deepen your trust in the Lord?

One curious detail contained in each of the Passion Narratives of the synoptic gospels (Matthew, Mark, and Luke), is that of the torn veil in the Temple. In Luke 23:45 we are told that the curtain of the temple "was torn down the middle". Luke's use of the passive form of the verb is a common way of referring to an action done by God and is called the "Divine Passive". Matthew 27:51 and Mark 15:38 indicate that the curtain was torn "from top to bottom" as a way of indicating divine agency. Regardless of the phrasing differences, the reality is that all three Gospels record the same important event and indicate it took place in response to, or as a consequence of, Jesus' death on the cross. Although much speculation has taken place in an effort to identify which Temple curtain is being referenced, it is a futile point to ascertain. It is commonly accepted that the Temple curtain was a general reference to the sanctuary. The meanings of the torn curtain may be manifold and not exclusive of one another. First, the torn curtain may be interpreted as a statement that the presence of God no longer resides in a physical temple but that the Lord is now to be worshipped in "Spirit and Truth" anywhere in the world (v. Jn 4:23–24). This interpretation could also contain allusion to Jesus' Exodus that He would accomplish in Jerusalem (v. Lk 9:31) and as discussed with Moses and Elijah. Second, the torn curtain may indicate that access to God is now available to all peoples including the Gentiles since the curtain served as a barrier to keep people out of various Temple areas. This second interpretation would be supported by the Centurion's statement of faith (a Gentile) in response to the death of Jesus. Paul alludes to the dividing and excluding effect of the Temple veil in Eph 2:14–15. Third, the torn curtain may be a symbolic statement of divine judgment on the Temple that initiates its destruction. This last interpretation would be particularly relevant for early Christians of the first century who witnessed the physical destruction of the Temple in Jerusalem by the Romans in the year AD 70.

> *Which interpretation of the torn Temple veil means the most to you and why?*
> *Why do you think the destruction of the Temple veil was associated with the death of Jesus?*
> *How do you think people responded when they saw the torn curtain and realized it was associated with the death of Jesus?*
> *How can Christians today unintentionally set up barriers that can end up preventing people from coming to God?*

Finally, only Luke tells us that the Centurion at the cross who witnessed Jesus' death exclaimed, "This man was innocent beyond doubt." The phrase used by the Centurion is a legal term and refers to a person who has been absolved of all guilt. This is not the first time in Luke's Gospel that Jesus has been declared an innocent person. Pilate declared Him to be innocent on three occasions (v.

Lk 23:4, 14, and 22). Herod found Him innocent as well (v. Lk 23:15). Even the Good Thief who was crucified with Jesus declared the Lord to be innocent of any wrongdoing (v. Lk 23:41). Throughout Luke's Gospel we have been introduced to people who were identified as being righteous, just, and innocent. They are presented as examples of discipleship for us to follow. Being innocent was an important quality for a Christian of the first century especially during the age of persecution. Luke goes out of his way to show how Christians are good law-abiding citizens and that the secular authorities have nothing to fear from Christian populations under their jurisdiction. Luke repeatedly encourages disciples to be found "innocent" of wrongdoing and exemplary in fulfilling their just civil responsibilities. The Centurion recognized that Jesus was a just person in how our Lord endured His passion and death. Jesus prayed with trusting abandonment to the Father, forgave those who persecuted Him, and reconciled the Good Thief. Jesus' death had a profound effect on the Centurion and evoked a response of faith that instructs us in our discipleship.

> *How does the story of Jesus' death affect you?*
> *If you were standing there and you had "seen what had taken place", what would be your response to it?*
> *What does it mean for Christians to be found "innocent" in today's world?*
> *What are ways in which Christians can try to excuse themselves from their civic responsibilities?*
> *How would the message of the Gospel be promoted if Christians were found to be "innocent" of wrongdoing on a massive scale?*
> *What industries would go out of business if Christians pursued innocent lives?*

SOLEMNITY OF EASTER (VIGIL)

Our scripture passage for this Sunday comes from the Gospel of Luke 24:1–12. The New Testament accounts of the Resurrection of Jesus are well known to us. Due to our familiarity with these texts we can easily overlook significant details by which each of the Gospel writers wished to communicate particular meaning. The Gospel of Luke offers numerous insights that are meant to inspire, encourage, and guide our lives as disciples.

In this passage we see the women who had accompanied Jesus from Galilee, and been present for His crucifixion, now going to the tomb to anoint our Lord's body. When they arrive, they see the tomb open and the body gone. They went looking for Jesus in the last place they had seen him, but He was not to be found there. Instead, two men ask them a question that is really a thought-provoking reprimand: "Why do you seek the one who lives among the dead?" (It should be noted that this phrase places the emphasis on "the one who lives" rather than on "the dead".) This reprimand is an important reminder for all of disciples who seek to find Jesus in the present by looking for Him as they knew Him in a past experience. Sometimes we can think that Jesus was more "real" in the past than He is in the present. We can look for Jesus as He "was" 2,000 years ago in history and fail to recognize Him present to us now in the Sacraments, the Holy Spirit, and the lives of faithful Christians. When we do that then we are like the women who return to a past experience of Jesus rather than learning to recognize Him present now in a new way. Luke emphasizes throughout His Gospel that today is the day of our salvation, not yesterday. Today the scripture is being fulfilled in our midst—not yesterday. Today is when we must pick up our Cross and follow Jesus—not yesterday or tomorrow. For this reason the Liturgy of the Word on Easter Sunday invites us to sing the antiphon taken from Psalm 118:24 "This is the day the Lord has made; let us rejoice and be glad." In this way, we are invited to celebrate the resurrection as a current event that is always relevant and significant.

> *What are typical past experiences of Jesus that people can be focused on in such a way that it prevents them from seeking Jesus in the present moment?*
>
> *When do you find yourself "looking for the living among the dead" and focused on a past event (retreat experience or prayer experience) rather than as the one who lives in the present?*
>
> *How do you seek the Living One present to you now?*
>
> *When we search for Jesus where He is not present we become frustrated and even doubtful; how can we as a faith community help people recognize Jesus (the one who lives) present in their lives today?*

The reprimand leads to a reminder as the women are challenged to remember the whole of Jesus' message including the necessity of His suffering, death, and subsequent glorification. That process of remembering Jesus' life and teaching transformed them and filled them with joy as they came to faith and believed in our Lord's word. They then understood the meaning of the empty tomb and the burial garments left behind. These things were statements that Jesus would never need them again because He would die no more. The problem is that we can sometimes suffer from a selective memory of Jesus' words and teachings. Obviously the disciples had the same problem or they would have understood Jesus' words. When we are selective in our faith then we don't embrace everything Jesus teaches but only those things we want to hear or that make sense to us. Sometimes we can even intentionally disregard the rest of our Lord's teaching. The women didn't understand what the empty tomb meant until they remembered Jesus teaching about "rising from the dead". Jesus' teaching interpreted their current situation and made them realize how much God was in control of all things. It is important for us to remember that we cannot enter into the mystery of Jesus until we understand the message of Jesus. (Note: In Christian iconography this essential truth of faith is represented by the four Evangelists [Gospel writers] represented on the four points of a Crucifix since the Evangelists teach us the Christian

Mystery that leads us to be united with Jesus in His suffering, death, and resurrection.) If we have neglected part of the message, we have reduced our ability to enter into the mystery of our Lord. We can't "remember" what we don't know. One of the necessary steps for discipleship is to learn what Jesus said and did by studying the Gospels; then we can remember it in the course of our daily lives so as to have a different perspective on how to understand and respond to the situations we face.

> *When has the teaching or lived example of Jesus helped you to understand your life in a new way?*
> *How have you been transformed by "remembering" the life and message of Jesus in a challenging time?*
> *When do people find it easy to focus on some things Jesus said and did but not on others?*
> *What part of the message do people tend to focus on and accept?*
> *What part of the message do people tend to disregard?*

The women then remembered His words, understood the reality of the resurrection, and took this message to the other disciples. In this action, the women became the first ones to announce the good news of the resurrection. These women were no newcomers to the ministry of Jesus. In Luke 8:1–3 we were told that there were some women who had been healed of "evil spirits and infirmities" who followed Jesus. Among these were Mary Magdalene from whom seven demons had gone out, and Joanna, the wife of Herod's steward. These two women are now present at the resurrection along with Mary the mother of James and some others. These same women stood by Jesus in His crucifixion (v. Lk 23:49) and witnessed His burial (v. Lk 23:55). Luke wants us to know that these women have been deeply immersed in the life and teachings of Jesus. They have been eyewitnesses of our Lord's actions throughout the Gospel. Now they are represented as becoming "Ministers of the Word" as they bring the fullness of the Gospel message to others by proclaiming the resurrection. For Luke, it is an important part of discipleship that "eyewitnesses" become "Ministers of the Word". Luke has already alluded to this necessary development in the very opening passages of His Gospel (cf. Lk 1:2). We are called to imitate the example of the women and to become ministers of the word as well. We become eyewitnesses to the presence and ministry of Jesus when we recognize the active presence of Jesus in our lives—an awareness we can only have when we are able to faithfully remember His words. Being a minister of the word means that we help others to understand the Christian mystery and to recognize Jesus, the One Who Lives, in their lives as well. It also means inspiring others to enter in the Christian mystery by our attractive witness of discipleship. The women in this passage took initiative in bringing the message to others; they didn't wait until they were told to do so. The same should be true for us. Also, we are told that the women in this passage "kept repeating" the message which indicates a repeated effort in a wide variety of contexts. Thus, the women are not only witnesses; they have become missionaries and so should we.

> *How does the transition from being an "eyewitness" to becoming a "minister of the word" change the way you understand discipleship?*
> *What can help you be a better eyewitness?*
> *What opportunities do you have to be a minister of the word for others in your family, friends, or professional life? Luke wants us to know that the same women who had previously been identified as suffering evil spirits and infirmities have now become the most courageous of missionaries. What temptations of unworthiness or unpreparedness can cause someone to dismiss the invitation to become a missionary of faith?*

One last note about this passage is the very frequent use of the word "tomb". A careful study of this section of Luke's Gospel indicates that the word "tomb" is used eight times (v. Lk 23:53, 23:55, 24:1, 24:2, 24:9, 24:12, 24:22, 24:24). Luke is making a very significant statement by using the term "tomb" eight times in connection with the death and resurrection of Jesus. The number "Eight" (8) was a symbolic way of referring to the eternal day of resurrection —the day that initiates eternal life. You see, while Jesus was in the tomb over the course of only three calendar days as calculated in Hebrew chronology (Friday, Saturday, and Sunday), Jesus actually rose from the dead on the first day of a new week (v. Lk 24:1). To call it the "first day", however implies that the resurrected life of Jesus is bound by time. In the resurrection, Jesus is no longer bound by time or space. Our Lord has opened the door to the eternal day that never ends —that is the "Eighth Day". There is no ninth day. For this reason, the number eight is associated with the resurrection of Jesus and has become a symbol for Jesus Himself as the "Eighth Day" incarnate. If you look at most baptisteries in Christian churches, you will notice that they have eight sides to them. The symbolism of the number eight being associated with the experience of Baptism is even represented in the very building of the baptistery of Saint John Lateran in Rome (dating to the fifth century). The eight references to the tomb in these passages from Luke's Gospel are telling us that our baptism is an immersion into the death and resurrection of Jesus and that we must enter into the tomb with Jesus in order to rise with Him as members of His body who share everlasting life. Saint Paul makes this clear in his teachings on Baptism and discipleship when he says that we must "die with Christ and be buried with him" (v. Rom 6:3–5 and Col 2:2). To phrase this teaching in a more poetic way, it could be said that the Tomb becomes the womb from which Disciples are born in the waters of Baptism.

> *How does this understanding of the tomb as a symbol for baptism deepen your appreciation of this passage?*
> *The tomb is the consistent symbol that connects Jesus' death, burial, and resurrection; in many ancient Christian churches the altar was actually represented as a tomb. What does that symbolism say about the Eucharist being the reality of our participation in the Paschal Mystery of Jesus and of His death and resurrection?*
> *Being a disciple means that we die to ourselves so that it is Christ who lives in us; what aspects of your life that you find it difficult to let go of so that Christ can live in you?*
> *The women were transformed by their experience in the tomb of Jesus and they become missionaries as a result of it; how is our baptism meant to be an experience of transforming grace that makes missionaries out of us?*
> *What can we do as a faith community to help people to better understand the reality and significance of their baptism?*

SECOND SUNDAY OF EASTER

Our scripture passage for this Sunday comes from the Gospel of John 20:19–31. The Church provides this same reading for us each year on this Sunday and so we have ample opportunities to reflect on the many rich aspects of this passage. In this reading, we hear the well-known account of Thomas who doubts the reality of Jesus' resurrection.

In this Gospel passage, we are told that the disciples are living in fear behind locked doors. Specifically we are informed that they were afraid of the Jews who had put Jesus to death. Perhaps their fear changed when Jesus stood in their midst. Just imagine what they must have thought? After all, here's their friend whom they abandoned and denied and left to die alone on the cross. The women came from the tomb that morning announcing that Jesus was alive. Now the disciples were probably more nervous than ever and wondered if Jesus would be angry with them. Rather than being vindictive towards the disciples, Jesus assures them that He seeks only their good and wishes them "peace". Our Lord does not want them, or us, to live in fear or condemnation because of our failures but in restored relationship. Jesus sought them out like the Good Shepherd going after the lost sheep. The disciples were embarrassed, afraid, isolated, and sorrowful. Jesus came to let them know that He still loved them and wished them peace, not fear or anxiety. There are times in our lives when we feel like the disciples in that upper room. These are times when we hide from the Lord and others out of our fear, shame, sorrow, and sin. Jesus wants to break into those locked rooms of our hearts and bring His peace and healing reconciliation to us as well.

When do you identify with the disciples behind the locked door and living in fear?
How have you experienced the truth that God's mercy is greater than your sin?

How can fear, shame, or sorrow keep someone from experiencing God's mercy in the presence of the Church?
When have you been surprised by someone taking the initiative to reconcile with you when you have been the one who offended them?

It's interesting that Thomas chose to remain with the other disciples even though he had not had the same experience of the risen Jesus that they had and did not believe. He stayed with them not because he shared the same belief as they did but because he saw something in them that attracted him: their lives were changed but Thomas didn't quite understand why. Thomas wanted what they had—joy, peace, and faith—but he didn't have it. Nonetheless, he persevered and, because he remained with the other disciples, he did eventually come to share their faith and experience the Risen Christ for himself. This is a great reflection for us as disciples because sometimes we don't fully understand the truths of faith that others do. Rather than walking away in disbelief, Thomas gives us an example of faithful perseverance when we struggle with matters of faith. Sometimes we only come to understand because we choose to remain a part of a community that understands. Thomas acknowledged that his failure to believe was his issue. He did not try to convince the other disciples that they were wrong; rather, Thomas just acknowledged his own limitation and remained in their company. It was Thomas' issue, not theirs.

What characteristics mark "people of faith" whom you respect and make you want to "have what they have"?
How has perseverance benefited you while you were searching in your faith life?
Had Thomas walked away in his unbelief then he might never have experienced the risen Jesus. How can we as a faith community help people persevere in the Church even when they experience doubt?

Thomas may have been the one who was singled out for his unbelief. However, he ended up making the most profound profession of faith found in the entire Gospel of John when he exclaimed: "My Lord and my God." Sometimes the most unlikely people become heroic in their witness of faith as they move from a situation of unbelief to a situation of exemplary faith. Even great Saints like Augustine and others had to mature in their faith lives so as to become heroic examples of holiness. The example of Thomas teaches us that discipleship is a process and that no one should be excluded from the real possibility of becoming a heroic witness of faith. That insight provides both encouragement for individual disciples in their own faith lives as well as hope for the faith lives of others. Thomas remained with the community of disciples because they welcomed him and continued to manifest lives that were transformed by resurrection faith. Little did they know that one day Thomas would surpass them by his confession of faith!

> *How have you seen the transformation from little or no faith to great faith take place in people you have known? Sometimes people say that converts make the best Christians. What do they mean by that statement and how can those who grew up as Christians develop a deeper appreciation for their faith on an adult level?*
>
> *The story of Thomas reminds us that we are all one family of God and that the experience of faith is both personal and communal. How has your experience of Church helped you in your faith life and how has your personal faith life made you a better member of the Church?*

The proclamation of Thomas "My Lord and My God" is worth pursuing in greater detail. It is important for us to remember that Thomas did not invent this greeting. Rather, the pagan Emperor Domitian previously preferred this greeting, but Thomas repeats it in reference to Jesus instead of the emperor. That was a very subversive statement! Thomas was saying that Jesus alone has the power to direct Thomas' life; not the emperor in Rome. That profession of faith in Jesus is exactly what Christians died for during the age of persecution because they refused to worship false gods, including the emperor. Thomas was not only acknowledging the presence of God in Jesus; he was also acknowledging the supreme authority of Jesus over all creation. Disciples answer to a higher authority when it comes to receiving direction and influence in our lives. In Acts 4:19 and 5:29 we see Peter, John, and the other apostles making this same great statement of faith: no one on earth has the right to ultimately govern our lives but only Jesus who is the Lord of heaven and earth. The Roman Empire considered anyone who did not worship Roman gods, including the emperor, to be a traitor. Today, people in our world are sometimes ostracized and regarded as "un-American" for not embracing and worshipping the values of a secular society. The proclamation of Thomas reminds us that no agenda, no cause, and no person has ultimate claim on our lives but only Jesus Christ.

> *What forces or influences try to control our lives, values, and decisions today?*
>
> *How do you think people would respond if we, like Thomas, made the same proclamation of faith in our workplace, family and social lives—that God alone has the power and authority to tell us who we are, to define our happiness, and to guide us in our decisions?*
>
> *How can Christians today be labeled as subversive in our world?*

THIRD SUNDAY OF EASTER

Our scripture passage for this Sunday comes from the Gospel of John 21:1–19. In this passage, we read about the Risen Lord directing the work of the disciples as they fish and then challenging Peter to be the chief shepherd of the flock. The image of fishing was used in scripture to describe the missionary activity of the Church while the image of shepherding was used to describe the pastoral activity of the Church. This passage is rich in meaning and offers some important details for our consideration as disciples who desire to carry on the missionary and pastoral work of the Church today.

One of the important clues in understanding this passage is found in the symbol of the "charcoal fire" (cf. Jn 21:9). This is an important detail because the last time the disciples were around a charcoal fire was in John 18:18 when Peter denied Jesus three times. Now, Peter will have a chance to affirm his love for Jesus three times around a similar charcoal fire. Jesus did not want Peter to be defined by his failure or to allow his denial to be the only thing Peter thought of every time he saw a fire. Rather, the Lord wanted to give Peter another opportunity to do the right thing. In providing this new opportunity, Jesus allowed Peter to "redeem" his failure. This symbol of the charcoal fire helps us interpret what takes place throughout this chapter of John's Gospel and to understand both the actions of fishing and shepherding through the lens of God's redeeming work in the world. Certainly Peter was grateful for the opportunity to be redeemed and in his gratitude could be both a great missionary and a great pastor. The reality is sometimes when we fail others, and the Lord, we are given opportunities to redeem our failure and demonstrate our love and fidelity just as Peter was. In God's great mercy, the Lord not only leaves the door open for our conversion but even sets us up with opportunities and invitations to pursue it!

> *In what ways have you been given opportunities to redeem*
> *situations of weakness or failure in your own life?*
> *What do you think was Peter's first thought when he saw*
> *Jesus standing around a charcoal fire?*
> *What situation or person are you avoiding because of a*
> *previous failure and how does passage give you encourage-*
> *ment to seek redemption?*

The first half of this passage focuses on the work of redemption that will take place through the ministry of Peter as the Chief Fisherman of the Church. The role of Peter as leader in this effort is demonstrated by the fact that he is the one who initiates the effort (v. Jn 21:3). Fishing is commonly understood as a metaphor for missionary activity (v. in Jn 20:21 where Jesus has just sent the disciples on mission). Thus, this passage is an important teaching on how the missionary activity of the Church will take place (Note: the image of a boat has been a symbol of the Church since the First Century; v. Jn 21:3). There are several elements in this passage that need to be considered:

- The disciples are taught the necessity of following the Lord's direction in order for their work to be successful (v. Jn 21:5–6). If they act on their own, without the Lord's direction, then their nets are empty and their efforts fruitless.
- The number one hundred fifty-three has a variety of possible meanings and there is no clear indication of what John intended, if anything, by including this detail. It is possible that this number is a symbol of the Hebrew phrase Beni ha Elohim which means "Sons of God" (in Hebrew, each letter had a particular numerical value and the value of this phrase totals to one hundred fifty-three). If this interpretation is correct, then the fish represent new Believers who have become "Sons of God" through the missionary efforts of the Church.
- Something interesting happens to these "fish" at various stages in this story. This change in status is indicated by the use of three diverse words in Greek to refer to fish. In verse 5, Jesus uses the Greek word *prosphagion* to refer to fish not yet caught. In verse 6, when the fish are in the nets, they are referred to as

ixthuon. Finally, in verses 9 and 13 when Jesus offers a meal of bread and fish to the disciples, our Lord uses the word *opsarion*. (Note: the same word for fish and bread is used in Jn 6:9 and 11 in the context of the Eucharist). The use of various terms is telling us that the missionary activity of the Church transforms people to become new realities through the Sacraments of Baptism (Sons of God) and Eucharist.

- It is only when the disciples are sharing the meal with Jesus that we are told the disciples knew it was the Lord (v. Jn 21:12). This revelation of Jesus in the context of a Eucharistic meal is similar to what the disciples experience on the journey to Emmaus in Luke 24:30–31.
- Of interesting note is the fact that Jesus wants the disciples to bring some of their fish to Him despite the fact that our Lord already has a meal provided for them. This element reminds us that there is an "offering" requested of us when we participate in the Eucharist. It is not that Jesus needs the fish; rather, it is that Jesus wants the meal to be a sharing of lives.

The above elements teach us much about the work of the Church today we strive to carry on the redeeming ministry of Jesus through missionary activity. It speaks to ministry leaders to remind them of the need to seek the Lord's guidance in their decisions. It reminds us that the Sacraments and ministries of the Church are meant to have a transforming impact in people's lives effectively making them "Children of God" (v. Jn 1:12, 21:5) and equal participants in the Eucharistic sharing of life. Finally, it reminds us that we have work to do because none of it will happen unless we, like the disciples, become the Lord's instruments and make it happen.

Which of these aspects of the redeeming missionary work of the Church speaks to you and why?
Given this passage as a model for evangelization, in which effort does the Church need to put more attention and effort?
The disciples had to work together in the boat in order to realize this great and important work. What is your role

in the "boat" of the Church when it comes to carrying out
missionary or evangelization efforts?

The second half of this passage focuses on the work of redemption
that will take place through Peter as the Chief Shepherd of the
Church. Three times Jesus asks Peter, "Do you love me?" and three
times Peter affirms his love for the Lord. Through this exchange,
Jesus is challenging Peter to grow in his ability to love. When Jesus
asks Peter "Do you love me?", He uses the word "agape" which is
the very love of God. Thus, Jesus is saying to Peter, "Do you love
me with the same love that I have for you?" Peter answers and says
"Yes, Lord, I love you" but Peter uses the word "*philos*" meaning that
Peter is only capable of loving Jesus with the love family members
have for one another. We lose the significance of this exchange in
English, but it is there in the Greek. Nonetheless, Jesus does not
reject Peter for his inability to love as Jesus loves. Rather, Jesus tells
Peter to put his love into action: "Feed my sheep ... tend my lambs."
A second time as well Jesus challenges Peter to love "agape" but
Peter can only love "*philos*". It is in the third question that Jesus asks
Peter "Do you love me?" and Jesus uses the word "*philos*". In doing
so, Jesus is showing that He is willing to work with Peter where
he is and in doing so will eventually lead Peter to where he should
be. Jesus will help Peter learn to love as God loves, but it will take
time. God is willing to work with us as well. We're not perfect or
perfectly holy but it is our desire to be what God wants. God can
work with anyone who's willing to work with God. That was true
of Peter and it is true of us.

> *How have you been challenged to grow in your capacity*
> *to love?*
> *When have you had to imitate the Love of God (agape) in*
> *a way that exceeded your natural ability (philos)?*
> *What was it like?*
> *What inspired you?*

After Peter affirms his love for the Lord, Jesus asks him to express
it through works of service and ministry to others. Thus, Christian
love is not an emotional experience only between the disciple and
the Lord. Rather, a disciple loves the Lord present in others and
serves Him in them. There is an expression that says, "Service is

Love made visible." Peter is to make his love for Jesus visible in how he cares for those entrusted to him. Peter is challenged to love all those the Lord puts in his life and not to love only those he wants to. Thus, Peter is to care for all who are in need with an unlimited generosity and compassion. Catherine of Siena lived during the 14th century and spent many years expressing her love for the Lord through her solitude and prayer. After a while she began to experience the absence of Jesus in her moments of prayer and so asked the Lord, "Where are you?" The Lord replied to her: "Catherine, from now on you will experience me in the dying, the condemned, the suffering, and the lowly." Thus began her remarkable life of heroic charity for others. The redeeming work of Jesus continues in our lives through the ministry of the Church even after we have become Christian. When we are hungry, we need to be fed. When we are wounded, we need to be cared for. When we are wandering in errant ways, we need to be called back to the flock. All of these pastoral actions of the Church are ways in which the work of redemption continues for those who are already Christians. Mother Teresa once said, "The hunger for love is much more difficult to remove than the hunger for bread."

> *What are the most common ways people express their love for God?*
> *How does the expression "Service is Love made visible" challenge you to grow in your discipleship?*
> *Whom has the Lord placed in your life that you find it difficult to love?*
> *What are the cultural forces today that want to define faith and love as private interior feelings rather than external expressions?*

In the end of the dialogue with Peter, Jesus tells him that being a disciple will require greater and greater surrender of his life. Literally, our Lord says that another will "lead you where you do not want to go" (v. Jn 21:18). Peter will eventually witness the self-giving love of Jesus by dying on a cross much like Jesus did. Peter may not be capable of such love now but he will be later. All he has to do is "follow Jesus". The journey of great disciples begins with a single step. We all hear that invitation from the Lord to "Follow Me" in concrete moments but we have to decide to do so by putting our love into action in concrete ways. Peter had to "feed the sheep" when it was easy and when it was difficult. He had to "tend the lambs" when they were cooperative and when they were uncooperative. Peter had to love the people Jesus put into his life and not just love the people Peter liked. This passage teaches us that being a Christian is not an emotion or sentimental feeling. It is a life-changing way of discipleship that is active and dynamic.

> *What does this discussion between Peter and Jesus mean to you?*
>
> *If Jesus said to you "Follow me", what would be the "next step" in your life of discipleship?*

As we celebrate the Easter Time, it is worth reflecting on how the ministries of "fishing" and "shepherding" complement each other for the work of the Gospel. When you think about it, Jesus could not have called a more unlikely character to be the key leader of the early Church. Peter was a simple fisherman from the remote regions of Galilee who denied the Lord three times and tried to deter Jesus from enduring the suffering of the Cross. Nonetheless, the Lord called Peter to love Him, serve Him, and give his life in witness of faith for Him. As leader of the early Church, Peter had to direct the ministries necessary to grow and sustain the Christian community. The Church today needs both the ministry of Peter as Shepherd (pastoral care of those already Christian) and the ministry of Peter as Fisherman (evangelization and mission outreach toward those who are not yet disciples).

> *What are the Church's primary ministries today of pastoral care and of evangelization and missionary outreach?*
>
> *Which dimension of ministry do you think is in greatest need of development?*
>
> *Who are unlikely people in our time that God has raised up to be disciples?*
>
> *Pope Francis is the successor of both Peter and Paul as the Bishop of Rome. How do you see the Holy Father carrying out today the two dimensions of Peter's ministry for the early Church?*

In which dimension of ministry (pastoral or missionary)
would you like to become more involved?

Lastly, it should be noted that love of Jesus is to be the foundation
of discipleship. There can be lots of motivations people have for
following the Lord but Jesus wants us to do so primarily and foun-
dationally out of love. Sometimes we can follow the Lord out of a
sense of duty or fear or hope for reward or to fulfill the expectations
of others. All of these motivations may help us take the first step
of discipleship but these motivations will not allow us to become
the disciples Jesus desires. Jesus didn't ask Peter, "Do you believe
me?" or "Do you respect me?" or "Do you fear me?" Rather, He
asked Peter "Do you love me?" Love of God in Jesus must be the
foundation of our discipleship as well. The challenge for us is to
grow daily in our love for the Lord as our Savior and friend. If we
are not motivated by love we do not have a solid foundation in our
discipleship.

What do you think are some of the false motivations other
than love that people can have for being Christian and how
do those false motivations manifest themselves in limited
discipleship?
What experiences in your life have manifested God's love
for you?
How do you foster your love for the Lord?

Fourth Sunday of Easter

Our Scripture passage for this Sunday comes from the Gospel of John 10:27–30. It is only a few verses long but has great meaning for our lives of discipleship. In these verses, Jesus speaks to us as the Good Shepherd and instructs us on some essential responsibilities as members of his flock.

In order to understand this section, we have to remember that this scene occurs during the Feast of Dedication while Jesus is in Jerusalem (v. Jn 10:22). On this Feast, the Jews celebrated and commemorated the re-dedication of the Temple in 164 BC following the desecration of the Temple by the Seleucid king Antioches Epiphanes in the year 167 BC. This Feast was an occasion when people called to mind certain themes related to both the experiences of desecration and re-consecration: God's presence, God's Protection, and what it meant to be faithful as God's people. It is in this context that Jesus reveals Himself as the "Good Shepherd" and offers His instruction on discipleship. For the Jews of Jesus time, the Temple in Jerusalem was the sign of God's presence and protection. To be "faithful" was understood as adherence to the Law of Moses. In this passage, Jesus is revealing Himself as the one who perfects the Temple: He is the sign of God's presence par excellence (v. Jn 10:30 "The Father and I are one."), His words are given to us as divine instruction for our lives and decisions (v. Jn 10:27 "My sheep hear my voice ... and they follow me."), and He offers eternal protection for those who belong to Him as His disciples (v. Jn 10:28–29 "They shall never perish. No one can take them out of the Father's hand.")

Sometimes it's easy to seek protection and security in materialism, relationships, ideology, or gratification but Jesus offers us His Word instead so that we can "Hear" Him and allow Him to be the most stable presence in our lives.

Where do we look for our "protection" when the storms of life come around?
How do you "hear" the voice of Jesus challenging you to place your trust in Him rather than in superficial or passing sources of stability?

What are distractions or obstacles to hearing our Lord that can prevent us from listening to Him?
When have you had to rely only on the Lord for your stability and protection and what was that like?
In what ways can we as the Church be tempted to rely on false senses of protection other than Jesus?

Jesus says that it takes more than just "hearing" to be a disciple. He also says that His sheep "follow" him. This teaching means that we must integrate into our lives the faith we believe and profess. It is always important to remember that John's Gospel never uses the word "faith" as a noun but only as a verb. That's because John doesn't want "faith" to become just a static set of beliefs for disciples. Rather, he wants us to remember that faith does something; it is an action that is dynamic and powerful in our lives. Faith is something that is lived out in our "following" and not only in our "hearing". Our secular culture wants to keep faith "private" and "personal"—more like a feeling than a conviction. That cultural expectation means that we can experience a subtle but real pressure to not put our faith into action lest we be seen as fanatics or dangerous (even something as simple as making the sign of the cross in a restaurant can evoke a hostile glance).

When do you find it difficult to "follow" what you "hear" from the Lord?
Who exemplifies for you what it means to live out their faith?
Remember, the promise of Jesus' protection is based only on the condition that we are following Him and not just thinking about him.
How can people today presume God's protection without seeking to follow God's will?

When Jesus says, "The Father and I are one," He means that everything He does is in perfect communion with the Father. We find that easy to believe when He does the nice, appealing works of forgiveness and mercy. However, this teaching can be more difficult to believe when our Lord suffers, dies, and is abandoned by those closest to him. Following Jesus means that we do His work and so share in the communion He experiences with the Father. The goal of the Christian life is to be one with Jesus so we can share in His communion of life and love.

> *What do you find personally appealing about the life of Jesus that draws you to desire that communion of life and love?*
> *What is the work God wants you to do in your family, community, or office?*
> *What work of Jesus do you find most difficult to carry out?*
> *As you think about the life and service of Jesus, when would you not want to be "in His shoes"?*
> *What practices help you to live your day in communion with Jesus?*

Jesus says in this passage that no one can "take them out of my hand." When He does so, He uses the same word previously used in reference to the wolf that "catches" and scatters the sheep (vs. 12). By using this image, Jesus is teaching us that we are safe only when we choose to dwell in the palm of God's hand and that we put ourselves in danger when we freely choose to wander away from God's protective presence. God doesn't force us to remain in His care. It is up to us every day to choose to place our lives in God's hands. It can be comfortable for us to think of how God needs to care for us but it can be upsetting to think of how we need to conform our lives to God's will so as to place ourselves in the Lord's care. This passage reminds us that we are not passive recipients of the Lord's protection but are active agents in placing ourselves under His care. We all want to experience divine protection but we don't always want to do what it takes to warrant that protection.

> *How do people today wander away from God's protective presence and put themselves at risk of being "snatched away" in the process?*
> *How can we keep ourselves in God's protective presence throughout the day?*
> *How can we keep our families and friends in God's protective care?*
> *Who is someone you know of who has wandered away and what can you do to help lead them back to the Lord?*

The image of Jesus as the Good Shepherd caring for His flock was commonly used in Early Christian iconography. It appears in the Catacombs (for example, the Catacombs of Priscilla) where the Good Shepherd leads His faithful sheep to eternal life as well as in the early basilicas of Rome where Jesus is represented as the Lamb of God calling the flock to Himself. It is this second image of Jesus calling the flock to Himself and forming the Church that is instructive to us as we study this passage. This image is usually depicted in the apse of a basilica and typically depicts six lambs coming from Jerusalem and six lambs coming from Bethlehem in order to be united in the one flock of the Lord.[4] Jerusalem represents the city of the Jews and Bethlehem represents the city of the Gentiles. Thus, the Church is formed from Jews and Gentiles who leave behind their former way of life in order to become a new reality as members of God's flock, the Christian people. This image was particularly instructive for the early Christians because it reminded them that following Jesus meant leaving behind their prior way of life and being converted to a new life in Christ. Sometimes we think that God exists to make our life better the way they are rather than calling us to conversion, transformation and change. When we have such a mistaken understanding of faith then we pray only for God to take away our difficulties and solve our problems. When we correctly understand that Jesus is calling us to conversion, and we hear that call, then we begin to pray for insight, courage, and opportunities to demonstrate our love for God even as God has demonstrated His love for us. That is a prayer God never leaves unanswered! Indeed, the Lord will lead us as long as we desire to follow. It is when we desire to remain the way we are that we become deaf to the Lord's voice leading us and inspiring us.

> *How does this image of early Christian art inspire and instruct your faith life?*
> *When do you find yourself praying only for God to make your life better the way you are rather than praying for conversion, transformation, and change?*
> *What part of your life do you have to leave behind in order to be drawn more closely to Jesus the Lamb of God?*

---

4.   See the Basilica of San Clemente and Sts. Cosmas and Damian.

FIFTH SUNDAY OF EASTER

Our scripture passage for this Sunday comes from the Gospel of John 13:31–33a, 34–35. It is a pivotal passage in John's Gospel in which Jesus gives His "new" commandment to love. It is this commandment that will define Christian disciples as people who embody the love of God present in the world and who bring glory to God through their lives. This reading offers several points for our reflection.

This passage is focused on the theme of "glory". John raises our attention to this theme by using the word "glory" five times in two short verses. John is trying to tell us something about what it means to glorify God. First of all, notice that the "glory" of Jesus begins when Judas leaves to carry out his betrayal—a betrayal that will lead to the Lord's arrest, trial, passion, and crucifixion. That action, Jesus says, begins the hour by which the Son of Man is to be glorified. In order to understand how the death of Jesus is connected to the theme of glory we have to remember that Jesus was sent to the world with the mission of making God known.

The process of making God known is to reveal God's glory. In order to make God known, however, Jesus had to make love known because God is love. In order to make love known, Jesus chose the cross as the means of His manifestation of God's love to the world. Only on Calvary could He show the world the depth of God's love for every person—even those who put Him to death, betrayed him, abandoned him, denied him, and cursed him. In John's Gospel, the cross is the highlight of Jesus' life and ministry. The love of Jesus shown on Calvary glorifies the Father. There are lots of ways in which we can try to give glory to God. Our efforts can involve verbal praise, bumper stickers, devotional areas in homes, prayer before meals, and so forth. This passage not only tells how Jesus glorified the Father but also directs us in our efforts to glorify God as well; namely, to witness the same sacrificial love for others that God has shown for us.

The cross was the highlight and purpose of Jesus' life. What would you say is the highlight and purpose of your life?

Jesus' mission was focused on doing the will of the Father and witnessing God's love for the world. What motivates you to work long days and nights?

The world of Jesus considered glory to involve grandeur, power, riches, and prestige but Jesus teaches us that true glory is found in the love of God on Calvary. What do people today think a "glorious" life looks like?

How do the values of the world differ from the values of the Gospel?

If Jesus were walking on the earth today, what would He do in our time to make the love of God visible for every man, woman, and child?

Next, Jesus gives us the new commandment of love. When Jesus tells His disciples to love one another He also gives them a definition of what love means. Namely, "as he has loved us" so "we are to love one another." All too often we try to define love on our own terms. When we do so, we tend to love those who are close to us (family and friends), or those who will appreciate our love and reciprocate it, or those whom we find it easy to love. In short, we like to choose the people we love rather than loving the people God places in our lives. The love of Jesus teaches us a different criterion. Jesus loved Judas—and Peter. To Judas He offered a sharing in the Last Supper even though He knew full well that he was about to betray Him. Jesus offered it to Judas anyway. To Peter, Jesus offered encouragement and friendship even though He knew that Peter was about to deny Him. Jesus offered it to Peter anyway. Jesus washed the feet of the disciples to give them an example of how to love: humble service for those who need it and not just for those who appreciate it. In this passage then, Jesus is teaching us both who we are to love (everyone) and how we are to love (complete self-giving in humble service). Our Lord's example has become the way of life for every disciple to follow and reaches perfection on the cross of Calvary. We may be happy to hear the commandment to love so long as we can define what love means but loving as Jesus loved is difficult and challenging.

Who do you find it difficult to love?
Who finds it difficult to love you?

When you look at a crucifix, can you see the love of God or do you only see unjust suffering?
How do our own definitions of love differ from the love of Jesus as expressed and defined at the Last Supper?
How can a faith community help people to better witness the love of Jesus and follow His example of humble self-giving sacrificial love for others?

Lastly, Jesus speaks about discipleship. He tells us that being a disciple is the result of loving as He loved. This is an important definition because it removes any possible misunderstanding that might lead us astray in our lives as disciples. Jesus didn't say that disciples would be known as people who "thought as Jesus thought" or memorized what Jesus said. He also didn't say that disciples are people who observe religious rules and acts of personal piety. No, disciples are more than just people who go to church on Sunday or someone who professes a particular creed. Becoming a disciple means more than just receiving the Sacraments of Baptism, Confirmation, and Eucharist. The singular identifying quality of disciples is that they "love as Jesus loved" which means living out the faith they profess and their baptismal identity in their sacrificial love for God and neighbor. Jesus is teaching us that we don't become disciples until we allow the love of God to flow through us to others ("all will know that you are my disciples if you have love for one another"). That is an active definition that is demonstrated on the cross.

Disciples, then, must follow Jesus in laying down their lives for others even as our Lord laid down His life for us. After Jesus ascended into heaven, the world could only know who God is when Love would again be made visible in the lives of disciples—that's us. When we allow the love of God to flow through us into the world then we are allowing others to know God through us. That is an awesome definition of evangelization! In 1854 the Danish philosopher Søren Kierkegaard criticized the attitude of his fellow Christians including the guilty silence of one of the bishops by saying,

It is the duty of a Christian, as an Apostle also enjoys, to be always ready to give answer concerning the hope that is in him. [...] But how does he comport himself? Pretty much like the boys on New Year's Eve, who when they see their chance

seize the opportunity to throw a pot at people's door, and
then make off, around by another street, so that the police
may not catch them.[5]

This hope that dwells in us is the truth of Jesus Christ, and those
who witness it, declare themselves true disciples.

> *If you were to describe what it means to be a Christian,*
> *what would be your definition?*
> *How have you come to know God through the love of some-*
> *one else?*
> *When have you been humbled by being an instrument of*
> *God's love for others?*
> *Love can turn the greatest sacrifice into a joy. When have*
> *you found joy in sacrificial love for others?*
> *While we may express our discipleship in a variety of ways,*
> *the commandment to love as Jesus loved challenges us to*
> *never exclude that essential witness from our daily lives.*
> *How does the New Commandment of Jesus challenge you*
> *to reconsider your daily discipleship?*

---

5.   S. Kierkegaard, *Attack Upon Christendom*, p. 67.

Sixth Sunday of Easter

Our scripture passage for this Sunday comes from the Gospel of John 14:23–29. In this reading, Jesus makes a great promise to His disciples even as He announces that He will be going to the Father. Everything our Lord promises is contingent on the fact that the disciples love Him and out of that love are obedient to Him. Therefore, they "keep his word". The event of Jesus' Ascension will be an occasion of blessing for those who do love Him and keep His word: They will receive the Holy Spirit and it will be a time of love, belief, joy, and peace.

One of the first things to note in this passage is that Jesus establishes the priority of love as the motivation and source of a disciple's obedience: "Whoever loves me will keep my word" (v. Jn 14:23). Jesus didn't say, "If someone fears me he will keep my word" and nor did He say, "If someone wants a blessing he will keep my word." By identifying love as the source and foundation of a disciple's obedience, Jesus is teaching us two things. First, the Lord is asking us to clarify and purify the motivations for our discipleship. When we think about the various reasons that can motivate us to attend Sunday Mass or to fulfill the other obligations of our faith lives, we can see how easily we could be motivated by factors other than love of God. Even works of charity for the poor can be motivated by a humanitarian desire for altruism rather than a holy desire to put our love of God into action. It is important for disciples to clarify and purify their motivations for faithful obedience. It's not enough to just "do the right thing," we are also called to do it for the right reason. Second, Jesus is teaching us that love is more than an emotion; it is a radical commitment to Jesus and that is lived out in visible ways. It is important to remember that there are many different kinds of love but that disciples are called to love God with the same kind of love that God has for us. In Greek, that kind of love is described by the specific term agape. In this passage, Jesus tells us that when we love Him with the same love that He has for us then we will want to be obedient to His will even as He was obedient to the Father's as a manifestation of their loving relationship. This kind of love is not a sentimental or emotional feeling and it is certainly not based on natural affections or similarities with others. Agape love seeks to do the will of God in every thought, word and action of a disciple's life.

> *How have you had to clarify and purify your own motiva-*
> *tions for discipleship?*
> *When are you tempted to be obedient because of some*
> *reason other than love of God?*
> *What loving actions of Jesus are most challenged to follow*
> *in your life?*
> *In what ways can people be tempted to disassociate their*
> *love for God from their need to live out that love in faithful*
> *obedience to Jesus' commands?*

Next, Jesus tells us that the Holy Spirit will "teach you everything and remind you of all that I told you." The reality is that Jesus had so much to reveal to the disciples but the fullness of that revelation was too much for them to receive all at once. Over the course of time, even centuries, the role of the Holy Spirit has been to unfold consistently and authentically the truth of the Gospel for people of every place and time. As the Church faced controversies and crises throughout the centuries, the Holy Spirit guided the faithful to an ever-deeper understanding of that Truth which is the person of Jesus (v. Jn. 16:13; 1Cor 12:3). We benefit from 2,000 years of ongoing teaching from the Holy Spirit. The work of Holy Spirit is a movement of constant renewal that seems to affect only the life of individuals, but ends up transforming human history. The IV century Christian author Didymus the Blind wrote, "Finding us in a state of deformity, the Spirit restores our original beauty and fills us with his grace, leaving no room for anything unworthy of our love."[6] In the renewal of people's hearts the understanding of the truth of Jesus is given as an ever new and ever fresh experience of salvation. We should never wish that our faith would remain only that of the first century Church to do so would be to ignore the gift of the Spirit who has taught us and brought to remembrance the truth of Jesus over the past two millennia. On the other hand, we do need to remain vigilant that our faith develops in an authentic

---

6.   See Didymus the Blind, *Treatise on the Trinity*, lib. 2, 12: *PG* 39, 667–674).

way and under the guidance of the Holy Spirit. Jesus taught His disciples while He was with them during His earthly ministry; now Jesus promises the gift of the Holy Spirit to continue His teaching ministry in the life of the Church.

> *What are some of the situations that we face today that the Church of the First century did not have to address?*
> *How does our rich knowledge of faith, developed over the past two millennia, help us and equip us to respond to these unique challenges?*
> *Have you ever had the opportunity to trace a Catholic belief from its origin in the scriptures and through its development over the past 2,000 years so as to better understand what it is we believe today; what was that belief and how did the experience of historical critical study illumine your understanding of that belief?*
> *How do we experience the Holy Spirit teaching us today and how do we know when it is truly the Holy Spirit?*

The last point is that Jesus will give us a peace that the world cannot give. So often we think of peace as merely the absence of violence. In reality true peace is much more than the absence of violence; peace is the presence of justice. Justice in the biblical sense meant that a person was in right or balanced relationship in a four-fold way: with God, with self, with others, and with the created world. When all those relationships were "right," a person was understood to be in peace. In the Gospel of John, Jesus says that His peace is a peace that comes from that communion and right relationship with the Father. This right relationship is only possible through the Lord's gift of the Holy Spirit who can draw us into the life and love of the Trinity. That is why the gift of peace follows from the gift of the Holy Spirit (v. Gal 5:22). When we know and experience communion with God then we know there is not power on earth greater than the Lord. In the words of Saint Paul we read, "If God is for us, who can be against?" (Rom 8:31). The confident peace Paul describes gives us courage and removes fear from our hearts when faced with adversity or opposition in discipleship.

> *When do you experience your deepest sense of peace?*

As you think about peace having its origins in justice, which of those four-fold relationships do you need to adjust in your life so you can be in right balance?
How does your awareness of communion with God give you a sense of enduring peace?
How does the world try to offer peace and why do those efforts lack enduring or satisfying success?

Let us pray with St. Francis of Assisi:

Lord, make me an instrument of Your peace. Where there is hatred, let me sow love; where there is injury, pardon; where there is doubt, faith; where there is despair, hope; where there is darkness, light; where there is sadness, joy. O, Divine Master, grant that I may not so much seek to be consoled as to console; to be understood as to understand; to be loved as to love; For it is in giving that we receive; it is in pardoning that we are pardoned; it is in dying that we are born again to eternal life.

Solemnity of the Ascension

Our scripture passage for this Sunday comes from the Gospel of Luke 24:46–53. These verses conclude the Gospel of Luke and prepare for the mission of the Church. There are several points worthy of our reflection as we read our Lord's final words to the disciples.

Before our Lord ascended into heaven, He first "opened their minds" that is the disciples to the meaning of His words and to the scriptures. It is significant that this appearance of Jesus to the disciples occurs in the midst of a meal (note that Jesus asked for something to eat and they provided Him with a piece of fish in Lk 24:41–43). The combination of Jesus' words, the scriptures, a meal and the breaking of the bread are all elements of our current Eucharistic Liturgy (Liturgy of the Word and Liturgy of the Eucharist). Luke is giving us an insight into what should be happening every time we gather to experience the Risen Lord in our community prayer: We should recognize Him both in the Word of God proclaimed in the Scriptures and in the Eucharist celebrated on the altar. The experience of Jesus in the context of the Mass is one of the significant themes of Luke's Gospel because he is trying to encourage his community to find Jesus in the present rather than only remembering Him as He was during his earthly ministry or how He will be when He comes again. Luke wants us to realize that we can hear the Lord speaking to us every time the scriptures are proclaimed, and we can experience deep communion with Jesus every time we break bread in the Liturgy. It is important to note that the disciples' could not grasp the meaning of scripture on their own. Rather, understanding required that the Lord interpret the scripture for them through the lens of His death and resurrection. Only from the perspective of Jesus' passion can the Law and the Prophets (Old Testament) be properly understood. With Jesus' instruction, the disciples are now able to see how the words of the prophets were fulfilled in Him. As disciples, we are called to continue using the interpretative lens of Jesus' suffering, death, and resurrection any time we read the Old Testament or the New Testament. Such a clearly defined perspective protects us from taking Jesus' words out of context or interpreting other passages of scripture in ways that are not divinely intended. This is an important message for us as disciples because it helps us properly unlock the scriptures and teachings of the Lord for our lives.

> *How can the suffering, death, and resurrection of Jesus change the way you will read or understand your favorite passages of scripture?*
>
> *What other principles or interpretative lens other than the suffering, death, and resurrection of Jesus can people be tempted to use when interpreting scripture?*
>
> *What is the danger of reading scripture through the lens of only one part of Jesus' Paschal Mystery—that is through His suffering, death, or resurrection only— but not all of it?*
>
> *How do you experience the presence of Jesus in the Liturgy of the Word?*
>
> *What can we do as a faith community to help "open the minds" of people to understand the meaning of the scriptures for their lives?*
>
> *How do you think the disciples were trying to interpret the scriptures and Jesus' words before our Lord opened their minds to the correct way?*
>
> *How do we know when someone is quoting or interpreting scripture in a way that goes against the divine intention?*

After the Risen One opened their minds to the meaning of the Scriptures, He then simply says to them, "You are my witnesses". This is a very powerful statement for three reasons. First, we usually understand "witness" in a passive sense meaning that a witness is someone who sees something occur. While it is true that the disciples did "see" Jesus teach, heal, lead, forgive, suffer, die and rise, there is more to being a disciple than just being a spectator. Being a witness means communicating to others the reality of Jesus that we have been blessed to experience. It is an active role, not a passive role. Eyewitnesses must become Ministers of the Word for others (v. Lk 1:2). Second, being a witness of Jesus means that we live out the same radical love and trust in our lives that Jesus demonstrated in His passion, death, and resurrection. The word for "witnesses" in Greek is martyres that gives us the English word

"Martyr". Indeed, Martyrs are people who witnessed their faith in Jesus' death and resurrection at the cost of their own lives. Virtually all of the disciples who encountered the Lord in this scripture passage were put to death because of their faith. By remaining faithful and being united to Jesus in a death like his, they manifested their hope to share in His resurrection as well. We may not be called to physically die because of our faith but there are lots of ways in which we are called to be courageous witnesses of Jesus' death and resurrection each day. Third, Jesus tells His disciples that they are witnesses and that their witnessing is to have a practical effect in other people's lives. Namely, Jesus is commissioning the disciples and sending them forth with the great task of proclaiming the Gospel to all nations so that the nations might repent and share in the forgiveness of sins. The message of Jesus has a purpose and that purpose is to change our lives (repentance) and lead us to holiness (forgiveness of sins). This great commission is not an invention of early Christians as some contemporary adversaries of the Church claim. This great commission of Jesus is actually part of the fulfillment of scripture just as much as the death and resurrection of Jesus is the fulfillment of scripture (Is 52:13–53:12 foretells the suffering messiah; Hos 6:2 foretells the resurrection on the third day; Is 49:6 foretells the message of salvation and repentance to all nations). With Jesus' commission, the early Christians understood that being a disciple required three things: that we share with others what we ourselves have received, that we live out in our lives the mystery of Jesus' death and resurrection, and that we show the world what a life conformed to Christ looks like so others can be inspired and invited to become disciples as well.

> *How does this understanding of being a "witness" change your reading of this passage?*
> *How can people witness the death and resurrection of Jesus?*
> *What would it mean for you to move from being an eye-witness to becoming a Minister of the Word?*
> *If Jesus told you in your prayer that He wanted you to be His "witness", what would your first thought be?*
> *When have you been inspired to grow deeper in your faith life because of another person's lived example of faith?*

Why do you think Luke connects the forgiveness of sins to the experience of repentance (change of life) and what does that require of you?

Jesus goes on to instruct the disciples to remain in Jerusalem until He sends the "promise of my Father" and they are "clothed with power from on high". It is important to note that these are our Lord's last words in the Gospel of Luke and as such they are an enduring instruction to all disciples. In using the phrase "Promise of my Father" (repeated in Acts 1:4), Jesus is calling to mind the great fidelity of Abraham who trusted that God's promises to him would be fulfilled (v. Acts 2:39, 3:24–26, 13:32, 26:6 for additional texts that speak about God's promise being fulfilled). Indeed, God's promise is fulfilled in the sending of the Holy Spirit for whom the disciples were taught to pray (v. Lk 11:13). The phrase "power from on high" is reminiscent of the words the Archangel Gabriel spoke to Mary in Lk 1:35 when he announced to her, "The Holy Spirit will come upon you, and the power of the Most High" would descend upon her. It is no accident that Luke uses the same phrase to describe both the creative power of the Holy Spirit, which overshadowed Mary to become the Mother of the Lord, and the creative power of the Holy Spirit overshadowing the disciples to become Witnesses of the Lord as the Church (v. Acts 1:8). It is the same Spirit who brings about the birth of Jesus and the same Spirit who brings about the birth of the Church! Thus, God's promises are being fulfilled not only in the sending of Jesus but also in the mission of the Church—that's us! We saw what this powerful work of the Spirit could do in the life and ministry of Jesus (v. Lk 4:14). To sustain us in our mission, the Spirit continues to bring about the Divine Presence in the Eucharist at every Mass. Indeed, God continues to fulfill His promises to us and through us to the world.

What do you think is the primary work of the Spirit in the Church and world today?
What do you think the disciples thought when they realized that they were going to receive the same Spirit that empowered Jesus?
God can do great things with those who willingly, eagerly, and openly receive the Lord's Spirit (for example, Mary,

Jesus, the Eucharist). Why is it difficult for us to be receptive to the Holy Spirit in our lives?

When we think about the promises of God, we usually focus on how those promises affect us but this passage indicates that the promise of God will be fulfilled for the world through us. How might God use your life to fulfill His promise to the world?

At the end of this passage we are told that Jesus "blessed them" and departed from them. With that, the disciples were filled with joy and blessed God (v. Lk 24:50–53). Christians today have little idea of how problematic the ascension of Jesus was to disciples of the 1st Century. They missed the Lord and for them the ascension was sometimes perceived as "bad news" rather than a cause for joyful celebration. In order to understand why it was a reason for joy, it is necessary to remember that as long as Jesus was physically with the disciples they allowed Him to answer challenges, to respond to questions, to help the suffering, the poor, the cripple. In short, the disciples didn't do much themselves or show much initiative because Jesus was with them. There was a point when the disciples had to become active agents in fulfilling the mission of the Church. The ascension of Jesus does not mean the Lord's absence from the life of the Church; rather, Jesus' enthronement in heaven means that our Lord will continue to direct the work of the Church through the Holy Spirit. With the eyes of faith, Jesus is actually more present to the Church in His ascended glory than He was in His early ministry and that is good news! When Catherine of Siena in the XIV century used the image of the bridge to describe our journey to God, she remembered the passage of Jn 12:32, "When I am lifted up from the earth, I will draw everyone to myself," which is a clear reference to the Ascension as the ultimate effort of Christ to bring to the Father what He has won with his sacrifice.[7] It is also good news that Jesus has confidence that we are capable of carrying out the mission entrusted to us thanks to the gift of the Holy Spirit. Sometimes Jesus knows our capabilities better than we do. Sometimes, too, we only discover our capabilities when we are required to fulfill a challenging mission.

---

7. See St. Catherine of Siena, *The Dialogue*, n. 26.

How are you an active agent in carrying out the mission Jesus entrusted to us?

In what ways do you feel ill equipped to fulfill our Lord's commission?

How do you seek the guidance of the Holy Spirit in your life? Sometimes when we hear of tragic situations we can find ourselves praying, "Lord, do something!" and if we listen carefully in our prayer then we can hear the response, "I did do something, I created you." How does this story of prayer challenge you to be a witness of Jesus in the world today?

What can the Church do to help disciples discover and fulfill their role in fulfilling the mission Jesus entrusted to us?

SOLEMNITY OF PENTECOST

Our scripture passage for this Sunday comes from the Gospel of John 20:19–23. It is the scene of the Risen Christ sending the Apostles and "breathing" on them the Holy Spirit (an allusion to Genesis 2:7 when God "breathed" life into Adam who was molded from the clay of the earth). It is an appropriate passage because this Sunday we celebrate Pentecost as the moment when the first disciples were enlivened by the Holy Spirit and filled with enthusiasm to continue the mission of Jesus.

Although our current usage of the term enthusiasm often includes derogatory meanings, the term itself is actually meant to be positive and inspirational when understood in a Christian context. The word "Enthusiasm" comes from the two Greek words meaning "God within" (*en theos*). It refers to the experience a person has when "filled" with the Spirit of God. To be enthusiastic is not only to be energetic; it is to be courageous, motivated, and committed. The disciples had that experience and thus began to carry on the mission of Jesus fearlessly as His witnesses even unto death. Because of their enthusiasm, they were able to do the things that Jesus did. The gift of the Spirit transformed their fear into faith. It motivated them from being self–preserving to other–serving. It changes the mission of the church from just a human organization into a holy endeavor. Wow—the Spirit can transform lives and communities!

> *When in your life do you experience "enthusiasm" in the religious sense of being "filled with God"?*
> *What works of faith, that is the Mission of Jesus, have you been led to do as a result of your enthusiasm?*
> *What fears can cause people today to be "paralyzed" in their witness of faith?*
> *How can people see their religious observances with a "self-preserving" attitude rather than an "other-serving" attitude?*

In John 19:22 we are told that Jesus "breathed on them." That is an important statement for several reasons. First, it is a direct allusion to the action of God in Genesis 2:7 when the Lord first created humanity with an infusion of divine life. This connection to the first creation is reconfirmed in Ezekiel 37:9–10 and Wisdom 15:11 and speaks to the power of the Holy Spirit to transform the individual Christian. Jesus' action of breathing on the disciples is a statement that a new creation is taking place in the life and mission of the Church and that humanity is regenerated by the life-giving action of the Holy Spirit. This life-giving spiritual regeneration occurs in the Sacraments through Baptism (v. Jn 3:5) and the gift of the Holy Spirit in Confirmation. Second, the gift of the Spirit makes the community of believers, the Church, a fundamentally spiritual reality that carries out the works of God and not just human efforts. When our Lord breathed on the disciples, He gave them the Spirit that will continue to mediate His divine presence even in His physical absence. The Church, then, is the mystical Body of Christ in the world through which Jesus continues His ministry (v. 1 Pt 2:5 for a similar understanding of the Church as a "spiritual edifice"). Third, the gift of the Holy Spirit draws the disciples into the communion of life and love, which is the Holy Trinity. This incorporation into the divine mystery is manifested by the ability to know the mind of Christ and speak with a prophetic voice in our time (cf. Jl 2:28, 1 Cor 2:6–16, Jn 15:26–27 and 16:12–15).

> *How is the prophetic ministry of the Church carried out today both in the lives of individual disciples and through the body of the Church?*
>
> *What ministries in our faith community most clearly carry out the work of Christ today?*
>
> *What is the work Christ wants to accomplish through our faith community?*
>
> *What prevents people from being able to fully receive and live the spiritual regeneration of Baptism and Confirmation?*

The Holy Spirit's presence in Acts 2:1–11 was manifested by the ability of people to hear the message of the Gospel despite "foreign tongues" (different languages). That means the Holy Spirit is able to bring about a deep communion of faith that crosses the divisions of language and culture. As Saint Paul teaches us, when one member of the body suffers, the other members suffer with it; when one member rejoices, all the members rejoice (v. Rom 12:15). That is a statement of deep communion of life lived on a global scale. Sometimes, however, we can have narrow vision and become shortsighted when it comes to determining with who we want to be in communion.

> *When have you experienced your faith as something that unites you deeply with those whom you have never met?*
> *When do you most experience the "universal communion" of the Church?*
> *What are some of the attitudes or actions that can cause us to lose sight of the universal nature of the Church?*
> *Jesus sent His disciples to be witnesses to the world and that meant they were to go beyond the safe confines of their own community so that others could experience the joy and peace they had received from Jesus. What parts of our world most need Christian witnesses today?*

Saint Francis of Assisi used to gather with His brothers every year on the Feast of Pentecost in Assisi to pray for the Holy Spirit to be with them and guide them. Francis believed the power of the Holy Spirit could change the world. Through Francis, the Holy Spirit indeed did change the world. The Holy Spirit is able to transform fear into courageous faith, anxious concern into peace, alienation into reconciliation, and disciples into missionaries. That's quite a powerful work!

> *When do you pray to the Holy Spirit?*
> *Through whom is the Holy Spirit working in a particularly powerful way to transform the Church and the world today?*
> *What do you feel prompted to do by the Holy Spirit in your own life of faith?*

In Paul's letter to the Corinthians (1 Cor 12:3b–7, 12–13), he specifies that there are many gifts given by the Holy Spirit to individuals but that those gifts are for the benefit of everyone and not just the personal benefit of the one who receives the gift. Thus, God equips us and asks us to work together as one body (the Body of Christ) so that the ministry of Gospel can be accomplished through the Church. Each of us is given some gift that we can contribute toward carrying out that mission. Remember: There are no spare parts on the Body of Christ! If we are not actively engaged in the work of ministry then it's because we haven't found our place and not because there is no place for us.

> *What are some of the gifts or talents or skills with which you have been entrusted and how can these be used for the common good and the mission of the Church?*
> *What gifts do we most need in the Church today to carry out our mission better?*
> *What gifts, talents or skills are you still looking for a way to place at the service of the Gospel?*

Jesus says to the disciples, "As the Father has sent me, so I send you ... Receive the Holy Spirit." Thus, the Spirit is given so that we can continue the mission of Jesus in the world. Jesus was sent to make God known and in order to do that He had to make love known (because God is love). To make love known, He died on the cross for us in an ultimate witness of self-giving, sacrificial love for others even in the face of hatred, rejection, and persecution. The Holy Spirit empowers us to carry on the mission of making God known in our world through the same demonstration of love. Others come to know God (who is love) through us. That is why Jesus was sent and that is the purpose for which He sends us.

> *Who in our time most needs to know the love of God?*
> *Who is it most difficult to love?*
> *When people encounter the Church, do they experience it as proclaiming the love of God first and foremost?*
> *How have you come to know about the love of God through the witness of someone else?*
> *What would be different about our parish if Jesus appeared to us this Sunday and said, "Receive the Holy Spirit ... as the Father has sent me so I send you?" How do you think that personal challenge of Jesus would practically affect our community and its ministries?*

Take time this Sunday to pray for the gift of the Holy Spirit and to be accepting and responsive to that gift when it is given.

Breathe into me, Holy Spirit, that my thoughts may all be holy. Move in me, Holy Spirit, that my work, too, may be holy. Attract my heart, Holy Spirit, that I may love only what is holy. Strengthen me, Holy Spirit that I may defend all that is holy. Protect me, Holy Spirit, that I may always be holy.

Saint Augustine

SOLEMNITY OF THE MOST HOLY TRINITY

Our scripture passage for this Sunday comes from the Gospel of John 16:12–15. In this passage, Jesus informs the disciples that He has much more to tell them but that they cannot "bear" it now. The promised gift of the Holy Spirit will be the ongoing source of revelation and understanding for disciples.

The word Jesus uses for "bear" refers to a heavy weight that someone must carry. By using this term, Jesus is telling the disciples that their commitment to follow Him will be an act of faith that requires trust rather than an act of knowledge in which they are fully aware of the details and implications for their future lives. That is an important lesson for us. Sometimes we are hesitant to accept responsibilities or tasks unless we fully understand the full scope of how those duties will impact our lives. When it comes to faith, such a prerequisite for our commitment will lead us to reject opportunities to follow the Lord because we don't know where that decision will take us. Jesus asks us to commit our lives to Him without such fore knowledge or predictability. Our Lord does assure us that He will be with us in whatever trials come as a result of our discipleship. The challenge for us as disciples is to make an irrevocable commitment to God with our lives and not to insist that the Lord reveal the details of all He will ask of us.

How has your life of faith unfolded in ways that have demanded unforeseen sacrifice that is dying to self?

In calling us to be His disciples, Jesus is asking us to sign a "blank check" with our lives based on the trust that He will be with us no matter what. When have you given someone a "blank check" with your life? What was that experience like? When have you given God a "blank Check"?

How does your desire for certitude and knowledge lead you to reject opportunities for discipleship?

When have you opened your life in an act of trusting com-
mitment to the Lord and been overwhelmed by God's gra-
tuitous providence and grace?

Jesus then promises the gift of the Holy Spirit who will "lead them
to all truth". For Christians, Truth is a person (Jesus Christ) rather
than an intellectual concept and so the role of the Holy Spirit is
to lead us more deeply into the life and mystery of Jesus Himself.
Literally, the Holy Spirit will help us to see the relevance of our
lives today through the living experience of Jesus Christ. That is the
"Truth" into whom the Holy Spirit wants to lead us. What a powerful statement! When we recognize and understand the presence of
God in the events of our lives then we gain hope, encouragement,
and insight. The gift of the Holy Spirit does not impose this recognition and awareness on us; rather, we must prayerfully seek the
Spirit's guidance and interpretative influence through sustained
prayer and spiritual counsel.

In what situations do you see your life most related to the
life of Jesus?
How does the understanding of "Truth" as the person of
Jesus Christ change your perspective on what it means to
be a "truthful" person?
When and how do you pray for the Holy Spirit to illuminate
and guide you in your life?
What situations are difficult to bear and in which are you
still looking of the "Truth" that is Jesus?

This reading speaks well of the dynamic of the Trinity and our
relationship to God. Note that the Father is the origin of everything
yet the Father freely gives all to the Son. The Son in turn freely
gives all to the Spirit and the Spirit in turn freely gives all to us as
Jesus' disciples. We believe that we are made in God's image and
likeness; therefore, in order for us to truly be ourselves, we have
to participate in God's great cascade of love by not only receiving
from the Holy Spirit but also allowing the gifts of the Holy Spirit
to flow through us to others. The Holy Spirit is also our access
to the divine life of the Father and the Son; when we love as God
loves and grow in "Truth" then we share in the life of the Father
and the Son. We can only love as God loves if we first allow the

love of God to enter our lives and become manifest to the world through us in everything we say and do. The Holy Spirit is the gift of God's Love to invite and unite us into that great communion. Thus, in everything we do, we are called to focus our lives on the Father, through the Son, and in the Holy Spirit. Every action of the Christian life is to be an expression of our faith in the Trinity since it is the Holy Spirit who draws us, the Son who unites our humanity with His own divinity, and the Father who receives us in the Son.

> *What aspect of this reflection on the life of the Trinity most inspires you?*
> *With which Person of the Holy Trinity do you relate most easily?*
> *How can your prayer more effectively draw you into the triune life of God?*
> *When it comes to receiving God's life and love, how does the image of being a conduit of God's love poured out through us to the world challenge you in your discipleship?*
> *How has God worked in your life so as to draw you into the divine life?*

We only know certain things about the life of God because they have been revealed to us. In the doctrine of the Trinity, we know that God is One in Three Persons—a relational life of loving communion. That is the deepest nature of who God is and we believe that we are created in God's image and likeness. This revelation of the Trinity means that we (as a human community) can only express our deepest nature and identity when we mirror God's relational life of loving communion. It also means that we can only become our truest self when we give of ourselves to another in an act of complete selfless love even as the three divine Persons of the Trinity share a complete and perfect loving communion. This revelation means that we cannot be our truest self as long as we live in individuality, isolation or disregard for the needs of others. In order to fulfill our identity, humanity cannot realize its deepest nature until we love all people with equality and justice. Also, it means that divisions of every kind are a fundamental sin against the unity of God. In short, the life of the Trinity is the model for our human lives and relationships.

*How does this teaching challenge you to live out the mystery
of the Most Holy Trinity in your personal life, your family
life, and your professional life?*
*When do you feel most connected to humanity on a pro-
found level?*
*In what experiences or moments do you feel that you are
living fully your truest identity?*
*When has the experience of caring for a stranger become a
holy encounter in your life?*
*How can we as a faith community help people to better
understand the truth of the Trinity and the implications
for the Christian life?*

Let us reflect on our own with these words of St. Augustine:

> Let us believe that the Father and the Son and Holy Spirit are
> one God, creator and ruler of the entire creature, and that
> the Father is not the Son, nor the Holy Spirit the Father or
> the Son, but that there is a trinity of mutually related persons
> and a unity of equal substance. Let us seek to understand this
> from that very one, whom invoking, we wish to understand;
> and to the degree that is given to us to understand, let us
> seek to expound with so much care and solicitude of piety
> that even if we say something for something else, we should
> say nothing unworthy.[8]

---

8.   St. Augustine, *On the Trinity*, Book 9.

Solemnity of The Most Holy Body and Blood of Christ (Corpus Christi)

Our scripture passage comes from the Gospel of Luke 9:11b–17. It is the story of the Feeding of the 5,000 people. Although on the surface this passage seems to be just a miracle about the multiplication of loaves and fishes, it is really much more than that. This passage is a profound insight into the early Church's experience and understanding of the Eucharist (notice how Jesus first speaks to them about the Kingdom of God and then feeds them; this is the movement from the Liturgy of the Word to the Liturgy of the Eucharist). These insights have implications for us as disciples and offer various points for our reflection.

One of the first points to note is the contrast between how Jesus responds to the crowds and how the disciples respond to them. Jesus welcomes the crowd, teaches them, and cares for their needs; He cures them. The disciples, on the other hand, wanted to send the crowd away and let them care for themselves. Our Lord corrects the disciples' errant desire and cares for the crowds Himself. This is one of the first lessons of this passage and invites us to reflect on how we respond to those in need around us. Jesus saw people in need as opportunities for ministry; the disciples saw people in need as a burden to be avoided and dismissed. The Acts of the Apostles teaches us that charitable outreach for those in need was a distinguishing quality of the early Church (v. the relief efforts in Acts 4:32–37, 6:1–6, and 11:27–30). The first lesson of this passage, then, is that disciples should welcome those who come regardless of their need and not turn them away. For the Church to reflect the hospitality of Jesus, we must learn to see the need of others as an opportunity for our ministry rather than a burden to be avoided or dismissed. The disciples reveal the source of their errant thinking when they speak the reason for their desire to dismiss the crowds: "Five loaves and two fish are all we have, unless we ourselves go and buy food for all these people" (Lk 9:13). The disciples mistakenly thought that what they needed was an abundance of money. However, what they really needed was the faith to rely on the authority and power of Jesus to work through them. As proof for the twelve disciples to trust in God's power the Gospel tells us they picked up twelve baskets of fragments —one abundant basket for each disciple.

The message of this teaching is clear: disciples are instruments of God but not the source of God's gifts. The ministry of the Church depends upon God and is not defined by the resources we muster. When disciples understand themselves as instruments rather than origins of all good gifts then disciples become more generous towards others and more reliant on God's providential grace. It is tempting to think that the success of our ministry efforts today depend on having the right building, vestments, decorations, and so forth but that is not the case. The success of the Church's ministry depends on God; it always has and it always will. What God can do through us is infinitely greater than what we can do by ourselves. This teaching is especially true when it comes to the Eucharist. We do not make the Eucharist; the Eucharist is the gift of God that makes us! While we strive to offer the Lord the best of our first fruits, the quality of our gift never determines the quality of God's gift. We are only the dispensers of God's grace but not its origin. If we trust in our own resources and our own liability to solve the needs of our world then we will give in to the fear of insufficiency; it is only when we learn to trust in the power of God working through us that we can courageously face the overwhelming needs of the world.

> *How can we today be tempted to turn away those in need because we see them as burdens rather than opportunities for ministry?*
> *How can we be tempted to rely on our own limited resources rather than faithfully trust in God's eternal greatness working through us?*
> *How can our faith community fall into the trap of believing that the effectiveness of our ministry relies on only our physical resources rather than on the Lord?*

The next thing to notice is how Jesus Takes, Blesses, Breaks, and Gives the five loaves and two fish to the crowds and it becomes more than enough for them. First, we need to realize that these four verbs are very significant and are only used in this combination in the context of Eucharistic scenes (cf. Mk 14:22–23, Lk 22:19, 24:30, 1 Cor 11:23–24). Anytime that Jesus uses these four verbs the reader automatically knows that our Lord is celebrating the Eucharist. This insight should change the way we read this passage because Luke is trying to tell us what should be happening during our celebration of the Eucharist as well. We have already detected the need to welcome those in need and to trust in God's power to minister through human agency. Luke wants us to learn something essential about the Eucharist and so he includes a very important additional detail.

This brings us to the second point: there is important symbolism in the giving of "fish". The image of a fish was an early Christian symbol used to discretely communicate faith in Jesus and identify Christians to one another. Each letter of the Greek word for "FISH" (the Greek word is "IXTHUS") stood for a word: I=**I**esus (Jesus), X=**X**ristos (Christ), TH=**Th**eon (God), U=**U**ios (Son of), S=**S**oter (Savior). Thus, "FISH" was an acronym and spelled out the following statement of Christian faith: *Jesus Christ Son of God Savior.* When Jesus gave the bread, and fish, He was giving the crowds Himself! Literally, He was giving them, in the bread, the presence of "Jesus Christ Son of God Savior". This is one of the profound ways in which the Early Christians of the first century professed their belief in the Real Presence of Jesus in the Eucharist. The use of the four primary verbs ("take, bless, break, and give") as well as the use of IXTHUS are intentionally used in this text so as to help us realize that the miracle of the Eucharist we celebrate in every Mass is meant to affect our discipleship and change the way we relate to one another.

> *When has the Real Presence of Jesus in the Eucharist made a difference in the way you approach the Mass?*
> *How has the Eucharist been a catalyst of conversion for you in how you relate to others?*
> *What are symbols that we use today (like the FISH) that help people to realize the Real Presence of Jesus in the Eucharist?*
> *How do you think Jesus wants to change our faith community at every Mass?*

By having the crowds sit down in groups of fifty, most scripture scholars see an allusion to Christian communities of the first century. When Christians of the early Church met, they gathered in people's homes to celebrate the Eucharist. Thus, the size of a Christian Community in the first century was governed by the size of the individual person's house. When a community became too large for one house then they started a second community. Some scripture scholars think that the groups of fifty in this Gospel passage represent all the Christian communities (parishes) of the world separated by distance but united in one communion of faith and being fed by Jesus. This is a beautiful image of the universal Church truly in communion with God and one another through the Eucharist! No matter where we are, we are always part of the 5,000. We may only see our own group of fifty persons (or five-hundred persons) but we are part of a larger Church nonetheless. Jesus is always the one who teaches us (Liturgy of the Word) and feeds us (Liturgy of the Eucharist). The priests are to dispense the gifts of God, but they are not the origin of those gifts—Jesus is. This is a powerful understanding of the essential identity of the Church today and explains why we always need to look beyond the boundaries of our faith community to identify and remind ourselves of our deeper communion of faith in the universal Church.

> *How have you experienced the universal nature of the Church?*
> *What harms the universal unity of the Church today?*

Jesus gives the bread to the disciples to give to the crowd, but it's not their gift; it's Jesus' gift. Sometimes we lose sight of that truth and put too much focus on the priest who celebrates the Eucharist rather than on Jesus who is present in the Eucharist.

> *At what point does an "attraction" of faith become a "distraction" from faith (that is when people's focus is distorted)?*

The people were satisfied with the Eucharist and the disciples collected twelve baskets of "fragments". The word used for "fragments" (Greek: "*klasmata*") is the same word used in other first century Christian writings to refer to the fragments (remnants) of the Eucharist. Today, we gather the "fragments", or remaining pieces, and place them in the tabernacle. Like the early Church, we treasure the gift of the Eucharist as an enduring gift of Jesus. We reserve the Eucharist in the Tabernacle for purposes of personal prayer and for the distribution of Communion to the sick and home-bound. In all of these actions, we are showing our respect for Jesus in the Eucharist. In addition to the reservation of the remaining Eucharist in the tabernacle, we also show our reverence for any fragments by placing special cloths on the altar (called "Corporals") to preserve any possible pieces of the Host or drops of the Precious Blood that may accidentally fall.

> *What signs of respect and reverence for the Eucharist have inspired your faith?*
>
> *How do you show reverence for the presence of Jesus (IXTHUS) in the Tabernacle?*
>
> *When has the presence of Jesus in the Tabernacle been a focus of your prayer?*
>
> *Have you ever been distracted by someone's lack of reverence for the Eucharist or for the presence of Jesus in the tabernacle and how was that lack of reverence demonstrated?*

Let us pray with St. Faustina:

> I adore You, Lord and Creator, hidden in the Most Blessed Sacrament. I adore You for all the works of Your hands, that reveal to me so much wisdom, goodness and mercy, O Lord. You have spread so much beauty over the earth and it tells me about Your beauty, even though these beautiful things are but a faint reflection of You, incomprehensible Beauty. And although You have hidden Yourself and concealed Your beauty, my eye, enlightened by faith, reaches You and my soul recognizes its Creator, its Highest Good, and my heart is completely immersed in prayer of adoration.

SECOND SUNDAY IN ORDINARY TIME

Our scripture passage for this Sunday comes from the Gospel of John 2:1–12. In this text we read of Jesus and His disciples participating in the Wedding at Cana and the miracle of water becoming wine. This passage is more than just a simple miracle story. It is really a teaching on discipleship that offers insights into the essential elements of Christian marriage and the necessity of obedience to the word of Jesus by "doing what he tells us." There are several points on which to reflect in this passage.

The image of wine is important to understand. In the scriptures, wine is a symbol of joy, happiness, friendship, celebration and blessing. Despite the best planning and human efforts of the couple, they could not sustain the "wine" in their marriage celebration. It is only when the wine runs out that what began as a human celebration (the result of human planning and effort) could become a truly holy celebration (the result of God's action and intervention). This is a very important message for all of us: We can't do it on our own. We need Jesus, and we need to remember that the wine He offers is always better than the wine we provide for ourselves.

> *When have you "run out of wine" in your life?*
> *Whom do you see running out of wine around you today?*
> *How can we as a faith community help people discover the new wine with which Jesus wants to enrich our lives?*
> *What are the ways in which married couples can try to provide for themselves rather than reaching out for the guidance, presence, and the gift of Jesus in their marriages?*

The couple at Cana had invited quality people of faith to their celebration and it is a good thing they did! They invited Mary who interceded for them and brought their concern to Jesus. They also invited Jesus who came because they asked Him to be there. With people like that in their lives, they were surrounded by an encouraging group of friends and family who could help them through any difficulty. The truth is that we are equally dependent on other people to get us through the difficulties of our lives as well. Oftentimes we hear about others who don't survive a crisis because they didn't have a supportive community around them that prayed for them in time of difficulty and encouraged them to remain faithful to their life commitments. This passage teaches us the importance of surrounding ourselves with people of faith who will pray for us, intercede for us, encourage us, and help us overcome difficult moments. This is a particularly important message for marriages.

Who are the people in your life helping you in your times of trouble?

How do you consciously invite Jesus to be a part of your life, your marriage, your family and your work each day (Remember, He wasn't there by accident; He was there by invitation)?

Who needs your encouragement and prayers to help them remain faithful to their commitments?

Whom do you identify with in this passage and why: Jesus, the servants, Mary, or the couple?

As you read this passage, notice how obedient the waiters are to Jesus' instructions. Mary was very specific on the need for obedience to, and utter confidence in, the word of Jesus when she said, "Do whatever he tells you." The Gospel passage goes on to tell us, "So they filled them to the brim." Because of their faithful obedience and cooperation with Jesus' instruction, the Lord was able to do incredible things that the waiters never could have accomplished on their own. It must have seemed strange to the waiters to be filling water jars when the problem was obviously a lack of wine but they followed Jesus' instruction nonetheless. The bottom line is that they trusted in Jesus' word and that our Lord understood the situation better than they did and so they willingly followed His direction in their lives even when they didn't understand it themselves.

Who is someone you know of who is an example of faithful obedience to God's word?

How do you seek to know God's will for your life?

When have you followed God's will when it didn't make sense to you and something wonderful happened as a result?

What teaching of Jesus in the Gospels do you find most difficult to live out in your life as a disciple?

Third Sunday in Ordinary Time

Our scripture passage for this Sunday comes from the Gospel of Luke 1:1–4 and 4:14–21. In this text we read of how Jesus returned to Galilee to start His public ministry by visiting the synagogue in Nazareth. As He did so, Jesus summarized His mission by reading from the Prophet Isaiah. The following are some points to note about this passage and how it applies to our lives as disciples.

Jesus begins by saying, "The Spirit of the Lord is upon me because he has anointed me." The Hebrew word for "Anointed" is "Messiah" and the Greek word for "Anointed" is "Christ". Jesus is introducing Himself as the Messiah and Christ who brings the Spirit of the Lord into the world. In doing so, He is stating that mission is not of his own choosing but is given to Him by God the Father. This has implications for us as Christian disciples because in our baptism we are incorporated into the Body of Christ and share in the "anointed" identity of Jesus (thus the name "Christian"). His mission is now our mission because we are members of his mystical body. Thus, we are not to simply read about Jesus carrying out His ministry in the Gospel; rather, what Jesus does is meant to guide us in how we should be acting. From the moment of our baptism our life is not our own; instead, it is Christ who lives in us.

How can you come to know more clearly your mission in Christ?
How do you know when you are carrying out the will of God?

Secondly, Jesus says that He is being sent, "To bring glad tidings to the poor." The word for "glad tidings" or "good news" is also interpreted as "Gospel". His message will be good news for those who are "the poor" because He will proclaim God's rich and generous mercy. He will also show in his actions and ministry that God has a preferential option for those who are powerless, poor, and suffering. The cultural world of Jesus' time believed that God rewarded the "good" and "favored" people with material riches. Thus, riches were a sign of God's favor and approval. Jesus changes the value system of His world to reflect a different set of values—the values of the Kingdom of God. In our poverty, we can know our need for God and welcome Jesus as our Savior. In order for the Gospel to be "good news" for us, therefore, we have to know our poverty. For example, the times when we can't do what we want for ourselves or for others, when we lack what it takes to make it on our own, or when we realize our need for God.

> *How does this passage help you to identify and articulate your own poverty?*
> *When do you most realize your need for God?*
> *When do you feel most limited or powerless in your ability to help others?*

Third, Jesus says that He will bring "Release to captives". The Greek word for "release" is actually the same as the word for "Forgiveness" (*apoluo*). In His ministry, Jesus will release so many people bound by sin, weakness, and destructive habits. He will set them free to become the people God intends them to be. However, He can only do that for those who know their need for freedom, own their sin, and seek His forgiveness. Sometimes people who are captive and paralyzed in sin cannot even imagine what their life could be like. Oftentimes, too, people lose hope and begin to believe that their sin is greater than God's mercy. When Jesus shares the gift of forgiveness with people, He not only gives them freedom to move on with their lives but He also gives them peace and healing so that they no longer define themselves by their failures or wounds.

> *Who do you know of who is "captive" in cycles of sin?*
> *How has the Sacrament of Reconciliation helped you experience the freedom, healing, and peace of forgiveness?*
> *When have you seen someone lose hope because of an experience of sin or failure in their lives?*

Fourth, Jesus says that He will bring "Sight to the blind." In the Gospels, people gain physical sight but they also gain spiritual insight to be able to see God present in their lives, other's lives, and the world around them. Their eyes will be opened to see God present in Jesus even on the cross. The ultimate sight Jesus gives us is the ability to see our lives as God sees us and to know God's love for us—something we don't always see in everyday experience but which is there nonetheless. We also begin to see others differently once we have that spiritual sight and, when we do, we love and care for our neighbor in need because we have come to recognize each of them as a brother and sister.

> *What has helped open your eyes to see the presence of God acting in your life?*
> *How have your eyes been opened to see others, even strangers, as brothers and sisters in Christ?*
> *What attitudes can cause us to become blind to God's presence or to seeing others as brothers and sisters?*

Fifth, Jesus says that He will let the "oppressed go free." Jesus freed those oppressed by unclean spirits; He healed those who were debilitated with physical injury and illnesses, and He even set free those who were condemned by others. In doing so, He helped people overcome their burdens and to move forward with their lives. He helped them to be better people, more capable people, and more grateful people. He helped them become people who could walk with Him in discipleship by removing those things that hindered them. Many of the people Jesus encountered were oppressed by the social and cultural world of their time. That list included women, gentiles, lepers, criminals, and tax collectors. They were all people who were not allowed an equal place in Jesus' time but to whom our Lord will give a place among His flock.

> *Who experiences oppression in our society?*
> *How are people held back or prevented from developing their potential today?*
> *How can you help liberate someone you know who is oppressed?*

Jesus ends His reading of the Prophet Isaiah by stating simply "Today, this scripture passage is fulfilled in your hearing." The emphasis in this passage is on the word "today." He's saying that this passage is being fulfilled for us right now and for Christians of all time. This is our "today." It is the message that we are the poor, the blind, the captive, the oppressed and that the Gospel has good news to bring us. That good news comes to us through the ministry of the

Church and sometimes we are called to be the ones who bring that good news to others as well. When Jesus said that the "Spirit of the Lord has anointed him," we need to remember that in our Baptism, the Spirit of the Lord anointed us as well! It's now our mission to carry on his mission. We must look to the world around us to see who is poor, who is blind, who is oppressed, who is captive and we do what we can to fulfill this passage for them today.

> *Who are the poor, the blind, the oppressed, and the captive in your lives, families, offices, and friendships?*
> *How can the Lord minister to them through you?*

FOURTH SUNDAY IN ORDINARY TIME

Our scripture passage for this Sunday comes from the Gospel of Luke 4:21–30. It may be helpful to read the complete scene beginning at verse 13 where we have the full account of Jesus' first action of His public ministry as He goes to the synagogue in Nazareth and announces His mission. Basically, He said that the Spirit has sent Him to bring good news to the poor, give sight to the blind, and set captives free. Who could argue with something as great as that? In today's Gospel passage we see that some people will resist Jesus' mission. As disciples, we need to study this passage so that we might be aware of the subtle ways in which we can end up resisting Jesus' mission as well.

The initial response to Jesus' proclamation is very positive. The crowds in Nazareth love it when Jesus says He's going to do these great things. In this week's passage, we find out why they loved it—because the crowds thought they could control Jesus as "one of their own" and keep His good works and blessings for themselves only. That's when Jesus tells them the story of the Prophet Elijah and the Widow as well as the story of the Prophet Elisha and Naaman the Leper. The basic message of these accounts is simple: God's mercy is for everyone, even the Gentiles. Sometimes others experience God's mercy even when we don't. That's what made the crowds angry and explains why they turned on Jesus. They rejected his teaching when He told them that His mission was for others, even Gentiles, and not just for the people of Nazareth. In their anger they sought to put Jesus to death. They didn't want to follow God when God didn't do what they wanted. There's a powerful teaching in that passage for us as well.

> *How many times do we find ourselves challenged by the Gospel and the teachings of Jesus?*
>
> *What do we do when we don't "like" what Jesus has to say to us?*
>
> *In rejecting his teaching, we are rejecting the Lord. What part of the Gospel message is most rejected by the today's world?*

What message of the Gospel do we find most difficult to
live and fulfill?
When has Jesus "acted" in our life in such a way that we
don't like it or maybe even wanted to reject it?
When have we been angry because others have been blessed
by God's mercy while we haven't been?

The response of Jesus to this experience of rejection and hostility teaches us how to respond to similar moments in our lives as disciples. Jesus did not shy away from speaking the truth even when He knew it was unpopular and people would be upset. He was not afraid to face hostility and even rejection. His response was to simply continue His way when such things happened. It is easy for us to be deterred by other people's negative reactions and to spend enormous time and energy trying to convince others of our perspective. Jesus simply spoke what was a truth and then continued with His mission rather than stay in Nazareth for the purpose of convincing the townspeople. As disciples, we will not always, or even often, be successful in our efforts to share the gift of faith. Sometimes the greatest witness we can give is to move on when faced with rejection so as to find other settings where our efforts will be successful. This is not an excuse for failure; rather, it is an encouragement for perseverance, creativity, and perspective. There are many ways in which a disciple can be impeded in following the Lord; one of those ways is when we allow anger, rejection, or failure to cause us to stop moving forward.

When do you know when it's time to move on from a par-
ticular effort of your discipleship?
When have you experienced hostility, rejection, or failure
in an effort to share your faith?
When have some people in your life been envious or resent-
ful because of the time and energy you spend with ministries
or doing good for others?

FIFTH SUNDAY IN ORDINARY TIME

Our scripture passage for this Sunday comes from the Gospel of Luke 5:1–11. In this passage, we hear about Jesus using Peter's boat to teach the crowds and then directing Peter's fishing efforts. When he follows Jesus' direction, Peter brings in an overwhelming catch. Peter realizes what has just happened and that Jesus was responsible for the success of his efforts. Peter is afraid and, after focusing on his inadequacy, asks Jesus to leave. Instead, Jesus asks Peter to follow Him and to "look forward" with trust, not backward on his faults. In the Gospel of Luke, Peter becomes the first disciple in this moment and Jesus tells him "from now on, you will be catching men." This is not the first time Jesus has met Peter in Luke's Gospel. In fact, Jesus had already been to Peter's home and healed his mother-in-law. Thus, it is within the context of an existing friendship that Jesus issues the invitation to deeper discipleship. This passage offers several points for our reflection.

It was one thing for Peter to let Jesus use his boat to teach the crowds, it's another thing for Peter to let Jesus direct his professional life and efforts as a fisherman. Jesus is slowly asking for more and more of Peter's life and for Peter to follow the Lord's direction more and more obediently. What began as a low-risk temporary borrowing of Peter's resources, that is using his boat, slowly moved into directing his professional efforts and finally became a life-long commitment of discipleship. This is how Jesus works with us as well. The Lord prepares us for greater commitments of faith by starting with lesser commitments. Sometimes we experience this deepening relationship of trust and commitment by getting involved in a low-risk ministry and then slowly increasing our involvement until we want nothing other than God's complete direction throughout our whole life. The individual steps of discipleship do not require us to take leaps beyond our capability, but the steps of discipleship oftentimes do invite us to move beyond our comfort.

*How has the Lord started to ask for more of your life in the
past year?*
*When have you experienced a moment when the Lord (or
faith) has sought to direct your professional life and actions
in a specific way?*
*How can our parish ministries provide realistic stepping
stones of discipleship that lead people deeper and deeper
into a committed life of faith?*
*Where are gaps in our parish ministries, which need to be
filled with "intermediate" stepping stones leading towards
deeper discipleship?*

Peter had been fishing all night using his own talents and abilities
but his nets kept coming up empty. Just imagine how Peter must
have felt at the end of his fishing expedition knowing that he would
return home with nothing to show for his effort. Think, too, of how
his family depended upon his daily success for their livelihood
and wellbeing. Those empty nets were more than just a personal
disappointment for Peter; those empty nets placed his life and the
lives of his family in distress. Certainly Peter was disappointed,
desperate, and searching for something to redeem his situation. It
is only when he follows God's will that his nets are finally filled. That
image of the empty net is something we all can relate to. Think of
how many times we experience that emptiness in life, relationships,
work, hobbies, and so forth. Emptiness craves to be filled and it is
easy to find superficial ways in which to temporarily alleviate our
craving for fulfillment. Sometimes people try to remove the pain
of their emptiness with unhealthy relationships, abuse of food and
drink, drugs, unhealthy entertainment, constant shopping, or over-
commitment to work. These false efforts only leave us unsatisfied
and emptier than before. Jesus allows us to experience emptiness
as a way of inviting us into deeper relationship with Him. Thus,
our emptiness is meant to be a motivation to seek out a life-giving
relationship with God who alone can fill us.

With what do we try to fill our emptiness?
*Peter never would have followed Jesus' direction had his
nets not been empty. How do you turn to the Lord in your
emptiness?*

What does the Lord direct you to do when you ask Him to fill your emptiness?
Peter would have not realized the power of Jesus had the Lord not stepped into his life that day and spoke to his emptiness. How can we as a parish reach out to people to help them fill their emptiness in a healthy and faithful way?

Peter was a fisherman. That was his skill, talent, profession, and business. Jesus does not tell Peter to walk away from those talents or skills. Rather, Jesus tells Peter that he is to use his professional talents, skills and abilities for the work of the Gospel: He is to "fish" for men. That is a message of stewardship for us as well. We are to use our time and talent for the work of the Gospel. Peter would have to apply the same hard work, perseverance, problem-solving, and teamwork skills that he used to catch fish in order to carry out his ministry in the early Church. God has gifted all of us with opportunities and abilities that are needed for the work of the Gospel and not just to enrich our personal lives. As disciples, we follow Jesus with our whole life and place our whole being at the Lord's service including our abilities and opportunities.

What are some of your professional talents, abilities or skills that you think could be of benefit to the mission of the Gospel and how might you put them to use as an expression of your discipleship?
When Jesus spoke to Peter, he told him "You will be a fisher of men" as a way of refocusing his professional skills. If Jesus spoke to you, what phrase would the Lord use to refocus your professional life into a mission of discipleship?
Who is someone you know who serves the Lord through his or her professional life?
As a baptized member of the Body of Christ, each of us is given a share in Jesus' ministry to the Church and the world. In which ministry do you most enjoy participating and why?

Peter was tempted to focus on his fear and failure so as to excuse himself from the invitation of Jesus. When it comes to being a witness of our faith, we can experience certain fears as well: fear of unworthiness, fear of being left alone, fear of failure, fear of insufficiency, fear of inadequacy, fear of sacrifice. As long as Peter was focused on his fear and failure he could not be a disciple who would follow Jesus with confidence and fidelity. Rather, his fears would hold him back from taking the risk of faith. Peter asked Jesus to leave him and withdraw the invitation to discipleship rather than ask Jesus for the grace and strength to accept discipleship. Jesus responds by telling Peter to focus on the future rather than being held back by his past. This is a powerful message for all Christians because we, too, can allow our inadequacies, weaknesses, and fears to hold us back from following the Lord. Sometimes we give in to feelings of unworthiness like Peter. Whatever our reason may be for shying away from the invitation to deeper discipleship, Jesus wants us to focus on the future and not the past.

> *How do you relate to Peter's desire to exempt himself from the call of discipleship?*
> *If Jesus were to say to you, "Come, Follow Me", what would you be afraid of?*
> *Peter was also concerned that his personal sinfulness and weakness would prevent him from being a good disciple. What are excuses people use today to excuse themselves from the challenge of faith?*
> *How can we as a parish help people to confidently focus on the future with God rather than being held back by their past?*

Lastly, when the text says that they "followed him", Luke uses the verb "to follow" in the imperfect tense. Luke does that a lot! The imperfect tense means that following Jesus is not something that happens only in a one-time moment but that discipleship is an ongoing decision, which must be lived out every day and every moment for the rest of our lives. Each hour of every day we are in the process of "following" the Lord.

> *As you look through the past week, when has it been most difficult for you to "follow the Lord" in the ongoing experience of discipleship?*
> *How can people mistakenly believe that being a Christian disciple is a momentary experience rather than an ongoing action that is lived out daily?*

Sixth Sunday in Ordinary Time

Our scripture passage for this Sunday comes from the Gospel of Luke 6:17, 20–26. This text contains the Lucan version of the Beatitudes. It is significant that in Luke's Gospel Jesus gives these Beatitudes on the Plain rather than the mountain (as in Matthew's Gospel). The plain is where life is lived and so Luke is telling us that these are to practical instructions for everyday life. These Beatitudes present a direct challenge to disciples of all times because of their blunt and radical demands. Although people are generally more familiar with the Beatitudes as they are presented in Matthew's Gospel, Luke's version possesses a starkness that prevents them from being spiritualized or reduced to mere platitudes. Let's look at these principles for discipleship and see how they are meant to guide and sustain the lives of Christians. Our study will focus on each blessing and the associated woe corresponding to it.

"Blessed are you who are poor / Woe to you who are rich"— Luke's Gospel is often referred to as the "Gospel of the Poor" because he has more teachings on the right use of material possessions and care for the less fortunate than any other gospel. The term "poor" can mean those who are marginalized and throughout the Old Testament there are various verses that identify God as the protector of the poor. It is not that God delights in people's poverty but that God does care for those whom society does not care for. Thus, God's preferential love for the poor is a statement of the Lord's mercy and compassion rather than a statement of poverty in itself. In Luke 18:22 Jesus will issue a challenge to a would-be follower to sell all he has, give to the poor and then follow Him; this is a challenge to use wealth in a way that manifests a true trusting dependence on God. The consolation of the poor is the reign of God's Kingdom in their lives (cf. Lk 2:25 and especially 16:25). The rich, on the other hand, are presented in Luke's Gospel as receiving their sense of security, value, and dignity from their wealth rather than God. In the time of Jesus, it was believed that material wealth was a sign of God's favor and blessing; Jesus challenges this understanding and calls His disciples to a radically-lived dependence on God and to find God's favor in their obedience to the Lord's will rather than their material blessings. The Early Christian community was a generally poor community in part because many people lost their possessions as a consequence of their faith. Thus, to be poor may well be the resulting sacrifice one faced when a person chose to adhere to their Christian decision. The Acts of the Apostles indicates that those members of the early Church who did possess wealth shared it with the community for the needs of all. Today we have the expression, "Live simply so that others can simply live" which may capture some of the message of this beatitude. The corresponding woe is a warning to those who trust in themselves and their own resources rather than living a practical trust in God alone and generously sharing their resources for the good of others. It may also be a condemnation of those who faltered in their faith commitment when required to make a choice between their faith in Christ Jesus or their material possessions.

> *When are Christians today faced with the choice between pursing personal material wealth or fidelity to Jesus?*
> *How can people today be tempted to find their security, value, and dignity based in their possessions rather than in their relationship with God?*
> *What does the phrase, "Live simply so that others can simply live" mean to you and how does it challenge you?*
> *How does God care for the poor today?*
> *Who exemplifies this beatitude in the world today?*

"Blessed are you who are now hungry / Woe to you who are now filled"—In Mary's *Magnificat* (v. Lk 1:46–56), we already heard similar words as we find in these Beatitudes when she said, "He has thrown down the rulers from their thrones but lifted up the lowly (poor); The hungry He has filled with good things; the rich He has sent away empty" (Lk 1:52–53). Jesus will "fill" the hungry with good things when He multiples the loaves and fishes in Luke 9:12–17. Jesus will also tell us a parable about a man named Lazarus who was filled after his own period of hunger in Luke 16:21. In the Acts of the Apostles, we are told that the early Church continued Jesus' ministry of filling people's hunger (v. Acts 2:45, 6:14, 11:28–30). It is important to understand these other passages in order to gain insights into how the hungry are blessed while those who are filled are not. As with the previous beatitude, the answer may lie in the early Christian experience. Those who cared only for themselves had plenty of food (cf. the parable of the Rich Fool in Lk 12:13–21) while those who cared for others often experienced personal inconvenience and sacrifice (v. the teaching on the Widow's Mite in Lk 21:1–4). The Early Christians who experienced hunger were the ones who had shared their food with the less fortunate or the ones who were dispossessed because of their faith decision. Jesus fills the hunger of those who trust in Him but those who care only for themselves are condemned to future emptiness. The Church is blessed to have received this mission of carrying on this work of filling the hungers and longings of Christians who suffer need because of their decisions of generosity and faith.

> *How do you care for those who are hungry?*
> *When has your generosity for others actually impinged upon your ability to pursue your own interests?*
> *What reasons lead people today to care only for themselves and their families rather than for the larger community?*
> *Who exemplifies this beatitude in the world today?*

"Blessed are you who are now weeping / Woe to you who laugh now"—Weeping is an expression of pain or sorrow. For the Prophets, the greatest reason to weep is that the people commit apostasy by turning away from God to pursue false idols or to reject the lived demands of the Covenant (especially justice and care for the less fortunate). Weeping is also presented as a sign of repentance and Saint Paul even says that in 2 Cor 7:10: "For godly sorrow produces a salutary repentance." In the Gospel of Luke, we have several passages where people are presented weeping in a virtuous and faithful way (v. the woman who washes Jesus' feet with her tears in Lk 7:32, 38, the moment of Jesus weeping over Jerusalem because of its failure to repent in Lk 19:41, and the women who weep when they see Jesus unjustly condemned and carrying His cross on the way to Calvary in Lk 23:28). All these scenes indicate that weeping is the appropriate action for those who mourn injustice, who desire to repent of their sins, who are saddened by others lack of faith, rejection of God, or disinterest in living the Gospel. Laughter also has a rich biblical background to it. In the Prophets we read of people who laughed in response to disaster (v. Hos 4:3, 10:5, Am 8:8, Is 24:4, Jer 4:8). That laughter demonstrated their entertainment at other people's misfortune. Later in Luke's Gospel we will read of a rich fool who "makes merry" (that is laughs) in the pursuit of his own temporary interests while ignoring the eternal priorities of the Kingdom of God (v. Lk 12:13–21). In the Letter of James, we read the admonition to change your laughter into Joy—an instruction that does not esteem sadness for its own sake but cautions against misplaced values and short-sighted concerns. When our values are out of order then we can find humorous what causes sadness to God. In Luke 8:52 we see the danger of wrong values when the crowd weeps for the wrong reason (the presumed death of the girl) and the crowd laughs for the wrong reason (the ridicule of Jesus' call to faith). Jesus proclaims Blessed those disciples who share the values of God and weep over the causes of divine sadness while rejoicing in the causes of divine gladness.

> *What makes you sad in the course of an average day?*
> *What typically causes you to laugh?*
> *How has the experience of sorrow led you to repentance?*
> *When have others' rejection of God and the values of the Gospel caused lasting sadness in you?*
> *When do you find it easy to laugh at other people's misfortune?*

"Blessed are you when they hate you, and when they exclude and insult you/ Woe to you when all speak well of you"—There is a strong emphasis on the experience of rejection in the beatitude that ranges from attitudes (hate) to actions (set you aside) and words (scorn you). Many early Christians did experience this rejection as they were expelled from synagogue communities, families, and other groups (social and professional) as a result of their decision to be disciples of Jesus. What was meant to be a punishment has become a cause of praise! Rather than seeing moments of rejection as a cause of humiliation, disciples are charged to see such experiences as a cause of honor and a reason for rejoicing. Jesus experienced such rejection (v. Lk 5:24 and 6:5) and following the Lord means being willing to embrace the same difficulties that He faced. Sometimes the proof of our true discipleship is only when others begin to react to it that is when it is no longer a private, personal, interior experience but something that is now being witnessed and affecting the world around evoking both a positive and negative response. We see this negative response to authentic discipleship in the crowds who put Stephen to death (v. Acts 7:52) when he carries on the prophetic ministry of Jesus in the early Church. False prophets, on the other hand, told the people what they wanted to hear and were praised for it. Oftentimes this false message led the people to dismiss the need for repentance and suffer disaster as a result. The goal of a Christian disciple is not to have a good reputation and win the praise of others but to faithfully and courageously speak God's word both when it is "convenient or inconvenient" (v. 2 Tm 4:2), when it is welcomed and when it is not welcomed.

> *When are you tempted to say what people want to hear ("keep the peace") rather than what they need to hear so they can be challenged to become the people God intends them to be?*
> *When has your decision to be a disciple cost you something because of other people's negative reaction?*
> *What are attitudes, actions, and words that are used today to marginalize or exclude Christians and Christian values from public life?*
> *Who is a person you know that has willingly experienced great sacrifice for their faith commitment?*
> *What does the statement "Sometimes the proof of our true discipleship is only when others begin to react to it" mean to you?*

SEVENTH SUNDAY IN ORDINARY TIME

Our scripture passage for this Sunday comes from the Gospel of Luke 6:27–38. Last Sunday's reflection on the Beatitudes in Luke's Gospel demonstrated that our Lord's teaching is directed to the practical actions of daily discipleship. This week's scripture passage continues this challenging teaching in what is commonly referred to as the Sermon on the Plain. There are several important lessons we can learn for our lives as disciples.

There are few verses in scripture more challenging than our Lord's commandment to love our enemies. This commandment becomes more powerful when we realize that the New Testament understanding of love requires actually acting in a way that seeks the good of the other person. This teaching reminds disciples that there is no place for retaliation or vengeance in the lives of disciples. It can be easy for us to limit our kindness and love based on how people will accept it, respond to it and even return it. Jesus' commandment to love challenges us to act in a way that is not based on how other people will respond. Rather, Jesus reminds us that we are to act in a way that reflects God's action to us. This is the "Divine Rule" (which is different from the Golden Rule): no longer are we to treat others as we would have them treat us; rather, we are to treat others as God would. Such a love requires us to be generous, proactive, and open toward others who are hostile and antagonistic toward us. This command is just as challenging today as it was when Jesus gave it to His disciples nearly two thousand years ago! When it comes to loving our enemies, we are usually content to simply not cause harm. However, this commandment calls us to be proactive in actually seeking the other person's good. For this reason, Jesus specifically instructs us to bless and pray for those who cause us harm (v. also similar teachings in the New Testament epistles of 1 Cor 4:12 and 1 Pt 2:23). It is also a love that calls us to practice a universal generosity and charity that does not discriminate or give in to favoritism.

When have you shown kindness towards those who are your "enemies"?
When have you been called to do what is "good" for another person even though they don't want it?
What are some of the excuses you use so as to dismiss yourself from showing selfless love for others in their time of need?

Through this heroic witness of God's love, disciples will be people whose actions are not governed by other people's response. Authentic disciples do not expect anything in return when they love, show generosity, demonstrate patience, or endure hardship. Rather, disciples are motivated to love by something beyond this world: They are motivated by a desire to be children of the Most High who demonstrate in their lives the same love God has for everyone. Being a "child of the Most High" means that we imitate the attitudes, values and actions of the Father. God loves us when we are good and bad. If we are God's children, then we will mirror that love. When Christians are motivated in this way then they are not frustrated, disappointed or angered when their love is not acknowledged, appreciated or returned. There are other scholars, both ancient and modern, who propose other reasons for loving one's enemies but the motivation Jesus specifies is unique.

Who loved you when you didn't expect it or deserve it?
Love forms us into the people we are. Who are the three primary people whose love has formed your life (even acts from a stranger)?
Who are the people who most need your love now to form them?
In your baptism you became a child of God. What resources are available to help you learn more about your Heavenly Father so that you can better imitate His values, attitudes, and actions?

Lastly, Jesus establishes the defining hallmark of Christian discipleship when He commands us to be merciful (compassionate) even as your Father is merciful (v. Lk 6:36). This commandment is very similar to that of Matthew 5:48 in which Jesus commands His disciples to be perfect as God is perfect and is based on the commandment given to Moses in Leviticus 19:2 to be holy as God is holy. For Luke, holiness is best expressed in mercy and compassion for others—regardless of who they are and especially when they don't deserve it. Luke's Gospel emphasizes the compassion of God toward the suffering, destitute and disadvantaged more than any other Gospel. For Luke, mercy is the defining characteristic of God and therefore it must also be the defining characteristic of a Christian disciple. This mercy is expressed in three specific ways: Disciples do not judge others, disciples do not condemn others, and disciples readily forgive others.

The motivation for a disciple to behave in this way is not based on fear of retribution from others or on the disciple's own moral goodness; rather, it is based on how God will respond. If disciples judge others, then God will judge them with the same criteria and standards! If disciples condemn others, then God will condemn them with the same severity! If disciples forgive, then God will forgive them—and that is something we all know we need. Disciples are motivated by their desire to experience God's mercy and so that motivation should guide how they express mercy for others. God will use for us the same standard we use for one another. This is a profoundly challenging teaching that should cause us to carefully reconsider our interactions with both friend and foe so as to be instruments of God's mercy in all situations we face.

> *Why do you think Luke chose the quality of mercy to be the defining hallmark of Christian discipleship?*
> *What is the difference between judgment and discernment for Christian discipleship?*
> *How can disciples remind themselves of their own need for forgiveness so as to motivate compassion and mercy for others and merit God's mercy in the process?*

EIGHTH SUNDAY IN ORDINARY TIME

Our scripture passage for this Sunday comes from the Gospel of Luke 6:39–45. In this text Jesus gives us some important requirements for becoming an effective disciple who is able to guide others to the Lord. Our Lord also identifies some important pitfalls to avoid in discipleship lest we become ineffective guides to authentic holiness. Let's study this passage so as to understand more clearly what challenges it offers for us as disciples.

The first thing Jesus cautions against is the temptation to be presumptuous in our leadership of others (v. the parable of the "blind leading the blind" in vs 39). Disciples are called to be leaders of others in the ways of faith, that is true, and we should not casually exempt ourselves from the responsibility of such leadership. However, neither should we assume initiative without carefully preparing ourselves for the task. If we ourselves are blind then we cannot very well lead others who are also blind. First, we must gain sight and only then we can help others to see clearly. In the Gospels, blindness is a symbol for those who are in "darkness" and do not have faith. In Luke 4:18 we were told that Jesus came to give sight (faith) to those who are blind (unbelieving). In various parts of the Gospel of Luke, we have heard Jesus sharing this gift of faithful sight with those who are blind and encouraging His disciples to do the same (cf. Lk 7:21–22, 14:13, 21 and 18:35–43). In the Acts of the Apostles we read about Peter giving the gift of insight to the Ethiopian Eunuch who could not otherwise understand the scriptures (v. Acts 8:31). Disciples gain "sight" when they become fully trained and teach as the Teacher (Jesus) does. For Luke, developing this likeness to Jesus is what discipleship is all about. These first two images ("the blind leading the blind" and the disciples who will be "like his teacher") teach us two things: that disciples must always be better trained in the ways of faith than those they seek to lead and that disciples should aspire to be like the Teacher (Jesus) in all things yet will never be greater than the Teacher. These lessons may seem simple but they have practical consequences for us. Because we are all called by virtue of our Baptism to lead others in the ways of faith, we have an obligation to understand well what we believe and must have the capacity and willingness to address challenges to our beliefs. It also requires real humility to acknowledge that the Lord always knows best and that when our opinions differ with Christian teaching then it is probably we who are mistaken and not the Teacher. Jesus does not want us to remain in blindness and so exempt ourselves from the responsibility of leading others; rather, the Lord wants us to become excellent students who learn the heart and mind of the Teacher and so can lead others to Jesus (v. Rom 2:19).

> *What opportunities exist for you to gain greater insight into your faith beliefs?*
> *In what particular area of Christian teaching do you feel like you are "blind"?*
> *What leads people to think that they know better than Jesus what is God's will?*
> *For whom are you called to be a leader in the ways of faith?*
> *What excuses do you use to exempt yourself from that leadership responsibility?*
> *What is the danger of one disciple trying to lead another disciple without being better trained in faith?*
> *If Jesus were to use an example from contemporary corporate culture, what do you think He would have said in order to communicate the same points?*

The second thing Jesus cautions against is that of judging other members of the Christian community (note: the term "brothers" refers to another disciple). Jesus refers to such people who engage in those actions "hypocrites". This term derives its meaning from Greek drama where an actor put on a mask to display a different persona. The term took on the meaning of pretentiousness, deception, insincerity, and false appearance. Jesus is cautioning that we need to correct our own weaknesses and faults before we can effectively help someone else deal with theirs. Hypocrisy occurs when we are blind to our own need for repentance but all too ready to see others' need for repentance. It can be easy for us to develop "blind spots"—areas of our lives in which we have grown complacent with human weakness and temptation. Jesus cautions us to look first at our own need for repentance before we can be credible guides for others in the community. As disciples, we have a well-founded desire to help others. Our Lord gives this caution not to stifle our desire but to help us be more effective in our desire. Part of the preparation for leadership of others, especially in the Christian community, is to carefully and honestly take an inventory of all the personal faults and weaknesses we individually possess and strive to overcome them through grace and virtue. That work of personal growth and sanctification will make us both credible and effective in our leadership of others.

> *What damage has been done to the message of the Gospel when disciples attempt to help others before they attend to their own faults?*
> *How does hypocrisy occur in our faith community today?*
> *How can this warning of Jesus be misused as an excuse to not help others?*
> *How can this warning be misunderstood so as to lead others into a mistaken spiritual complacency?*

Lastly, Jesus speaks to the motivation disciples should have in their desire to lead others and grow in holiness. By using the image of a good tree that produces good fruit, Jesus is telling us that the character of a disciple is always primary and foundational to a disciple's actions. Disciples are called to be people of a genuine goodness that motivates them to improve their own lives and the lives of others. That same goodness inspires them to desire likeness with the Teacher and greater insight into God who is the ultimate good. Being a disciple means much more than just someone who corrects a few faults; it is about fostering a creative and generative goodness of heart that underlies all other actions of leadership for self and others. Our brother (or sister) will more willingly allow us to help them correct their faults if they know we are motivated primarily by goodness. Others will be more receptive to our leadership in the ways of faith if they know we are motivated primarily by goodness. Jesus doesn't want disciples who just "do good things"; rather, our Lord wants disciples who are people of integrity, consistency, and purity—disciples who do good things because they are first and foremost good people.

Sometimes as disciples it can be easy for us to settle for doing good things without taking the time and effort it takes to become truly good people of solid and faith-filled character. Likewise, it can also be easy for us to become lazy by believing that we are good people who are exempt from the need to manifest that goodness in concrete deeds. Jesus wants us to observe a delicate balance between faith as an interior reality and faith as an exterior work. It is also significant that Jesus identifies good deeds and not good words as the necessary fruit of a good person. Actions, not speech, define someone's true convictions. It is important to periodically take an inventory of our actions as an indicator of our character. The question is not "do I produce good fruit?" but rather "do I consistently produce only good fruit?" It is too easy to look only at the good we do and ignore the bad; Jesus tells us that a truly good tree produces only good fruit.

> *If someone were to ask you, "How can I become a good person?", what would you say?*
> *What leads someone to think they can be a good person without manifesting that goodness in practical actions?*
> *What resources are available to help someone grow in goodness of character?*
> *When has your growth in goodness inspired others to grow in goodness as well?*

All of these teachings of Jesus are meant to address a false notion of discipleship that would settle for less than total commitment to the Lord and the dedicated pursuit of growth in holiness. Great damage is done to the Church and to the message of the Gospel when people who are not truly committed to the Lord present themselves as trustworthy guides for others.

> *What does this statement mean to you?*

NINTH SUNDAY IN ORDINARY TIME

Our scripture passage for this Sunday comes from the Gospel of Luke 7:1–10. In this scene Jesus meets the Roman Centurion who demonstrates an ideal example of faith and trust in our Lord's word. This example of faith is meant to inspire us to us ever-greater trust as well. There are various characteristics about the Centurion and his faith that are worthy of our reflection.

We should not overlook how many exemplary characteristics are represented in the Centurion. Luke introduces this man not only as an example of faith but as an example of the virtues all disciples should strive for. Of interesting note are the following aspects of the Centurion's character.

- Although the Jewish delegation of Elders has described the Centurion as deserving of Jesus' intervention, the Centurion himself acknowledges his unworthiness to have Jesus enter his home (v. Lk 7:4–6). This intentional juxtaposition of the flattery of the crowds with the Centurion's own honesty (expressed through his messengers) demonstrates that he is not someone who is deluded by others' praiseworthy opinions of him. Rather, he knows who he is and who he is not. His humility is particularly noteworthy because he was a person of position and power. This is an important message for disciples. It can be easy for us to believe the deceptive values of the world around us and to evaluate our worthiness or unworthiness based on the acceptance or rejection of others. Jesus wants disciples who are people of honesty and integrity and have a clear understanding of their identity rooted in their relationship with God. In that relationship, we are always unworthy.

When are you most susceptible to the praise or criticism of others?
Where do you go for an honest awareness of who you are and you are not?
How do you express your unworthiness to be in the presence of Jesus in a healthy and holy way?

How can people react to a sense of unworthiness in an
unhealthy or unholy way?

- The Centurion is presented as a person of compassion who is
  concerned about the needs of others. He does not seek Jesus'
  intervention for his own needs but for those of his servant.
  This demonstrates the importance of caring for others as a
  part of our discipleship as well. Disciples are to be people of
  compassion who look out for the needs of others and seek to
  alleviate their suffering. It can be easy for us to think we are
  responsible only for ourselves and those closest to us. Throughout the Gospel of Luke, Jesus will instruct us on the need for
  disciples to "Be merciful, just as your Father is Merciful" (v. Lk
  6:36). This mercy and compassion actively cares for the needs
  of those whom God has placed in our lives and not only those
  whom we choose.

How do you express mercy or compassion for others who
are not your family or friends?
When have you actively become involved in alleviating the
suffering of someone else for whom you are not responsible
or with whom you are not connected?
How does this witness of the Centurion's compassion chal-
lenge you to grow in your willingness to assist others in
need?

- The Centurion is also someone who contributes to the needs
  of the larger community for the common good. This quality is
  demonstrated because we are told that he built the synagogue
  in Capernaum. Throughout Luke and the Acts of the Apostles,
  Christian Disciples are presented as model citizens who are
  upright and enrich the society in which they live. This man certainly captures that spirit of altruism that fosters what is good
  for the community and not only what is in his own self-interest.
  As disciples, we are called to contribute to the common good
  as well and to enrich our societies as part of our Christian witness. Through involvement in various organizations, disciples
  can make a difference for the better in the world around them.

In what organizations are you involved so as to improve the larger community for the common good?
Who for you is an excellent example of community service and civic responsibility?
How can we as a faith community better encourage and facilitate works that benefit the common good?

- It is important to note that the Centurion never actually meets Jesus in this passage. In the first place, we are told that the Centurion only heard about Jesus from the crowds who had listened to the Lord teach in Capernaum. This initiative of the Centurion demonstrates his readiness to turn to Jesus for help despite the fact that he has only heard about the Lord. Thus, the Centurion is presented as a person of faith who accepts the testimony of others about the Lord, trusts that testimony, and acts on it. This, too, is an important message for us as disciples. Like the Centurion, none of us will ever hear the Lord personally teach or witness His ministry of healing and other such works but we are called to trust in Jesus' word nonetheless. The Gospels show us repeated scenes in which the word of Jesus is powerful and effective in healing the sick, calming the storms, and overcoming the forces of evil (cf. Lk 4:36, 39, 5:13, 6:10). When we trust that Jesus cares for us and is moved by compassion for those who suffer, then we will not hesitate to call out to the Lord with our limited faith.

The Centurion acted on very limited faith; what doubts or fears can prevent people from acting despite on limited awareness of Jesus?
When do you find yourself not approaching Jesus in prayer because you don't think the Lord is concerned about your issue?
What past situations do you wish you had brought before the Lord but didn't and why didn't you?

- Lastly, the Centurion is presented as someone who is sensitive to the cultural realities of others. This quality is demonstrated by the Centurion sending additional messengers to inform the Lord that He does not need to come "under the roof" of the Centurion. In the time of Jesus, it would have been a cultural and religious prohibition for a Jew to enter a Gentile house. The Centurion is sensitive to this cultural norm and is considering Jesus and our Lord's situation as well as that of his servant. As disciples, we inevitably face a variety of different cultures each day. We can either show cultural sensitivity to others or we can show cultural indifference. This characteristic of a disciple fosters esteem and respect among others in the workplace and society. Rather than requiring that others conform to our cultural expectations, a disciple who truly cares for others is also sensitive to their cultural needs.

Life situations are unique for each person. When have you been ennobled and honored by another person's respect for your personal culture or situation?
How can you create a better culture of respect and sensitivity for others in your professional, personal, and family life?
Why do you think this characteristic (cultural sensitivity) was recorded in the Gospels as an example of discipleship and great faith?

Jesus closes this scene by commenting on the Centurion's great faith. Although he may have been presented as a person of exemplary character, the Centurion is a person of faith first and foremost because of his utter trust in the word of Jesus. Using the example of military command, the Centurion states his confidence that what Jesus says will, in fact, be done. In response to this confidence Jesus says to the crowd that He has not found such faith in all Israel. Our Lord has found this faith in the humble, honest, compassionate, benevolent, responsive, and respectful Centurion. The Centurion did not require that Jesus be present in an extraordinary way but trusted in Jesus' compassion and care even without the Lord's visit to his house. Before we receive Communion at each Mass, the priest announces the presence of Jesus in the Blessed Sacrament as the Lamb of God and the One who takes away the sins of the world. In response to this announcement, we respond with the words of the Centurion and say, "Lord, I am not worthy that you should come under my roof but only say the word and my soul shall be healed."

How does this simple refrain take on new significance and meaning for in light of the above reflection?

The Centurion had many positive qualities, but it was his utter trust in Jesus' word for which the Lord recognized his faith. In what word of Jesus do you need to trust more deeply?

How can people today be tempted to make their faith contingent on Jesus' personal attention or response to their needs rather than trusting in His word in the absence of His presence?

Which aspect of the Centurion's character or faith inspires you the most and challenges you grow in your character or faith?

TENTH SUNDAY IN ORDINARY TIME

Our scripture passage for this Sunday comes from the Gospel of Luke 7:11–17. This reading contains the moving story of Jesus restoring to life the only son of the widow at Naim. This is a fascinating passage for so many reasons and it challenges us as disciples to imitate our Lord's unbounded compassion for those in distress.

The first thing to notice is that Jesus is never asked to get involved, to perform a miracle, or to make any other intervention. This scene is the only time in Luke's Gospel when Jesus performs a miracle entirely of His own initiative or without discussion. The Gospel tells us that He was "moved with pity" which is also translated "compassion" (v. Lk 7:13). Because Jesus was moved with compassion, He took initiative and acted so as to alleviate a situation of distress. It is important to note that it was not anyone's faith that warranted this intervention and neither was it anyone's request nor even that anyone deserved it. Rather, it was simply that Jesus was moved with compassion when He saw someone else's suffering and sorrow, and He chose to do something for the widow. This is powerful instruction for us as disciples because so often we consider "compassion" and "mercy" to be emotions we feel rather than actions we do. Jesus didn't wait to be asked to help alleviate the sufferings of others; rather, He demonstrated initiative and took the first step to reach out when He saw someone in distress. His experience of compassion became a motivation for practical works of mercy.

This initial point challenges us in two ways. Sometimes we can wait until we are asked before we help others. Oftentimes we can even be thankful when we are not asked to assist with another's need. Jesus gives us an example for how disciples should show initiative rather than waiting to be asked. Also, Jesus is challenging us to experience compassion as a virtue that motivates us to action and not just as an emotional response that "feels sorry" for people. It is easy to pray for people when they are in distress, but it is a Christian virtue when we actually do something that helps them.

Why has compassion become primarily just a feeling or emotion for us?
What in our society has so de-sensitized us and paralyzed us that we are not moved to action when we see another's needs?
How does it challenge you that Jesus is willing to take initiative rather than wait for others to ask him?
What situations of human suffering or distress do you see on a regular basis but have not yet demonstrated initiative in helping to alleviate it?

The second thing to notice is that it was the sight of the widow that evoked Jesus' deep feelings. In the time of Jesus, women had a place in the socioeconomic systems primarily through the men in their lives. To be a widow meant that her only means of support was her son. Now we are told her only son has died (v. Lk 7:12), which means she has no one to care for her. Not only is she alone in the world, but she is also destitute and vulnerable. It is important for us to imagine the fragility, the fear, the powerlessness, and the deep agony of this woman. We were told that Jesus was moved with compassion for her, but He also must have been angered by the social and cultural world that caused much of her suffering and rendered her so vulnerable. Jesus was making a statement that He would not allow the social and cultural systems of oppression to have the last word that day. Rather, He did something to keep this woman from experiencing such a state of distress and uncertainty. As disciples, we are called to be active agents in addressing the cultural and social world in which we live so as to provide for the security and safety of others—especially the vulnerable and those who cannot defend or provide for themselves. We must become the voice that speaks on their behalf so as to ensure that indifference or neglect never have the last word. It is important to remember the challenge issued in James 1:27: "Religion that is pure and undefiled before God and the Father is this: to care for orphans and widows in their affliction and to keep oneself from being unstained by the world."

Who are the people in our society who are like the widow (the powerless, the ones without rights, the vulnerable, the ones who don't have access to the economic or social systems necessary to survive and thrive)?

How can you be moved with "compassion" for these individuals in light of today's gospel passage so that systematic oppression or prejudice does not have the last word and what can you do?

What would Jesus say to our cultural and social world?

How can we become polluted by the world and deceived into thinking we are not responsible for addressing the social or cultural systems that cause distress in peoples' lives?

The third thing to notice is that Jesus touched the funeral bier. To touch anything associated with death in the time of Jesus was to be rendered "unclean". That's why the procession stopped when He reached out to touch the coffin! The people of Jesus' time believed that the power of death contaminated a person and that anyone who came into contact with items associated with death (even the items used to carry the body) were rendered unclean as well. In touching the funeral bier, Jesus is making the statement that He is not concerned about being contaminated by the "unclean" aspects of our lives. Rather than us causing Jesus to become unclean, our Lord has the power to make us clean —and whole—and alive! It is important to understand that this passage is about more than just the physical restoration of life; it is really about a spiritual restoration as well. That is the grace of conversion. This spiritual awakening is indicated when Jesus uses the command to "Rise" which is the same verb used to describe the resurrection. Thus, Jesus is bringing the grace of the resurrection into the life of this otherwise dead son. Jesus has nothing to fear from reaching into our lives and neither should we fear His healing, life-giving and spiritually-restoring touch. This teaching is a challenge for us and encourages us to prayerfully and explicitly invite the Lord to come into our lives and heal what is unclean, what is sinful, and what is causing spiritual death within us. It is through this grace-filled presence of Jesus that we are awakened to new life through the experience of conversion. Sometimes in our prayer we only want God to see the good sides of our lives; the reality is that God waits for us to invite Him into the dark sides as well because it is there that we most need Him.

What are some of the dark sides or unclean aspects of people's lives today that most need to be touched by Jesus?

Who is someone you know of who has been brought back to spiritual life by the power of God and how did God "touch" them?

How does the power of evil try to keep us from inviting Jesus into the dark parts of our lives?

When the dead son is brought to life through the grace of the resurrection then others are brought to faith as well (see the response of the crowd that acclaims Jesus as a great prophet and acknowledges that God has visited His people in verse 16). How have you seen one person's conversion influence the faith lives of others?

ELEVENTH SUNDAY IN ORDINARY TIME

Our scripture passage for this Sunday comes from the Gospel of Luke 7:36–8:3. It is the story of the Sinful Woman who washes Jesus' feet with her tears and dries them with her hair all in the context of a dinner with the Lord and a Pharisee. This passage offers several challenging teachings for us as disciples who gather regularly for the Lord's Supper.

Jesus speaks up to confront Simon's erroneous thoughts when the Pharisee criticizes the woman and dismisses the Lord in his heart. By doing so, Jesus shows that He protects the weak and the vulnerable on their journey of faith. The woman was obviously someone who had a reputation of being on the "outs" with society. People looked down on her and those attitudes of judgment and condemnation were now manifesting themselves in the context of the dinner with the Lord. Surely the woman must have wondered if even God looked down on her as well. Jesus does not push her away or tell her to stop because of her reputation or past sins. Instead, the Lord allows her to perform her action of love and devotion for Him. It is her need to show her love that the Lord accepts. In doing so, Jesus is helping her on the journey of reconciliation and redemption. He does not need her kindness; rather, she needs to show it. When the Pharisee rejects her in his heart, Jesus stands up for her and defends her journey of reconciliation of love. In all of these actions, Jesus is showing how He protects the weak and the vulnerable in their journey of faith.

When have you been weak and vulnerable in your journey of faith?
Who helped and protected you? Who criticized you or made your journey more difficult?
Who do you now protect in their weakness and vulnerability?
What might the Pharisee have done to help the woman rather than hinder her redemption and reconciliation?
Who are the weak and vulnerable closest to us?

How do we protect and help them?

By allowing the woman to touch Him and by speaking to her with familiar language, Jesus is showing that He is not afraid of being contaminated by the world and that He is confident of His ability to change the world. By being known as a "sinful" woman, she was also perceived as being "unclean". The Pharisee believed that by touching Jesus, the woman would make Jesus unclean as well. Thus, the Pharisee believed that Jesus would be contaminated by coming into contact with unclean people in the world. Instead, Jesus knows that He has the power to make all people clean. Thus, Jesus is not afraid to be associated with those whom others reject and neither is He afraid that it will "damage" His reputation if He is seen with sinners (Note: He even talks to her directly; a sign that He engages her in relationship). The Lord does not base His self-worth on those with whom He is associated. Rather, He sees all people as children of God who are in need of love and redemption. With His love, that redemption is possible. Jesus associated with the lowly not because He wanted to be lowly like them but because He wanted the lowly to be exalted like him.

> *How do we fall into the trap of thinking like the Pharisee who believed that contact with others might hurt our reputation or make us unclean?*
>
> *When have you been ennobled by someone else choosing to be associated with you?*
>
> *"We can change the world but first we have to be willing to be part of it." What does that statement mean to you?*

When Jesus tells the story of the two debtors He is revealing an important relationship between love and forgiveness. In the story itself, our Lord teaches how a person's experience of forgiveness (debts) leads them to love in a proportionate way that is those who are forgiven more love more. In the application of the story to the situation of Simon and the woman, Jesus reveres the relationship. Rather than moving from forgiveness to love, our Lord starts by looking at love as the indicator of forgiveness. In doing so, Jesus is instructing us to examine our lives based on our love of God and neighbor as well. We know we are forgiven much when we love much. Love does not earn our forgiveness but is the sign and result of that forgiveness. Simon did not love much because he did not know his need for forgiveness and there was not forgiven much. The woman knew her need for forgiveness and so was forgiven much, which led her to love much.

> *How can this dual basis of evaluation be helpful for your life of discipleship?*
> *Why do you think Jesus identified love as the manifestation of someone who is forgiven?*
> *How can people seek forgiveness out of a selfish motivation? How does the experience of forgiveness help you to love more?*

At the end of the passage Jesus says to the woman that she can go in peace because she has "faith that saves". Although other people have been introduced in Luke's Gospel as having "faith", no one has ever been introduced as having "faith that saves". That is a powerful kind of faith! We need to look at this woman's actions carefully to see what kind of faith we need as well—faith that can "save" us. Her faith was demonstrated by the fact that she allowed nothing to separate her from coming to the Lord. For example, in the cultural world of Jesus, it was forbidden for women and men to be in the same room unless they were related. She broke that rule to be with Jesus in the home of the Pharisee. It was also forbidden for women to touch men in such a way. She broke that rule in order to anoint the feet of Jesus. It was forbidden for women to have their hair uncovered. She broke that rule in order to dry his feet, and Jesus let her do it! Sometimes we have to go against the social conventions of our world in order be close to Jesus. When we do so, we are showing that being with the Lord is more important to us than anything else—even our cultural norms and rules. Saving faith is faith that overcomes barriers.

> *When have you seen people demonstrate "saving faith" by going against social norms? What did they do?*
> *When has your faith called you to act contrary to the social conventions of your world? Which rules did you break?*
> *What are some of the other "barriers" we have to overcome today so as to be in the presence of Jesus?*

Like many passages of scripture, this story can be read on different levels. Luke has included some important comments to help Christians of his community better understand what this passage might mean for their lives. For example, anytime we are told Jesus is having a meal we should automatically think of a Lord's Supper setting. That is always a Eucharistic context. Also, we are told that the woman is at the "feet of Jesus" which is a statement of discipleship (v. Lk 10:38–42 for a similar image of discipleship). Her actions demonstrate her dedication to Jesus and she is presented as a fervent disciple. However, she is also someone who has a difficult past and there are members of the community who continue to define her based on her past sins rather than her present conversion.

Simon the Pharisee does not want to welcome her at the meal because he does not recognize her repentance and conversion as having really changed her. It does not take much reflection to see how the attitude of Simon the Pharisee is alive and well in virtually every Christian congregation! Every time we refuse to welcome with love someone who has been welcomed and reconciled by Jesus then we are playing the role of Simon the Pharisee. Sometimes being a disciple means more than just accepting the Lord's invitation to us personally to be at His Supper; it also means accepting all those other people whom the Lord has called to His Supper as well. When we distance ourselves from "them", we are distancing ourselves from the Lord Himself. The celebration of the Eucharist is always a celebration of reconciliation between God and all His people; we become an obstacle to that reconciliation when we forget our own need for forgiveness and focus on other people's sin or past mistakes.

> *How do you see the attitude of Simon the Pharisee present in our community of faith?*
> *Simon didn't do anything to overtly alienate the woman; he just didn't do anything to actively welcome her. How can we end up alienating people by our failure to actively welcome them?*
> *Simon was content to be associated with Jesus as long as it didn't mean being associated with the woman; Jesus teaches that He desires communion with all God's children, especially those who are on the journey of conversion*

and repentance. How is Jesus asking you to join Him in befriending someone on a similar journey today?
What do you think is the central message of this scripture passage for a faith community?

Twelfth Sunday in Ordinary Time

Our scripture passage for this Sunday comes from the Gospel of Luke 9:18–24. This is the passage in which Jesus first asks His disciples the question, "Who do people say that I am?" and then proceeds to ask the more personal question, "Who do you say that I am?" Peter gives his famous response, "You are the Christ of God." Peter could answer that question because he had spent time with Jesus and had come to know the Lord through His actions, teachings, and experiences. (Note: versions of this passage are contained in Mt 16:13–20 and Mk 8:27–35. Additional insights regarding common elements can be found in the reflections on those gospel passages.)

It's one thing for Peter to give an intellectual answer to a question but it's another thing for Peter to live out the ramifications of his answer. That is the movement from experiencing faith as a set of beliefs into the lived experience of faith as a personally committed relationship with Jesus Christ. Peter was given certain insights into Jesus' identity and Peter could articulate those insights. The challenge for Peter was whether or not he would be able to follow where Jesus would lead. In our lives as disciples, we also have to make the move from "faith" being just a matter of intellectual beliefs to faith being a radical commitment to Jesus Christ as the Son of God and the Lord of our lives. Like Peter, the practical implications of our beliefs only become apparent to us as the Lord opens our minds to understand what following Him means in the practical details of daily life. For this reason, Jesus goes on to explain to Peter the full meaning of His identity as the Anointed One of God (translated as "Christ" or "Messiah"). Jesus also explains to Peter what it will mean for him to follow such an Anointed One: Peter will be called to lose his life for the sake of following Jesus. The experience of Peter teaches us that it is much easier to give the right answer than it is to follow where that answer leads us!

What has helped you understand the practical ramifications of your faith?

> *How have you experienced the shift from faith just being*
> *information (something you were taught) to faith being*
> *something personal (something that emerged within you*
> *because of your committed relationship with Jesus)?*
> *What can we do as a faith community to better help people*
> *understand clearly who Jesus is and what following Him*
> *means?*
> *What is a ramification of faith that you have difficulty*
> *living out?*

This passage opens with the statement that Jesus was in praying and the disciples were with Him (v. Lk 9:18). Luke tells us this detail for a reason: he wants to teach us that our ability to understand divine revelation and to live discipleship are only possible within the context of prayer. Luke presents Jesus at prayer especially during significant moments in our Lord's life and ministry (v. Lk 3:21, 5:16, 6:12, 11:1, 22:40–41, and 23:46). The context of Jesus' prayer teaches us what our Lord says and does is part of God's redemptive plan—that includes the call to pick up our cross and follow Him. The context of prayer adds significance to our Lord's teaching as something that reveals privileged insight into the divine will. Jesus manifests God's redemptive will when He uses the word "must" (Greek: dei) in verse 22: "the Son of man 'must' suffer." This means that our Lord's passion (suffering and death) is the way in which the Father will accomplish the salvation of the world. It is oftentimes difficult to understand how innocent human suffering can be part of God's will. This passage provides important insight into the way our Lord perceived His own suffering in a faithful way. Certainly the story of the Maccabean martyrs and the redemptive value of their suffering would have been common knowledge during the time of Jesus (cf. 2 M 7:38 and the Apocryphal writing of 4 M 17:21–22). As disciples, the significance of Jesus' prayer and His teaching on redemptive suffering should encourage us. There are times when we need God to reveal for us the true identity of Jesus, the implications of faith for our lives, and the redemptive value of suffering. All of these teachings successfully take place in this passage in the context of prayer. When we try to understand Jesus apart from a living relationship (prayer) then we are like the crowds who easily misunderstand His identity and misinterpret His actions. When we try to fulfill the implications of faith without prayer then our actions of discipleship become burdensome obligations rather than loving expressions of commitment. When we try to make sense of innocent suffering without prayer and the lived experience of Jesus then it is easy for our reasoning to spiral into absurdity and mistaken conclusions. There are some things that must take place in our lives and our world; the teaching of Jesus assures us those things are not signs of God's absence and that we can only, through the context of prayer, understand those experiences as being part of divine will.

> *What are some of the erroneous opinions about the identity of Jesus that you have heard?*
> *When have you gained insights of faith in the context of your prayer?*
> *How does prayer help you understand and desire to fulfill the implications of discipleship for your life?*
> *How can innocent suffering lead a person to absurd or misguided conclusions about God?*
> *How can the teaching of redemptive suffering give hope to those in the midst of distress?*
> *How can you participate in the ministry of redemptive suffering each day?*

Lastly, only in Luke's Gospel do we find Jesus adding the adverb "daily" to His command to "take up one's cross". We see the importance of daily discipleship in several places of Luke's Gospel (v. Lk 4:21, 19:9, 23:43). The need for ongoing vigilance in the life of discipleship is also demonstrated by the use of present tense in the command to "follow". This emphasis on the ongoing nature of discipleship is meant to counter any false belief that following Jesus involves a one-time action. While there are decisive moments in our journey of faith, every day presents new opportunities and challenges to our discipleship. We cannot be satisfied with accomplishments of the past as a way of excusing ourselves from responding to the challenges of the present. Rather, we are called to yield to the will of God every day even as Jesus did. In the sixteenth century, Marguerite Naseau, the first member of the Daughters of Charity died after contracting herself the disease she was trying to cure in a sick woman. As a true disciple of charity Marguerite said upon her deathbed, "I wish I could have done more."

How can disciples be deluded into thinking that they have "done enough" in their faith life and so exempt themselves from future daily challenges and opportunities?

How can you practically remind yourself each day of the necessity of taking up the cross as part of your discipleship?

What actions or habits can help you throughout the day to remember the importance of ongoing discipleship in the "present"?

Jesus calls us to "follow" Him as His disciple. In what daily situations are you finding it difficult to be a faithful disciple who imitates Jesus?

THIRTEENTH SUNDAY IN ORDINARY TIME

Our scripture passage for this Sunday comes from the Gospel of Luke 9:51–62. This is a very significant passage that marks the beginning of the second half of Luke's Gospel. In this scene Jesus begins His ten-chapter journey to Jerusalem. This journey is no ordinary trip. These chapters are filled with Jesus' most important teachings about discipleship as He progresses on His "Way" to fulfill His mission through His death, resurrection, and ascension into heaven. (Note: Some translations of the New Testament use the word "road" instead of "way".)

It should pique our interest when the Gospel tells us that Jesus is on His "Way" (v. Lk 9:57). That is because the very first Christians did not call themselves "Christians"—that name wasn't developed until the Church was already established and functioning in Antioch (v. Acts 11:26). Rather, the first followers of Jesus Christ referred to themselves as Followers of "The Way" (v. Acts 24:14). Thus, when Jesus undertakes His ten-chapter "Way" to Jerusalem, He is really leading us as Followers of "The Way" as well. These chapters, then, offer deep insights into what it means to be a follower of Jesus. The first thing Jesus does in this journey is to identify the obstacles of discipleship that can prevent someone from having the freedom to follow the Lord. Let's study each of these obstacles to discipleship. The first obstacle is anger demonstrated by the disciples who want to stop their journey in order to take out revenge on the Samaritan town (v. Lk 9:52–56). They want revenge for the rejection they have experienced and they are willing to do terrible things in the name of religious righteousness. Jesus cautions the disciples that anger is really an anchor that will hold them back from following him. He also wants the disciples to know that His mission is about reconciliation and conversion rather than destruction and punishment. Jesus will accomplish the Father's will only by confronting those who oppose the Gospel in a non-violent way. Sometimes it can be easy for us to justify our actions based on how others have treated us or what others have done, but Jesus teaches James and

John that true disciples do not stop following the way for the sake of retribution, anger, or vengeance.

> *When have you found anger to be something that distracts you in your life of discipleship that is causing you to turn your eyes away from Christ and be filled with violent disdain for others?*
>
> *What situations in our world today show how people can use religion as justification to carry out violence?*
>
> *Have you ever known of anyone whose faith has been eroded by anger?*
>
> *How have you experienced anger as something that takes away your freedom to follow Christ?*

The second obstacle to following Jesus with freedom is the desire for personal comfort and security. The first would-be follower of Jesus is cautioned that the animals live with greater security than the Son of Man and that's true for His disciples as well. Those who would follow Jesus on His way must be prepared to be vulnerable and endure less comfort than others. When our priority concern is our self-preservation rather than our self-offering to God, then we cannot be a very good disciple because we will falter when we are called to make a sacrifice of faith or to endure some hardship for the sake of the Gospel. Many Christians of the first century endured such vulnerability as they suffered the loss of material comforts and financial security because of their discipleship.

> *How can the desire for comfort and security today present an obstacle that prevents people from being good disciples?*
>
> *What are the dangers Christians experience today as a result of being faithful?*
>
> *When have you felt the Gospel asking "too much" of you?*

The third obstacle to following Jesus with freedom is the desire to make the Gospel anything less than the top priority in our lives. While the statement of Jesus can appear harsh and insensitive, it is important to notice that nowhere in this passage does it say that the man's father has actually died. It is possible that the man was most likely saying to Jesus, "Let me stick around until all my other responsibilities are done and then I'll think about following you."

Sometimes that's how we can approach our response to faith as well. Jesus cautions us that we can always find excuses to exempt ourselves from living the Gospel. When we do so, the Gospel will be the last thing in the world for which we give our time, talent, or resources. Sometimes it's easy to give God what's "left-over" in our lives rather than making God the priority of our lives. If God is our priority, then all other obligations and responsibilities will fall under that one, over-arching duty to serve the Lord. We will only have the freedom to follow Jesus if He is the most important person in our lives.

> *What are some of the good excuses people use to exempt them from responding to the Gospel?*
> *When have you felt yourself "putting the Lord on the back burner" because something else was more important to you?*
> *Sometimes people can approach their lives in such a way that their faith is more ornamental than foundational to who they are. What does "ornamental" faith look like? What does "foundational" faith look like?*
> *What otherwise good priorities have you had to sacrifice in order to follow Jesus?*

Finally, Jesus says to the last would-be disciple that whoever puts his hand to the plow and looks back is not fit for the Kingdom of God. When Jesus uses the word "fit", He is not referring so much to a person's moral character but rather to the stamina needed to face the challenges ahead. That's because the man wanted to fulfill his social and cultural obligations before he would follow Jesus. In short, he wanted to be polite and courteous according to the customs of his time. Jesus warns him that a disciple cannot conform to the social and cultural world around him. Rather, a disciple must have the courage and fortitude to follow Jesus even when it means being perceived in a negative way. As long as we are governed by political correctness, the expectations of polity, and other social norms, we will never really have the freedom necessary to be a disciple. Instead, we will make the Gospel subservient to social expectations.

> *When do you feel that your faith calls you to go against the social conventions and culture of your world?*

When do the expectations of others become an obstacle to your following of Jesus?

Who are some Christians you admire who have gone against their cultural norms in order to witness to Christ?

In the midst of challenging times, Archbishop Oscar Romero said, "Each one of you has to be God's microphone. Each one of you has to be a messenger, a prophet. The church will always exist as long as there is someone who has been baptized... Where is your baptism? You are baptized in your professions, in the fields of workers, in the market. Wherever there is someone who has been baptized, that is where the Church is. There is a prophet there. Let us not hide the talent that God gave us on the day of our baptism and let us truly live the beauty and responsibility of being a prophetic people."

FOURTEENTH SUNDAY IN ORDINARY TIME

Our scripture passage for this Sunday comes from the Gospel of Luke 10:1–12 and 17–20. In this passage, Jesus sends out the seventy-two disciples to continue His mission. As He does so, some interesting teachings emerge and are worthy of our reflection and prayer.

The image of the harvest is both powerful and deeply rooted in the prophetic books of the Old Testament. In Joel 3:13 and Micah 4:11–14, the harvest was a metaphor for the time of judgment. Jesus uses the harvest in this passage to describe the work of the Gospel and the mission of the Church. By using the image of the harvest, Jesus is communicating a sense of urgency and the need for everyone to be involved. The harvest waits for no one and the magnitude of the work is seemingly greater than the workers can handle. It requires the efforts of everyone, each in their own capacity, for the harvest to be successful. If we wait, or if we choose to not be involved, then the ripe harvest will be in jeopardy and what was intended to be a bumper crop could be a lost crop. This sense of urgency, all-encompassing work of the harvest, and need for everyone to be involved is communicated through the opening verse of this passage when we are told that Jesus sent seventy (or seventy-two as some translations indicate) disciples on mission. Although scripture scholars differ on which is the correct number, the significance remains and indicates that the mission of the disciples is to encompass the whole world.[9]

In addition to the universal mission of the disciples, the number also indicates how important it is that everyone be involved in the work of the harvest. In Nm 11:16–17 Moses selected seventy elders to share in his work with the people and in Ex 24:1, 9–24 the seventy go with Moses to the mountain; the number seven-

---

9.   See Gn 10 where the entire earth is divided among the descendants of Noah; the Hebrew copy of Genesis indicates that there were seventy nations that were formed while the ancient Greek translation of Genesis [Septuagint] indicates there were seventy-two nations.

ty-two also has a tradition of including everyone because when the Hebrew scriptures were translated into Greek in the third century BC, it is related that seventy-two scholars spent seventy-two days working on the translation —six people from each of the Twelve Tribes of Israel.[10]

> *What are some of the "harvest" moments you run across in your daily life (family, profession, and other social encounters) when situations are "ripe" for a message of faith or an expression of Christian charity?*
>
> *The harvest requires everyone but sometimes we find it easy to dismiss ourselves from the task while waiting for others to step forward, and the opportunity of the harvest is oftentimes lost. What are some of the excuses we use to exempt ourselves from working in the harvest?*
>
> *By using the image of the harvest, Jesus is stressing that there are opportune moments of faith that do not last forever in people's life. What is the harvest the Church is missing out on today and who are the workers the Lord wants to send into that harvest?*

In the face of such great need, it would have been easy for the disciples to think their first action should be that of organization, planning, and travel. However, Jesus is very clear about what their first action should be. After explaining the huge work they have to do, the Lord simply commands them to "Pray". Prayer is essential in the life of a disciple and is necessary before we begin an effort so that whatever work we do may be in accord with God's will and guided by the Holy Spirit. It does not matter what we accomplish if it is not in accord with God's will. In fact, disciples sometimes act with good intentions but end up working against the Gospel rather than for it. Prayer keeps us focused on our purpose, open to the Lord's inspiration, and aware of the sacredness of our efforts. Without prayer, we risk doing our own will rather than God's will. Jesus sent the disciples to proclaim the Kingdom of God and in order to do that, the disciples had to know clearly what the Lord wished to occur in every situation they faced.

---

10. See *Letter of Aristeas* as found at Christian Classics Ethereal Library: www.ccel.org/c/charles/otpseudepig/aristeas.htm.

What prayer do you use to start your day so you can be guided by the will of God and responsive to the harvest you will encounter?

One of the prayers at Mass reads, "Lord, may everything we do begin with Your inspiration, continue with Your saving help, and come to completion in Your Kingdom." How does this prayer speak to you?

What happens when we begin doing without first praying?

When Jesus sends the disciples on mission, He tells them to basically do three things: Foster community (table fellowship and staying in one place), take care of people's physical needs (heal the sick), and deepen their faith lives (proclaim the Kingdom of God). These three tasks continue to be essential elements of the mission of the Church today. In order to foster community, the disciples had to "eat what was set before them." That would have been very difficult for a Jew going into a Gentile world where Kosher food laws were not observed! Jesus was telling the disciples to meet people where they are and to remove all social barriers that would prevent them from effectively ministering to others. Sometimes we like to minister to people on our terms that is when it is convenient for us, in the way we want, and so forth; this admonition of our Lord tells us that the setting for preaching and ministry is to be set by those we minister to and not by us as the ministers.

Also, when Jesus tells them to not move about from one house to another He is doing so because He does not want the disciples to give the appearance that their ministry is about seeking personal comfort or to prolong their stay in a particular community when the Gospel needs to be preached elsewhere. Such pursuits of personal comfort and self-interest can compromise the witness of the Gospel. (The prohibition against carrying a money bag is most likely intended to address a similar concern so that the disciples are not perceived as using their healing ministry for a source of personal profit as did other miracle healers of their time.) As a parish, we are responsible for fulfilling each of these tasks as well. It takes creativity and flexibility to meet people where they are. It takes selflessness and detachment to be free of the desire for personal comfort and self-interests. It takes courageous witness to speak a message of faith that is relevant for people's lives. It takes initiative and compassion to alleviate the suffering of others.

> *How do we currently foster a healthy community life?*
> *How can the desire for personal comfort and the pursuit of self-interest compromise the witness of the Gospel today?*
> *What are opportunities to increase our community life so that all social barriers are overcome?*
> *How do we currently take care of people's physical needs and what are opportunities to do more in our outreach efforts for those in need?*
> *How do we currently deepen people's faith lives and what more could we do?*

When the disciples returned, they were filled with joy because they were victorious over the forces of evil. Jesus, too, shares in their joy but He also cautions them to rejoice more in the fact that God has given them a share of His ministry rather than in their ability to overcome evil. This is an important lesson for us as well. You see, sometimes we can find ourselves rejoicing in our own victories and personal credit for our accomplishments. When we do so we lose sight of what those victories mean in God's overall plan and that we could do nothing if it were not given to us by God. Our deepest joy should be rooted in the fact that God believes in us and has confidence in us so much that the Lord actually entrusts to us a mission. We should rejoice, then, that we have been found worthy to be co-workers with the Lord. That is a joy that will endure regardless of success or failure, acceptance or rejection. If, on the other hand, our joy is only based on our success and victory, then life will be a roller coaster as we move from happiness to sadness based on how our day is going. Jesus wants disciples who have a deep and abiding joy—a joy that is rooted in their relationship with God meaning their names are written in heaven and not just in their daily successes.

> *What are the daily experiences that bring you joy and sadness?*
> *When has your relationship with God given you peace and joy even in the midst of troubling moments or situations of seeming failure?*

In our American society, we tend to see people in terms of their accomplishments rather than their relationships. When do you find yourself evaluating other people that way?

When do you find yourself evaluating your own self-worth in that way?

How will you take the necessary step of faith that roots your identity first and foremost in your relationship with God?

Fifteenth Sunday in Ordinary Time

Our scripture passage this Sunday comes from the Gospel of Luke 10:25–37. In this text we read the famous story of the Good Samaritan. Because most of us are very familiar with this passage we may actually miss some of the subtle teachings Jesus wants to communicate. Let's study the passage in depth to see what insights can be offered for our discipleship.

The passage begins with a Lawyer asking Jesus what must be done to inherit eternal life. Although the Lawyer already knows the answer, the question is posed in an effort to test Jesus. The malicious questions of the Lawyer demonstrate a serious dichotomy in his faith life: although he may know the correct answer (love God and neighbor), he is not acting on that knowledge as is demonstrated by his repeated attempts to test Jesus. In response to the Lawyer's actions, Jesus commands him to start acting on his knowledge of the Law. Certainly the study of the Law was important, but what good is it to know the right answer but not live it? A person who knows the right thing to do and doesn't do it is more culpable than the person who lacks knowledge of right and wrong. For disciples, it is important to have an integrated faith that seeks to live out in concrete deeds what we know to be true and revealed by God. If we fail to integrate our faith into daily action then we are like the Lawyer in this story who may have known the way to eternal life but wasn't following it. Christian love is not a mere sentiment but rather a movement toward action to do the good for another person that Jesus wants. To love God with all our heart, soul, might and mind is to give the Lord a complete sovereign claim on every aspect of our lives. If any part of ourselves is held back from the Lord then we have not fulfilled the commandment to love.

What part of people's lives can they be tempted to keep from God and why?
What happens when a person loves God with only a part of their being?

> *When have you seen a Christian accumulate knowledge of faith without living it?*

The Lawyer wanted to limit the scope of his duty to love and so he asks Jesus to define for him who is a neighbor. Some people thought that a person's neighbor was limited to someone who was a member of their family, friends, community, or nation. The Lawyer wanted Jesus to draw the boundaries of who was his neighbor because that would determine whom he had to love. Of course, the answer would also determine whom he didn't have to love. It can be easy for us to follow the example of the Lawyer and to seek ways in which we limit our responsibility to care for others as well.

> *How do we tend to limit our responsibility for others today? Who are the groups who "don't deserve our love" in our society?*
>
> *If you were to identify the hierarchy of groups in your life that is family, relatives, friends, business associates based on their "right" to your love, what would be the relative order?*
>
> *Who is someone you think exemplifies love without limitation and what does it look like?*

We oftentimes think the parable of the Good Samaritan is just a teaching about being kind to people but it's much more than that. You see, the whole parable is told from the perspective of the man who is half-dead on the road. We are meant to see ourselves as that person and to see the parable unfold through his eyes. Two people passed by him and both of them had reasons why they should have stopped and helped but didn't. Instead, they focused on their excuses for not helping. The priest and Levite might become ritually "unclean" if they touched a half-dead man, and it was dangerous to wait around in that region longer than necessary. The wounded man's hopes were dashed as each of these two religious figures left him to die. Then, the Samaritan comes by—the one person who had every reason not to stop but the one person who is moved by compassion to help the man. The injured man did not care that a Samaritan helped him. He was grateful for anyone who would come to his aid. Whoever helped the injured man was a "neighbor" to him. If the injured man would allow the Samaritan to be a neighbor to him, then the injured man had to consider the Samaritan his neighbor and love him in return. This perspective turns our reasoning upside down because it asks us to see ourselves in a position of dire vulnerability and need. In such a position, we have to ask ourselves the question, "Who would you allow to help you if you were half-dead on the roadside?" Then that person is our neighbor, and we have an obligation to help them just as we would accept help from them. The very question of the Lawyer has been reversed. Rather than asking, "Who is my neighbor?", the Lawyer should have been asking, "How can I be a neighbor to those in need?" Rather than patting ourselves on the back every time we do a good deed for someone we love and saying, "I helped someone", we need to also ask, "Who did I not help?"

> *How does this understanding of the parable broaden your perspective of who is your neighbor?*
> *Who have you been a neighbor to this past week? Who have you failed as a neighbor?*
> *Who are the Samaritans in our world?*
> *How can people today use religious principles as an excuse for not helping someone in need?*

Jesus ends by saying to the Lawyer, "Go and do likewise." This is almost the exact same commandment Jesus gave the lawyer at the beginning of this passage. Our Lord is trying to help the lawyer, and us, understand that compassion must translate itself into self-giving that takes risks for the good of others. The compassion of the Samaritan moved him to delay his journey in a perilous part of the wilderness solely for the sake of helping another human being. The compassion of the Samaritan also led him to use his own resources to pay for the man's care and even to provide future generosity based on his need. That kind of compassion helps others even when sacrifice is involved. Lastly, the Samaritan made no claim on the wounded man in exchange for his kindness but simply moved on with his life and allowed the wounded man to move on with his life. That is true detachment that does not need to be thanked, recognized, or praised for doing good for someone. This entire passage began with the Lawyer asking a very self-centered and self-serving question about his own salvation but the passage ends with the story of the Samaritan who acts with complete selflessness. If the Lawyer shows mercy only for the sake of gaining heavenly reward then he will not be imitating the selfless generosity of the Samaritan. Rather, only when the Lawyer knows his own need for mercy and out of that awareness shows mercy to others can he then trust in God's mercy for eternal life. Eternal life is not for sale and it is not a reward for doing good. Eternal life is a trusting relationship in a good and merciful God who asks us to share that goodness and mercy with others even as we seek it from Him. Mother Teresa once said, "We ourselves feel that what we are doing is just a drop in the ocean. But the ocean would be less because of that missing drop."[11]

When have you risked something to help another person? What is the most profound compassion you have experienced?

What situation in your life right now is calling you to show the compassion of the Good Samaritan for someone? How do you know when you have enough knowledge and it is time to do something?

---

11. As quoted in Mother Teresa, *Reaching Out In Love—Stories told by Mother Teresa*, Compiled and Edited by Edward Le Joly and Jaya Chaliha (Barnes & Noble, 2002), p. 122.

SIXTEENTH SUNDAY IN ORDINARY TIME

Our scripture passage this Sunday comes from the Gospel of Luke 10:38–42. It is the story of Jesus going to the home of Martha and Mary. This scene should be read in the context of the lawyer's question from last week (v. Lk 10:25) because it demonstrates what love of God looks like just as the Good Samaritan parable demonstrated what love of neighbor looks like. As this encounter with Mary and Martha unfolds, it becomes a teaching moment for all disciples about the need to stay focused in the midst of our busyness.

This story tells us that Martha was so busy doing things for Jesus that she actually ends up ignoring Jesus. When that happens relationships suffer. This is an important insight for us as disciples because it addresses how we relate to our families, friends, and co–workers. Jesus reminds Martha, and us, that only one thing is necessary when it comes to hospitality and that is to pay attention to the guest. Everything else we do for the guest is secondary. Sometimes we get our priorities out of balance and end up spending hours doing things for other people but not spending time with those people. Our deepest longing is for love and that is the one thing necessary. It is true with out human relationships and it's also true in our relationship of faith.

How can people today end up working so much that they don't spend time with the ones they love (and for whom they are actually working)?

What are some of the ways that you make time to just be with the people you love?

What are some of the temptations that try to lure you away from time with your family/ spouse?

What are some of the ways in which we find it easy to "do" religious tasks rather than spending time in the loving presence of God?

Jesus doesn't say anything to Martha until she complains. The Lord allows her to do her works of service and intervenes only when she expresses anger and frustration. It is then that He can speak to her and refocus her heart by helping her see what is out of order. Martha's works of service should have been an expression of her love for Jesus; instead they became a source of anger, judgment, and hurt. What could have been a blessing for Martha (the opportunity to serve Jesus) became nothing more than a burden. Imagine how many people would have been honored to have Jesus visit their homes, but Martha lost sight of the honor and the opportunity to experience the Lord's wonderful presence. Sometimes that happens to us as well when we are motivated more by duty than by love. Think of how quickly the opportunity to attend a sporting event with your child can become the burden of an additional demand on your schedule. Also, think of how the opportunity to care for an ailing parent can become an imposition on your personal freedom.

> *What are some of the blessed opportunities in your life that could easily become burdens for you?*
> *How do you respond when you feel like you are overburdened with duties?*
> *What practices help to keep you joyful, grateful, and focused in the midst of very busy and burdensome situations?*
> *Have you ever prayed about feelings of being overburdened and what insights has the Lord given you?*

When Martha complains, she reveals what happens to all of us when we lose our focus on the Lord's presence in our lives. As we listen to her list of comments we can readily understand how easily we experience these same errors in our faith. First, Martha accuses Jesus of not caring about her troubles. Oftentimes in the scriptures we hear similar cries of people in distress who accuse God of not caring. Second, Martha tells Jesus what the problem is as though He couldn't figure it out for Himself. Third, Martha assigns blame to someone else for her situation —it is obviously Mary's fault that Martha has ended up busy and distracted. Fourth, Martha tells the Lord what is the solution to the problem (like He couldn't figure that out either). Fifth, rather than listening to what Jesus has to say, Martha does all the talking: she interprets, accuses, assesses, and recommends without ever letting Jesus say a single word. Sometimes we can find ourselves praying like Martha. It can be easy for us to have feelings of self-pity and self-righteousness in the midst of great efforts. It can also be easy for us to complain to the Lord about what others aren't doing while reminding God of how much we are doing. When our prayer is more a monologue than a conversation then we have become a Martha who is more interested in telling Jesus what to do than listening to what Jesus wants us to do.

> *Which of the above erroneous attitudes affects you most regularly in your prayer?*
> *When do you pray more to listen rather than to speak?*
> *What do you think Martha should have said to Jesus?*

When Jesus speaks to Martha, notice how He has to call her name twice. In the scriptures, when a name is called twice it is often done in order to wake someone who has fallen asleep. By calling out "Martha, Martha!" Jesus is telling us that Martha has fallen asleep in her faith and that is what ultimately led her to lose focus. The Lord has to "wake her up" so she can once again have right relationship. Lots of things can cause us to fall asleep in our faith life. For some people, it is the routine of daily prayer or even the liturgy that becomes so ordinary that they stop reflecting on what they are doing. A good rule is this: our religious works probably don't mean much to God if they don't mean much to us! Other people can fall asleep because of a fundamental disinterest in their faith life. When that happens they can perceive prayer as fruitless and stop spending time with the Lord.

This Gospel passage specifically says that it was "busyness" and the distractions of much serving that led Martha to fall asleep in her faith life. That means we can become so preoccupied by our tasks that we end up in an obsession with completing our duties. Sometimes people have to be awakened from such a state. Lastly, some people fall asleep in their faith due to simple carelessness and lack of discipline when it comes to observing simple religious practices (Sunday Mass attendance, daily prayers, regular Confession). By allowing these good and regular practices of faith to slowly deteriorate, people can actually find themselves in a non-practicing state of faith.

> *What have been some of the "wake up" moments in your faith life?*
> *How does God "call your name" when He wants to get your attention?*
> *What makes you fall asleep in your faith life?*
> *What are indicators that help keep you from falling asleep in your faith?*

One other aspect of this reading that should pique our interest is that Martha becomes overwhelmed with much "serving". The actual word that is used in Greek is *diaconia* and is also translated as "ministry." This passage, then, has a particular message for those who are involved in various ministries of the Church. One of the pitfalls of ministry is that a person can become preoccupied by what others aren't doing. Such an attitude of comparison, and even competition, can be detrimental to the spiritual benefits offered through works of ministry. The risk of being overwhelmed with much activity is also a reminder that better ministry doesn't necessarily mean more ministry. Sometimes it is the faithful and responsible task of the Church to discern which ministries are important and which ones are not. Since we are limited in our human abilities, we have an obligation to use our energies wisely and efficiently in order to accomplish the tasks entrusted to us. In order to do something well, we will inevitably have to say "no" to doing everything.

> *How can people become overburdened by being involved in ministries in our faith community?*
> *How can we best discern what ministries are essential to our mission and which ministries are not essential to our mission?*
> *When have you seen organizations attempt to multiply their efforts rather than to discern their best efforts and what has been the result?*

The final comment about this passage concerns the statement of Jesus regarding Mary having chosen the "better part". Scripture scholars have debated what that comment means. Most believe that it is a reference to Mary's decision to become a disciple of Jesus (she "sat at his feet" and "listened to his word"—all references to discipleship). Mary had to leave behind her social obligations to be in the kitchen preparing food for the guest so that she could be with the Lord. Others looked down on her for ignoring these duties customarily assigned to women. Mary had to enter the room with Jesus and His disciples and share their company —something not permitted in the time of Jesus. In all of these actions Mary has demonstrated a courageous willingness to choose Jesus rather than be trapped by the social expectations of her time. That is the "better part." She may have offended some, but she pleased the Lord. Jesus will not interrupt such a commitment of faith and discipleship despite the complaints of those around Him. He sees Mary as an example for others to follow. In addition, the development of Christian spirituality attests that the figures of Martha and Mary, despite their obvious differences in attitude and disposition, have also become the ideal for what we call in the Church "contemplation" and "action." The integration of Mary (contemplation) and Martha (action) is for a true disciple the perfect balance in the service to the Lord.

> *What social expectations do people have to leave behind to be a disciple of Jesus today?*
> *Mary's decision for discipleship did not bring about harmony in the household. How can a person's radical decision for discipleship today end up causing disharmony among family and friends?*
> *Jesus had to intervene to defend Mary's decision for discipleship; how does the Lord speak up today to defend and esteem decisions of discipleship?*

SEVENTEENTH SUNDAY IN ORDINARY TIME

Our scripture passage for this Sunday comes from the Gospel of Luke 11:1–13. In this text Jesus instructs the disciples how to pray by giving them the Lord's Prayer. Jesus then goes on to teach the disciples about the need to pray with boldness, perseverance and trust for the gift of the Holy Spirit. Jesus gave this prayer to be the one prayer that would form Disciples throughout history. That is why the Lord's Prayer is of greatest importance in the Christian tradition: our lives are supposed to be changed by it.

The text of the Lord's Prayer appears in two different versions in the New Testament. In addition to this passage from the Gospel of Luke, the more familiar and more extensive version is contained in the Gospel of Matthew (cf. Mt 6:9–13). Interestingly, however, the Matthean version of the Lord's Prayer does not appear in the Lectionary readings for Sunday. Because of the importance of the Lord's Prayer for Christian disciples, this Gospel reflection will incorporate elements from both the Matthean and Lucan versions.

In the Gospels of both Matthew and Luke, Jesus presents the Lord's Prayer as an explicit instruction for the disciples so that we will pray for the "right things" and in the "right way". Jesus prayed many of the same petitions found in the Lord's Prayer during His life and ministry. The Gospel of Matthew specifically instructs Christians to "not heap up empty phrases as the Gentiles do" (v. Mt 6:7). This is an important perspective on the purpose of Christian prayer as distinct from certain forms of prayer in the ancient world. In pagan temples, prayer was intended to change the minds of the gods so as to get them to do what people wanted. That is why the multiplication of words and phrases was important—it was all designed to convince the gods. However, Christian prayer is very different. Its purpose is not to change God's mind but to change us as disciples. Our heavenly Father knows what we need better than we do! The purpose of Christian prayer, then, is intended to open our minds and hearts so that we can know the will of God and do it with eagerness, generosity, and trust. Prayer reminds us of our dependence on God and allows us to more clearly recognize the presence of God in our lives.

> *What do you pray for? Who do you pray to?*
> *Is your prayer an attempt to change God, or are you seeking*
> *to be changed by God?*

Jesus gave us this prayer for a reason. It has the power to change us. But this can occur only when we are conscientious and intentional about our prayer. Let's study the Lord's Prayer for a moment and see what Jesus wants to teach us about being a Disciple. The following reflection will hopefully help us to appreciate this prayer more deeply and is based on the more complete version found in the Gospel of Matthew which incorporates all the elements of the version found in the Gospel of Luke.

"Our"—Both the Matthean and Lukan versions of the Lord's Prayer are presented as the communal public prayer and not the private prayer of an individual. This is an important statement because it reminds us that disciples always pray as members of the Family of God. If we are only interested in our own needs or if we seek to exclude others from our lives and faith then we cannot authentically say "our". Jesus did not each us to say "My Father" or "give me my bread" but to make our prayer inclusive of others and their needs. This prayer is meant to form the way we understand our relationship with God and the openness disciples necessarily have for the needs of others as fellow members of the Family of God.

> *How are you tempted to be self-centered in your prayer?*
> *How can disciples put limits on whom they are willing to*
> *consider their "brother and sister" in Christ?*

"Father in heaven"—This is an interesting combination of images. Jesus prayed with the word "Abba" which connoted an intimate relationship with God the Father. Our Lord wanted us as disciples to share in that intimate trusting relationship He enjoyed and witnessed. The term "Father", then, brings out the immanent and intimate relationship into which we are invited. It also calls us to willingly open our hearts to others as brothers and sisters of one family of faith. The phrase "who art in heaven" emphasizes God's transcendence and power as Lord of heaven and earth. It also reminds us that that there is more to life than our current experience and that God calls us to choose the values of heaven over those of earth. God is both immanent and transcendent; the Lord cares for us with the tenderness of a Father and as the sovereign Power over all creation. As we prayerfully express our needs in an act of trusting confidence, the Lord asks us to understand and accept His plan for our lives including our ultimate destiny to with God in heaven.

> *When do you most readily relate to God as immanently and intimately present in your life?*
> *When do you relate to God as the transcendent Lord of heaven and earth?*
> *What is the danger of relating to God only as Father (immanent presence) or as "in heaven" (transcendent presence)?*

"Hallowed by thy name"—God's name is already holy. This petition is a prayer that the holiness of God be respected, honored, and manifested in the lives of disciples. We show to the world the holiness of God by how we live and by the reverence we show for divine affairs. We proclaim the holiness of God by how we act in God's presence while in both the sacred space of a church and the secular environment of the word. If we are not actively witnessing to the holiness of God in our actions then we are not living out this petition in our lives and our prayer has become just a multiplication of words.

> *How do you show reverence for the holiness of God while in the sacred space of a church?*
> *How do you honor the holiness of God in your office and your home?*
> *How do you honor the holiness of God in your friendships?*

"Thy kingdom come"—This petition reminds us that disciples seek the active and practical reign of God in every part of their lives. Jesus came to establish the Kingdom of God and that requires us to seek the Lord's direction in our marriages, families, offices, friendships, hobbies, and other interests. It can be easy to compartmentalize our faith so that we only seek the Lord's direction in some parts of life but not others. This petition expresses the desire to accept the Lordship of God in every part of our lives.

> *When do people usually find it easy to accept God's Lordship?*
> *When do people tend to have difficulty accepting God's Lordship?*
> *How do you express the desire for more complete submission to God's reign in your life?*

"Thy will be done on earth as it is in heaven"—This petition is found only in Matthew's version of the Lord's Prayer and is an explicit extension of the previous petition for the coming of the kingdom. Christian disciples are to pray first and foremost for God's will to be done in all things rather than only trying to convince God to grant our own desires. Jesus expressed this same prayer on the night of His betrayal and arrest (cf. Lk 22:42 and Mt 26:39). While Jesus encourages disciples to pray for our perceived needs, the Lord's own example and this passage remind us to always end our prayer by expressing our hope for God's will to be done and for our ability to accept and desire that divine will. God's will can be perfectly manifest in heaven because of the spiritual harmony that exists among the angels and saints. It is human free will and weakness that obstruct God's will from taking place on earth.

> *What space do you provide in your prayer so that you can hear and know God's will for your life?*
> *When do you find it easier or more tempting to do your will rather than do what you know to be God's will?*
> *How does the prayer of Jesus in the garden help form the way you will pray about your personal needs or wishes?*

"Give us this day our daily bread"—This verse is difficult to translate and can have various layers of meaning. On the surface, it functions as a prayer for the communal needs of daily sustenance. It should be emphasized once again that this is a collective prayer and not an individual prayer. As such, the human family prays for those resources needed by the entire human family for daily survival. This challenges us to also recognize that we bear the responsibility of being good stewards of the resources we have received so that we will distribute God's generosity to those in need throughout the world. The blessings we receive are not only for our individual benefit but so that we can be instruments of blessing for others. On a deeper level, however, this petition is about much more than just the needs of daily sustenance. This deeper level is identified by the word used to translate "daily". The Greek word *epiousioun* is very difficult to translate but the most literal meaning would be "supernatural" or "higher essence" or "being from above". All these terms point to a more spiritual meaning for "daily bread" and indicate that it refers to a specific type of bread that is "supernatural" and has the ability to give us our "being from above". That, of course, is the Eucharist. The Eucharist is what makes us the Body of Christ; it is the supernatural bread of heavenly being that forms the Church. This petition then is a prayer to be formed into the Body of Christ through the regular gift of the Eucharist—the very presence of Jesus.

> *How does the interpretation of charitable distribution for the world's resources challenge you?*
> *How does the spiritual interpretation of "daily bread" as the Eucharist affect the way you will pray the Lord's Prayer?*
> *This petition is really praying for us as disciples to be changed in our attitude and identity; what can prevent that change from actually taking place in a disciple's life?*

"Forgive us our debts (sins) as we forgive our debtors (those who sin against us)"—Jesus has offered several teachings on the interconnection between personal forgiveness by God and willingness to forgive others (cf. Mt 6,14, Mt 18:35, Mk 11:25 and Lk 6:37). There are two dimensions to this petition as well. The first dimension has to do with the action of forgiving and implies that divine forgiveness cannot take place when an individual is unwilling to forgive others. In refusing to forgive others we are actually closing ourselves off to God's forgiveness. The second dimension concerns the quality of our forgiveness and reminds us that if our forgiveness is half-hearted and full of conditions then that is how God will forgive us (cf. Mt 7:2 also Mk 4:24). We want God to forgive us completely and to give us second chances to move forward in freedom. Accordingly, that is how the Lord wants us to forgive others.

Why do you think Jesus had so many teachings about forgiveness?
What are typical conditions people place on their forgive-
ness of others?
What can lead someone to refuse forgiveness to another
person and what does that do to the spiritual life?
What can lead a person into despair and erroneously think-
ing that their sin is too great for God to forgive and what
would you say to that person?

"Lead us not into temptation"—Jesus instructed His disciples to pray for similar protection during His agony in the Garden (cf. Lk 22:40, 46, Mk 14:38, and Mt 26:41). Temptation and testing were experienced in the life of Jesus as challenges to His identity and mission. This challenge was true both in the desert after our Lord's baptism and on the cross. It is only by remaining faithful to His identity as God's obedient Son that our Lord could pass these tests even to the point of enduring suffering and death. Jesus knows that we are weak and that our human condition all too often leads us to give in to the desires of the flesh rather than remain obedient to God's will for our lives. For this reason the Lord encourages us to pray for protection from temptation lest we succumb to disobedience and reject our identity as children of our Heavenly Father. Part of the growth in Christian maturity is the development of self-awareness so that we know areas of personal weakness and can avoid placing ourselves in situations of temptation. Thus, when we pray "lead us not into temptation" then we should be prepared to practice the self-discipline it takes to avoid known occasions of sin.

What are typical ways in which people put themselves in
known situations of temptation?
Who do people tend to blame when they fall into sin?
What are practical ways in which people have altered their
behavior in order to avoid known occasions of sin?

"Deliver us from evil (Evil)"—This petition is contained only in the Matthean version of the Lord's Prayer and can be interpreted to mean either deliverance from situations of evil or from the power of Evil personified that is Satan. It is important to remember that disciples are not exempt from the confrontation with evil in the world. The reality is that we live in a world that is weakened by sin and that we are called to fight daily against the forces of evil within us and around us. This prayer does not seek preservation from the Christian confrontation with evil; rather, this prayer seeks protection from being overwhelmed by the evil we face. Christians are called to confront and eradicate evil in whatever form we find it: institutional, national, personal, cultural, professional, or relational. Sometimes it is easier to become complacent with the presence of evil than it is to continue the fight to eradicate it. When we become complacent with evil in our midst then we have been overcome by it.

> *How can people be tempted to tolerate sinful behavior rather than pray for the grace of authentic conversion?*
> *How does this final petition challenge you to confront evil?*
> *What cultural values can encourage a person to become complacent with evil?*
> *As you read this reflection on the Lord's Prayer, which of those phrases offer new insights for you?*

Teresa of Avila said, "prayer in my opinion is nothing else than an intimate sharing between friends; it means taking time frequently to be alone with Him who we know loves us".[12]

> *What is the personal change this prayer can effect in your life as a result of praying it intentionally and persistently every day?*

---

12. See *Life of St Teresa*, 8, 5.

Eighteenth Sunday in Ordinary Time

Our scripture passage for this Sunday comes from the Gospel of Luke 12:13–21. In this passage, we hear Jesus teach about the need to become rich in the things of heaven rather than the things of earth. While this passage has a message that is of enduring meaning for all people, it has particular meaning for disciples who are immersed in a materialistic society. The Gospel of Luke has more teachings about the right use of material wealth than any other gospel. This parable introduces the topic of stewardship and discipleship in such a way that we cannot help but see ourselves in it and reflect on the many challenging points it contains.

One of the most shocking parts of the parable is that the rich man never considers anyone else's needs or that the blessing of his harvest was meant to enrich anyone other than himself. In the ancient world, when one person was blessed then the whole community rejoiced because they presumed that the blessings given to one person would be shared with everyone. That is not the case in this parable —the man keeps everything for himself and in doing so reveals his lack of compassion, lack of faith, and overwhelming greed. Greed was understood in the ancient world as the insatiable desire from acquiring more possessions.[13] It is one of the vices listed in various New Testament passages that are contrary to Christian discipleship and the Gospel way of life (v. Mk 7:22, Rom 1:29, Eph 4:19, 5:3). Paul even goes so far as to equate greed with idolatry (v. Col 3:5). The basis of greed is the mistaken belief that life is a matter of having rather than being. Jesus identifies this teaching on the nature of true life as the primary focus of the parable when He corrects the man who seeks the Lord's intervention to secure his share of inheritance (v. Lk 12:15). Jesus knows that possessions can become a source of false security for people. People seek such a sense of security especially in times of fear or vulnerability. For Christians, however, security of life is to be found in God and not

---

13. See Plutarch, "De Cupiditate" in *Moralia*, 3.

in their possessions. When a disciple correctly establishes their security in God then they are able to let go of false securities in an expression of generosity. Thus, the virtue of generosity is actually a sign of true faith and a witness of spiritual freedom.

> *When are you preoccupied with possessions?*
> *The man in today's parable believed the myth that "Whoever dies with the most toys wins." How has that lie affected your life?*
> *How do you see it played out in the world around you?*
> *The myth of materialism tells us that possessions equal happiness and that the more we have the happier we will be. What experiences have shown this myth to be false?*
> *When you experience fear or vulnerability, in what do you seek security?*
> *What does it look like when people value possessions over persons?*
> *How does greed destroy individual persons, families, careers, institutions and nations?*

The second negative quality of the rich man is his failure to consider the consequences his current actions will have for eternal life. Instead, his primary concern is for the pursuit of pleasure and self-indulgence in this life. When a person believes that pleasure is the goal of life then they have given in to what is known as hedonism. The pursuit of pleasure and self-indulgence is exemplified by the rich man's statement, "take your ease, eat drink and be merry." This very phrase was used in Sir 11:14–19 to describe the thoughts of someone corrupted by their possessions and whose interests are only focused on present life (v. Sir 11:14–19). Such an attitude is an affront to God who in His mercy created us for eternal life in heaven (v. Is 22:13). Paul goes so far as to say that such a hedonistic approach to life is an implicit denial of the resurrection (v. 1 Co 15:32). Jesus personally condemns hedonism and its power to blind disciples when He commands His followers to avoid concern for the vain and fleeting pursuits of this life (v. Lk 12:29). It is easy to become focused on our own pleasure and comfort. Sometimes all we think about is a future of freedom, leisure, recreation, and surplus. When that is only what we are working for then we are not planning wisely because we are planning selfishly. When a person becomes hedonistic, they have practically excluded God from their daily decisions. Such an atheistic attitude exists when our decisions and management of resources takes place without considering the divine will for our lives.

> *How does the hollowness of hedonism afflict us and how is it communicated in our culture?*
> *How do you prepare for others in your future and not just your own self or your own family?*
> *What difference does your faith in God make in the practical matters of life?*
> *How do you use your possessions differently because of your faith in God?*
> *What can help a person better understand the connection between their present decisions and the eternal consequences of those decisions?*

The third negative quality of the rich man is that of egocentrism. This is the inability to understand or assume any perspective other than an individual's own perception. This attitude is reflected in the rich man because of how he constantly speaks about himself: "I will do...", "I will pull down", "I will build....", "I will store....", "I will say to myself....". He never considers what God may desire for his life or what others may need from him. His self-absorption prevents him from understanding anything other than his own desire. His self-absorption and egocentrism continue to unfold as his desire for a greater personal kingdom is manifested by his preoccupation to retain and increase his possessions. What was meant to be a blessing (an abundant harvest) has become a problem because he now has to find a way to keep it all for himself. This self-absorption is demonstrated by the use of such phrases as "My crops", "my barn", "my goods", "my grain", and "my soul". Such self-absorption can affect us as well and cause us to become very self-centered in our decisions. Egocentrism can also lead us to believe that we are self-sufficient and do not need other people. The man in this parable didn't think he needed anyone else—family, community, or God and so he doesn't include them in his deliberation and planning for his future.

When do you find it most tempting to live your life without
responsibility for others or fidelity to God?
When are you tempted to believe that you are secure in
your self-sufficiency?
How does our American culture foster an unhealthy sense
of self-sufficiency and egocentrism?
What can we do as a faith community to help people break
free from the trap of self-sufficiency and egocentrism?
How often do you pray about self-concerns in your prayer?

The wake-up call to rich man occurs with an interesting phrase:
"You fool, this night your life will be demanded of you." The identification of the man as a fool is meant to demonstrate the false
perceptions that dominated his decisions and actions: he wanted
to be perceived as "merry" but in reality is perceived as a "fool", he
thought he had "many years" to enjoy his life but in reality it will
last no more than "this night". He enjoyed self-absorption with his
own soul and now his own soul is being taken from him, and he
believed his possessions would be his security but now they can
offer him no help. In fact, his possessions could very well be the
active agent of his demise as is indicated by the curious phrase
"your life will be demanded of" (v. Lk 12:20). A more accurate
translation of this phrase would read, "...they are demanding of
you your soul." This translation is rarely used, however, because it
begs the question of who is meant by "they" demanding his soul.
One interpretation is that "they" refers to the man's possessions.
Thus, his possessions are actually taking the man's life away from
him. St. Francis of Assisi once said, "Remember that when you
leave this earth, you can take nothing that you have received...but
only what you have given."

What are foolish thoughts people have today?
What has helped you see the foolishness of some of your
pursuits and preoccupations?
How can the preoccupation with possessions actually rob
people of their lives?
How does greed take away people's ability to deeply enjoy
life?

When has a misguided value taken away a part of your life and how can you help someone who is currently caught in a similar misguided pursuit?

The Catholic Church teaches a principle called the "universal destination of goods". That means God provides for the needs of all humanity by entrusting to all humanity the goods of the earth for our common use. Thus, the blessings we receive as individuals or nations are meant to be blessings for all people and not just a few. The world does have enough resources for the needs of humanity. What we lack is generosity and compassion for others who are in need and the sense of justice to distribute those resources accordingly. The man in the parable never considers what he could do for others. He has no sense of his responsibility to use wisely and responsibly the blessings he has received so as to help others. Indifference to the needs of others has eroded any compassion he might have had.

How does this teaching of the universal destination of goods challenge our culture of absolute consumerism and unbridled capitalism?

NINETEENTH SUNDAY IN ORDINARY TIME

Our scripture passage for this Sunday comes from the Gospel of Luke 12:32–48. This text is a continuation of Jesus' teaching on the need to place our trust and security in Him and not in our material possessions. The right use of material possessions is an essential response of faith for disciples and Luke's Gospel contains more references on this topic than any other Gospel.

Jesus begins this section by specifically addressing the fear of insecurity and insufficiency that can lead a person to care only for themselves rather than generously caring for the needs of others. In the verses immediately preceding this passage the Lord instructed the disciples about God's care for the ravens, lilies, and grass of the field. If God cares for these created things so well then the Lord will care even more for disciples who seek His Kingdom. Jesus teaches the disciples that they can trust in the Father's loving and caring providence over their lives because God is in control of all things. With that blessed assurance, there is no need to fear. Rather, disciples who have received the Kingdom must be disciples who freely give the Kingdom to others. For this reason, the sharing of resources becomes a witness of faith in God's protection and providence.

How can the fears of insufficiency and insecurity cause people today to care only for themselves and not for the needs of others?
What other fears can cause people to fail in generosity?
Why do you think the phrase, "Do not be afraid..." is one of the most common statements of Jesus?
What has helped you overcome your fears so as to be guided by faith and trust in God?
Who is an example of someone who focuses more on heavenly treasure than earthly treasure?

This teaching on the right use of material possessions then moves into a series of parables that describe different people's actions concerning accountability and good stewardship. It should be noted that the accountability Jesus refers to is not just a once-for-all experience at the Last Judgment, the end of the world, or the death of the individual Christian. These parables are used in the Gospels of Matthew and Luke to communicate such an apocalyptic understanding of the Master's return but the Gospel of Luke implies that the Master's return to check on his servants occurs in the course of every day and is an ongoing experience of discipleship (v. apocalyptic use of similar images in Mt 24:42, Mt 24:43–44, Mt 24:45–51, Mt 25:1–13, and Mk 13:33–37). The emphasis on more regular accountability and daily judgment is a distinctive theme in Luke's Gospel.

The first parable is about servants who wait for their Master's return from a wedding. They are the ones who are "watchful" meaning they are prepared by prayer and faithful fulfillment of their duties. The Master's return for them is a cause of joy and they are invited to participate in a great banquet in which the Master serves them. We should not be surprised by such an action because Jesus said in the Last Supper that He was among them as "one who serves" (Lk 22:27). The meaning of this parable is that faithful servants have nothing to fear. The Master's return will be a time of great blessing as God's greatness is revealed in humble service. The servants were eager for the Master's return; it was what they were living for. Obviously, this parable is about the return of Jesus and our need to be servants who are watchful that is praying and faithfully fulfilling the responsibilities God has given us. It can be easy to fall asleep in our faith every day and to forget the tasks the Lord has entrusted to us —especially the right use of material possessions. The Master of the household may come at any time in the course of our day to see how faithful we are in generously caring for the needs of others. When we "fall asleep" in that duty then we fail to act according to the Master's will (v. Lk 12:47).

> *As you hear this parable, whom do you think most looks forward to the coming of Jesus in our time?*
> *When have you been most faithful in your use of material possessions?*
> *Have you ever felt uncomfortable because someone "greater" than you was actually serving you?*

How would you feel to have God be your servant at the eternal banquet? How does the image of God as Servant motivate you as a disciple today?

The second parable is slightly different but continues the theme of faithful stewardship of material possessions. Rather than the coming of Jesus being a positive event people would look forward to, for those who are unprepared the coming of Jesus will be like a thief in the night. That is an interesting image: If we are mindful that the household belongs to the Lord, then His return is a cause of great joy; but if we begin to deceive ourselves by thinking the household is ours, then the return of Jesus will seem like a thief coming to take back what we falsely believe to be ours. This image of the return of Jesus being like a thief in the night was deeply rooted in the mind of the early Church and is used elsewhere in the New Testament (v. Mt 24:43, 1 Thes 5:2,4, 2 P 3:10, Rev 16:15). Whether we eagerly await the Lord as the Master of the House or fear the Lord as the Thief depends upon how we are living our discipleship. To be "ready for the Lord" in Luke's Gospel requires that disciples have the following characteristics. They trust in God and not in possessions (v. Lk 12:13–21), they live out the petitions of the Lord's Prayer (v. Lk 11:1–4), they are to be generous in caring for the needs of others (v. Lk 10:25–37), they are to stay focused on the presence of God and remain attentive to the Lord's word (v. Lk 10:38–42), and they are to remain watchful and perseverant in their prayer (v. Lk 11:5–9). The coming of Jesus in these parables is not just an event that will occur at the end or time or at the end of an individual disciple's life; the coming of Jesus for each of us can happen on a daily basis as we encounter the Lord in others and are challenged to assist them in their need.

Which of these aspects of discipleship are most difficult for you to live? Which are easiest?
If the Lord came to you this night, would you welcome with joy as the long-awaited Master or would you feel "cheated" as though a thief had broken into your life?
How do you think Jesus has been present to you this past week in the people and situations you have faced?

The third parable is prompted by the question of Peter: "Lord, is this parable meant for us or for everyone?" Most probably, this third parable is addressed to those in positions of Christian leadership or ministry responsibility. The image of a household manager is interesting. The household manager was a fellow slave who was given two responsibilities: first, to oversee the activities of the other slaves and make sure they were doing what was asked of them and, second, to serve the needs of the other slaves by providing their food and materials. Thus, the household manager was accountable both to the Master and to the other slaves. That's dual accountability.

It is said that the true measure of a person's character is what they will do when no one is watching. The manager in this parable thought the Master wasn't watching, so he treated the other servants badly. God does pay attention to how we treat others. One of the morals of this story is that disciples cannot be faithful to God if they are abusing their roles and responsibilities or the other people in their lives. Although the parable is directed towards those entrusted with leadership responsibility, we should be careful to not define those roles too narrowly. Christian leadership is not only for those who are employed by the Church or ordained for ministry. It includes many others as well. Parents are responsible for the Christian development of their children. Husbands and wives are responsible for the spiritual development of their spouses. Parish volunteers are responsible for serving those in their ministries. Teachers are responsible for giving good witness to their students. Each of us has some responsibility for others and so each of us faces this dual accountability. It is important for disciples to evaluate how well they are fulfilling their responsibilities to others and not just their responsibilities to God.

> *How do you keep yourself from becoming like that manager when it comes to handling situations of leadership and responsibility in your life?*
>
> *To whom are you accountable for your Christian leadership?*
>
> *What practical examples can you think of in which people abuse their position and authority today for self-gain?*
>
> *How often do you pray for those who are accountable to you?*

Imagine that both God and those for whom you are responsible gave you a report card on how well you are fulfilling your responsibilities of discipleship; what would be your grade from each?

How can you seek to be spiritually accountable to those for whom you are responsible?

TWENTIETH SUNDAY IN ORDINARY TIME

Our scripture passage for this Sunday comes from the Gospel of Luke 12:49–53. In many ways it is a strange teaching in which Jesus speaks about fire, baptism, and the divisions caused by faith. We should remember that our Lord's words in this passage follow up on His caution to the disciples when He said: "Much will be required of the person entrusted with much." (v. Lk 12:48). When a disciple faithfully carries out the will of the Master (v. last Sunday's reflection) it will lead to an all-encompassing commitment of life. This commitment of life may bring harmony between the disciple and the Master but it will oftentimes cause division with others. All of these points are worthy of our study and prayer so that we can better understand and respond to the challenges we face as disciples.

First, Jesus says that He has come to throw "fire" on the earth. Fire is a symbol with various meanings. Some scripture commentators think this image of fire refers to the experience of judgment that burns and punishes sin (cf. Mt 5:22 and Mk 9:48 for the "fires of hell" or Gehenna, Lk 3:17 for the fire of judgment). Even the disciples of Jesus wanted to call down fire on the Samaritan town for rejecting them as they made their way to Jerusalem (v. Lk 9:54). In the Old Testament, Elijah threw fire from the Lord against the prophets of the pagan god Baal (v. 1 Kgs 18:36–40) and the soldiers of King Ahaziah (v. 2 K 1:10,12,14). Fire was also an image of purification as in the melting process for gold and silver that are "tested" in fire—references exist for this meaning both in the Old Testament and the New Testament (cf. Sir 2:6, Wis 3:5, Wis 3:6, 1 Pt 1:7). This purification allows a disciple to follow the Lord with readiness and freedom (v. Heb 12:1). Fire is also a symbol for faith both in the Old Testament and the New Testament. The Prophet Jeremiah said that the Word of God is like a "fire" in his bones (v. Jer 20:9 and 23:29). In the New Testament, Paul writes to Timothy and instructs him to deepen his commitment of faith with these words: "...stir into flame the gift of God that you have through the imposition of my hands" (v. 2 Tm 1:6). In the Acts of the Apostles, the gift of the Holy Spirit (and the faith that is born of the Spirit) is symbolized by fire as well (v. Acts 3:16 and 2:3).

This final image of the Holy Spirit and the connection to fire is particularly important because in Luke 3:16 John the Baptist announced that the "mightier one" (Jesus) would baptize with fire and the Holy Spirit. When Jesus says He came to cast "fire" on the earth, He is drawing on all of these images. He came to destroy the power of evil, to purify us of our sinfulness, to sanctify us with the gift of the Holy Spirit, and to awaken within us the gift of faith and obedience to His Word in our hearts. What a powerful image! And how our Lord wishes it were already ablaze! It is often said that faith is "caught" more than "taught". We catch the fire of faith from those around us who are "on fire" for the Lord and whose hearts burn with love. This image of faith as a fire that burns within our hearts was also experienced by the two disciples on the way to Emmaus (v. Lk 24:32).

> *Which aspect of the symbol of fire strikes you in a particularly meaningful way?*
> *How can each of these images of fire inform and inspire your discipleship?*
> *From whom have you "caught" the fire of faith?*
> *How do you "fan into flame" the gift of faith you have received?*
> *How can you continue to "fuel" the fire within you?*
> *What can cause the fire of faith to diminish and smolder?*
> *What is the purification we need to pray for so we can grow in holiness as a community of faith?*

Second, Jesus cautions us that being on fire with faith will not necessarily make our lives easier. Although we may bring joy to the Master of the household, other members of the household may not be so happy because not everyone will share in our passionate love for God and neighbor or agree with our decisions of discipleship. As a result, the gift of faith sometimes can become a cause of division and rejection rather than a source of communion and peace. In the early Church of the first century, many people were disowned by their families for becoming Christians and choosing to persevere in their commitment to Jesus. Oftentimes this meant that they lost their possessions, positions, and economic standing in society. Many people today can experience rejection, persecution and disharmony for their decision to follow Christ. Such an experience can cause bewilderment in a disciple's life because we sometimes think that faith only brings peace and good will. This passage cautions us of the reality that faith doesn't always make life easier and that sometimes those closest to us will not agree with our decisions of discipleship.

> *Who do you know that has experienced difficulties because of their decision of faith?*
> *When has your commitment of faith brought about division with others (even a clear difference of values)?*
> *How can we as individuals and as a community support those who are isolated or rejected because of their decision of faith in Jesus?*
> *How can we encourage one another to persevere in our faith even when it means risking alienation or going against the values of those closest to us?*

Lastly, Jesus is reminding us that, as disciples, we are called to follow our Lord's own example and experience. That is why Jesus says that He has a baptism to undergo and that He is anxious until it is accomplished. The baptism that Jesus speaks of will occur in His passion and death when He is washed in suffering and the shedding of His blood and our Lord has made it clear that disciples will be called to follow Him in picking up their cross if they are to be faithful (cf. Mk 10:38–39 and Lk 9:23). Our baptism derives its meaning from the baptism of which Jesus speaks (Holy Spirit and Fire v. Lk 3:16) and is an immersion into our Lord's Death and Resurrection so that we live no longer for ourselves but for Christ. This connection between faith, baptism, and sharing in the cross of Jesus reminds us that sacrifice is essential to discipleship. Certainly the apostles experienced persecution, rejection, and hatred from many people of their time because of their commitment to Jesus. It is important to remember in these moments that the Church is not founded on human relationships but on our relationship with Jesus Christ and that there will always be tension in our lives when we try to please others and God at the same time. Sometimes we will have to choose who is of greatest priority. Rather than being surprised when these moments come, we should expect them and see them as necessary opportunities for purification and deepened faith. This passage is a sobering reminder that faith and baptism are a serious commitment that will encompass every aspect of our lives. If we try to contain, restrict, or tame the gift of faith we risk extinguishing the fire of God's word within us. Jesus wants us to be washed in His own passion and commitment to the Father's will that marked His life.

> *How do people try to contain, restrict, or tame the message of faith?*
>
> *If baptism is an immersion into the death and resurrection of Jesus then why are people surprised when the challenge of discipleship involves sacrifice?*
>
> *When have you found yourself in the difficult situation of having to decide whether you act to please God or to please others and what has helped you act in a faithful and courageous way?*
>
> *Who is an example of someone who is passionate about living out his or her baptism?*
>
> *How does the meaning Jesus gives to baptism in this passage differ from what most people think they are doing when they accept baptism?*

TWENTY-FIRST SUNDAY IN
ORDINARY TIME

Our scripture passage for this Sunday comes from the Gospel of Luke 13:22–30. In this scene, someone poses a question of faith that manifests his or her religious curiosity. Jesus responds not by answering the question but by redirecting the person's focus to where their attention should be placed. Following Jesus requires more than just knowledge of religious information; following Jesus involves a transformation of life. Therefore, Jesus responds to the question by telling the person they should be striving now to enter the "narrow door" and not just wondering how many will get in. If they are not striving now, they will not enter. Let's study this passage in detail to better understand what it means for us as disciples.

The person who posed the question to Jesus was someone who heard Jesus as our Lord made His way to Jerusalem. The person addresses Jesus with the title "Lord" which indicates that the person was favorably disposed to Jesus and may have even been a disciple. Their question reflects the religious curiosity of someone who is exploring the details of faith and discipleship. It also reflects the curiosity that seeks ever-greater knowledge and can even become an unhealthy pursuit of religious trivia. Sometimes it's possible for a person to become infatuated or distracted with religious things while being deterred from a committed relationship with the person of Jesus Christ. Jesus does not answer the man's question. Rather, our Lord redirects his attention to actively trying to live out discipleship. This interchange invites us to reflect on the nature of discipleship and what it means to be a person of faith. Faith is not just a matter of knowing more but of our ability and willingness to act on our knowledge and pursue a transformed life (repentance). No one has ever been declared a Saint (canonized) because of what they knew but because of how they lived. Such transformation is an ongoing challenge in a Christian's life. If a person is not striving for holiness each day then they have become complacent in their discipleship. Saint Paul challenged the Christians of his community similarly when he said, "Work out your salvation with fear and trembling" (v. Phil 2:12).

> *What religious fascinations in our world today can distract*
> *people from the daily task of real discipleship?*
> *How do you know in your life when a religious interest or*
> *religious curiosity has become a distraction?*
> *What aspect of your faith do you find difficult to live out*
> *in practice?*

Jesus then presents the image of the "Narrow Door" and challenges the man to strive to enter it (as opposed to the wider doors). Some ancient cities actually did have very narrow passageways that would allow individuals to enter only if they dismounted their horses, shed their armor, and let go of their excess baggage. The narrow door was meant to prevent enemy soldiers from entering in such a hostile way. It also meant that the people had to reorient themselves so as to fit through that narrow passageway. That is a very good image for what it means to be a disciple! This instruction becomes more challenging when we remember that in the Gospel of John Jesus identified Himself as the door through which we enter to become a member of His flock (v. Jn 10:9). To enter through the "Narrow Door" is to enter through the person of Jesus. That is the challenge to reorient our lives to become like Jesus. This process involves shedding what should not be part of the Lord's kingdom, letting go of our false senses of security, and dropping the baggage that weights us down and keeps us from following the Lord in freedom.

> *What is the armor we hide behind that God wants us to get*
> *rid of so we can be more authentically ourselves?*
> *What is the baggage we carry with us that has no place in*
> *the Kingdom of God?*
> *What are the means of aggression we need to leave behind?*
> *Entering the Kingdom of God means becoming vulnerable*
> *to the Lord. How does the image of the "Narrow Door" fit*
> *with your experience of Christian Discipleship?*

The final image of Jesus' teaching is that of a man who "rises" (the same word used for the Resurrection) and shuts the door. Those locked outside cry out but the Master of the House says that he "does not know them." Those outside say in response: "We ate and drank in your company; you taught in our streets," but the Master replies: "I do not know where you are from. Depart from me, all you evil doers!" This exchange is fascinating and troubling. It is a powerful warning to Christian disciples. You see, we "eat and drink" in the Lord's company and Jesus "teaches in our streets" every time we attend Mass that is the Body and Blood of the Eucharist and the Word of God proclaimed in Scripture. Jesus says that it's not enough to receive those gifts of grace; we also have to respond to those gifts of grace. The faith experience isn't complete until we have become "Doers of Good" rather than "Doers of Evil". The people "locked out" in the parable received much (Eucharist and Scripture) but didn't respond so as to become the living presence of Christ in the world. Rather, their understanding of faith and discipleship was a matter of what God could do for them rather than doing what God was asking of them. They remained "evil doers" despite all the blessings and graces they had received. It is also important to note that the Master of the House specifically says that he does not "know where you are from." This implies that those locked outside were relying on their physical proximity to Jesus rather than their spiritual closeness. This verse reminds us that discipleship is not a matter of our association with others, status in the community or the Church, ethnic background, or geographical proximity. Discipleship is the challenge to actively conform our lives to Christ each day and never tire of the challenge to grow in holiness.

> *How does this final image of the parable challenge you?*
> *How does this understanding of faith change the way you approach the Mass?*
> *If we were to find ourselves "locked out", what would we say to the Master of the House as a reason to let us in?*
> *What false senses of security can people erroneously rely on today to ensure their place in the Kingdom of Heaven?*
> *In all of these teachings, Jesus is instructing us as His disciples on how to be people of better faith—a faith that is manifested in an active transformation of life striving to be more like Christ every day. What can you do as part*

*of your daily life to foster such a radical and committed
"following" of the Lord?*

TWENTY-SECOND SUNDAY IN ORDINARY TIME

Our scripture passage for this Sunday comes from the Gospel of Luke 14:1, 7–14. In this passage, Jesus is once again in the home of a Pharisee and sharing a meal. This happens a lot in Luke's Gospel and it's for a reason. Luke is not only telling us about something that happened during the historical life of Jesus. Rather, Luke is really speaking to the early Christian community and addressing issues taking place in the life of the early Church. Thus, Luke is telling us that there are certain attitudes and behaviors that can be divisive in the Christian community. Let's study this passage to see what the Lord may be saying to us as disciples.

At the dinner in the home of the Pharisee, Jesus notices how people were competing with one another so they could be seated in privileged places. In doing so, they were claiming honor for themselves and hoping that others would admire them because of their position at the table. Jesus lived in an honor-based society and there were a variety of ways in which people tried to seek honor. Other examples of ways in which people sought honor included displays of material wealth (homes, clothes, lavish dinners), causing others to be socially embarrassed or ridiculed, confusing or baffling another person with questions, or even physical assaults (especially slaps to the face). In response to this endless competition for self-honor, Jesus offers an instruction about the nature of honor itself; real honor is not that which we claim for ourselves but what we are given by another, especially God. The dinner guests were concerned about the "externals" of life (exclusive positions, fine clothes, pricey toys, nice house, being invited to the best social events, appearing better than others, and so forth) and so they competed for those things in order to be the center of attention. How familiar that sounds for our world as well! The message of Jesus is just as important for us as it was to the people of our Lord's own time. The competition for honor creates an endless addiction that is never satisfying for very long. It causes people to have a false image that is based on the externals of life rather than a deeply rooted relationship with God. It also causes a person to base their self-worth on other people's opinions. Jesus wants disciples who willingly and intentionally choose to not pursue the false honors of the world.

> *What are the status symbols that most tempt people today to claim honor for themselves so as to be admired/respected by others?*
> *Some people become so wrapped up in the externals of life that those "things" become their identity. When has that been true in your life?*
> *How can the competition for honor be harmful to a community of faith?*
> *What happens today when a person bases their self-worth on the opinions of others?*

Next, Jesus instructs the guests to seek a place of lower status and thus be "honored" when they are called to a higher place. Remember: true honor is not that which we claim for ourselves but that which is given to us by another, namely God. Our Lord is instructing us in what God finds honorable; the humility to put others first. Humility is the remedy that breaks the endless competition for honor. The Christian virtue of humility is not an act of self-degradation or deprecation; Christian humility is based on the truth of who are and who we are not. The very word "humility" comes from the Latin word "humus" meaning "earth". As human beings, we come from the dust of the earth yet we receive life through the Spirit of God who creates us. Who we are, then, is a complete gift of God. Such an honest awareness both prevents us from developing a falsely exalted view of ourselves and acknowledges the great dignity inherent to our nature.

> *Who is someone you know that manifests such a truly humble life? What are their characteristics?*
> *When have you been honored by someone else in a way you were not seeking and why?*
> *What was that like to have unsolicited honor given to you rather than seeking it for yourself?*
> *What does unhealthy humility look like?*

After offering His teaching on how to behave at a dinner, Jesus then moves on to offer the more challenging teaching of who to invite! In doing so, He is no longer addressing actions; now He is addressing relationships. He says, "Stop inviting your friends". The implication is that enough friends have already been invited; now it is time to invite some others—namely, the ones who need to be included because they live their lives on the margin of society. It's interesting that in this passage, Jesus uses four different words to describe the various settings in which His teaching applies; reception, lunch, dinner, and banquet (Greek = *gamous, aristos, deipnon, doche*). By referring to these four different settings, Jesus is including all social events in His command and the Lord is teaching us to open all our life to others and not just one part of our lives. Basically, the inclusion of the marginalized is to be a way of life for a disciple. Each of us knows marginalized people who would love to be included in the events of our lives. They may be members of our families, friends, professional associates, neighbors, and even fellow parishioners. They are the ones who may be a little different from the rest—the blind, lame, deaf, and poor. They are also the ones who may not be able to return our kindness and so our generous welcome becomes a truly selfless act of mercy and compassion. Jesus tells us that God honors those who make a place in their lives to care for the marginalized. After all, in the eyes of God we are all blind, lame, and poor. When we care for one another with mercy, compassion and acceptance then, Jesus says, God will care for us in the same way. Sometimes it is our invitation and welcome that gives dignity to the marginalized and restores them to fullness within the community.

Who in your life, for example, family, friends, professional associates, needs to be dignified by your welcome and hospitality?

In what part of your life do you find it easy to practice a welcoming mercy and compassion?

In what part of your life do you find it difficult to practice mercy and compassion?

When do you find yourself doing nice things for other people because you are hoping they will reciprocate your kindness?

*When have you invited a truly marginalized person into
your life as an equal and what was that experience like?*

All of the above reflection has been applied to the experience of our
personal lives. However, we should not miss that Jesus offers His
teaching in the midst of a "Meal" with the Lord. Thus, everything
on which we just reflected could also be applied to our Church
community as well. The celebration of the Mass is not meant to
be a celebration for the privileged few but an experience of God's
mercy and welcome that heals and restores human dignity to the
wounded and marginalized in our midst.

*As members of a parish, how can we be tempted to focus
on externals?*
*When can we seek honor for ourselves rather than giving
honor to those who need it?*
What does the challenge of humility mean for our parish?
*Who are the marginalized you need to welcome into our
community (or your pew)?*
*What is the ministry of mercy, compassion and acceptance
Jesus wants us to undertake in your community?*
*Why do you think Jesus was so concerned that Christians
not participate in the competition for honor?*

Let us pray with St. Thérèse de Lisieux:

And yet, dear Lord, Thou knowest my weakness. Each morning I resolve to be humble, and in the evening I recognize that I
have often been guilty of pride. The sight of these faults tempts
me to discouragement; yet I know that discouragement is
itself but a form of pride. I wish, therefore, O my God, to build
all my trust upon Thee. As Thou canst do all things, deign to
implant in my soul this virtue which I desire, and to obtain
it from Thy Infinite Mercy, I will often say to Thee: "Jesus,
Meek and Humble of Heart, make my heart like unto Thine."[14]

---

14. St. Thérèse de Lisieux. *The Story of the Soul* (New York: Cosimo,
     2007), p. 283.

TWENTY-THIRD SUNDAY IN ORDINARY TIME

Our scripture passage for this Sunday comes from the Gospel of Luke 14:25–33. It is a surprisingly harsh teaching in which, at first glance, Jesus appears to be telling His disciples to "hate" those closest to him. This passage is challenging, indeed, and offers many points worthy of our reflection.

For background information it is important to note that we are told there were "many crowds" following Jesus. That is a peculiar phrasing. It means that there were many different kinds of people with Jesus—those committed, those interested, and those who were just curious. They are all sharing the same journey with the Lord to Jerusalem. Jesus issues them a wake-up call in today's passage. To be a disciple might sound nice, but it means there will come a time when they will have to choose between Jesus and the other people and priorities in their lives. It is then, in that moment of decision, that the challenge of discipleship will become real. True discipleship is not a matter of convenience but of strong conviction in, and commitment to, the person of Jesus Christ. It will require great sacrifice to faithfully persevere to the end with Jesus. Many will not be able to endure the trials and tests that will inevitably occur because they will be unprepared to make the necessary sacrifices so that Jesus can be the highest priority of their lives.

> *If you were to describe the "many crowds" that compose our faith community, what would they be?*
> *How does the sacrifice required for committed discipleship differ for each group?*
> *When have you been surprised by the sacrifice required of you in your discipleship?*

The first challenge Jesus gives us is that of "hating" our father and mother, brother and sister, even wife (and husband) for the sake of following him. This is strong language. The word "hate" in this passage refers more to action than to emotion. The best way to interpret this passage is to think of times when we are called on to do something that others don't like or that goes against their wishes. Following through on such an action means that we can sometimes be accused of "hating" them for going against their request and expectation. Many parents have heard the words "You hate me" from their children because they made them go to bed at the appointed hour. Loving God and our Neighbor does not mean that we always do what our neighbor wants. Sometimes our love for God can actually challenge us to acting in a way that our neighbor does not want. Historically, Christians had to sometimes be willing to face rejection from their families (parents and siblings) as well as their own spouses (v. 1 Cor 7:15) for the sake of their Christian discipleship. Following Jesus sometimes meant putting the Lord first even above the most foundational human relationships of our lives. That's not easy.

> *When have you felt the call of discipleship challenging you to act in a way contrary to the wishes of your spouse or family?*
> *When have the values of the Gospel and your commitment of faith caused you to differ with your co-workers?*
> *When have your friendships been strained because of your discipleship?*
> *What relationships have most helped you in your discipleship?*
> *When have core relationships actually been an impediment to your discipleship?*

Next, Jesus challenges those who would follow Him to bear their cross. In our contemporary Christian piety, we have used the phrase of "bearing the cross" to refer to any situation of human suffering, weakness or distress. However, such an interpretation is broader than our Lord's instruction. To "carry the cross" is not so much an action of accepting a general human condition (weakness, illness, and so forth) but rather of voluntarily taking on a difficulty as a direct consequence of our commitment to Jesus—deliberate sacrifice, exposure to risk and ridicule. The "cross" is the suffering we knowingly accept as the consequence of our decision of faithful discipleship.

When have you had an unpleasant consequence for a decision of faith you made?
What decision are you facing now that is calling you to embrace sacrifice in order to follow Jesus more closely?

Who inspires by their fidelity in carrying the cross of discipleship? Jesus then tells two parables about situations that require total commitment—the man who builds a tower and the king who goes into battle. In both parables, the message is clear; calculate the cost because it will require everything in your life to be a successful disciple. If you are not willing to accept the consequences of discipleship then do not pretend to be a disciple. Jesus tells us these two parables for a reason. He is not looking for superficial disciples. Rather, He is looking for people who are totally committed if they are going to follow Him at all. Just think for a moment about how much damage is done to Christianity when someone claims the title "Disciple" but does not witness the reality! Discipleship is not easy.

When have you been disappointed by someone claiming to be a "Christian" but who acted in very "un-Christian" ways?
What is the most "un-Christian" behavior you need to address in your own life?
Who is someone you know who has given all for the sake of being a disciple of Jesus?

Jesus ends this passage with a simple statement regarding the attachment to possessions. He says, "Unless you relinquish all your possessions, you cannot be my disciple." Luke has more teachings on the right use of material possessions than any other Gospel. It is not that disciples are called to reject their possessions but rather that they are called to relinquish any claim their possessions have on them. In the age of persecution, Christians were sometimes stripped of their possessions as a consequence of their faith. Unless those early Christians were willing to relinquish "all their possessions," they could not remain faithful to Jesus. Today, we do not face the same persecution as those who lived during the time Luke was writing his Gospel. Our challenge is to be good Stewards who are willing to freely and wisely use our material possessions for the mission of the Gospel.

The important question is this; do our possessions control us or do we control them?

Do we see our possessions as the source of our life or do we see them as tools with which we can do good for God and others?

Following Jesus means that we put our possessions at the service of the Gospel. How has the practice of sacrificial generosity grown in your life because of your growth in discipleship?

When did you start being truly sacrificial in your service of the Gospel?

What have been some of the challenges you have faced along the way?

What have been some of the rewards that have encouraged and sustained you in your commitment of faith?

How do you know when possessions begin to dominate your life?

In all of these teachings, Jesus is reminding us that He wants disciples who are committed to following Him and who hold nothing back from Him. The cost of discipleship is different for each person, but it will be all consuming for everyone. For some, it will require their time and energy; for others it may mean a change in personal relationships; still for others it may mean pursuing a different vocation; and, finally, for others, it may mean a sacrificial commitment of our resources.

What is particularly challenging about the call to discipleship for you at this point in your life?

Twenty-Fourth Sunday in Ordinary Time

Our scripture passage for this Sunday comes from the Gospel of Luke 15:1–10. (Note: for an additional study on the Parable of the Prodigal Son, see the scripture reflection for the Third Sunday of Lent.) This chapter is the heart and center of Luke's Gospel and in it we hear three parables of divine mercy and reconciliation. We also hear the reaction of those who disapprove of God's generous and merciful love. This reading challenges us to embrace the values of God and to cooperate with the work of reconciliation the Lord is trying to effect in our lives and in the lives of others.

The chapter begins with the Pharisees and scribes complaining because Jesus is welcoming sinners and eating with them. To share a meal in the ancient world was more than just a way to satisfy hunger. It was a way in which people shared their life and celebrated relationship among the participants. The English word "companion" communicates this meaning since it is derived from the two Latin words *cum* ("with") and *panis* ("bread") and refers to a person with whom we share bread (meal). The objection of the Pharisees and scribes, then, was focused on the fact that Jesus was becoming friends with people who were regarded as sinners. This action of Jesus was scandalous and unacceptable to the Pharisees and scribes because they believed it was honorable to separate oneself from those who were considered less holy. Jesus teaches us that God desires reconciliation and the conversion of others. In fact, God not only values openness to a sinner's conversion but also actually takes initiative in seeking that conversion.

The Pharisees and scribes may have welcomed sinners to their table at some point but only when those sinners had proven themselves worthy of such an honor. Jesus teaches us that God honors those who reach out to reconcile and welcome the wayward rather than waiting for them to first correct their lives before they receive love and attention. The attitude of the Pharisees and scribes can be divisive in a community because it creates a world in which some people see themselves as better than others and restrict their associations to those they considered like themselves. Of course, others who are deemed unworthy are excluded from such associations. Rather than facilitating or encouraging conversion, such a divisive and condemnatory attitude actually frustrates and impedes conversion. Jesus came to seek out and save what was lost and He expects His disciples to assist Him in that effort. This passage challenges us to examine our attitudes and judgments of others so as to take initiative in seeking their conversion rather than frustrating it. The fact that the tax collectors and sinners were drawing near to listen to Jesus indicates that they were receiving our Lord's word and becoming disciples with a corresponding change of life. Such a delicate moment of grace needs nurturing and acceptance lest it perish from indifference or rejection.

> *As you think about the differences in attitude expressed by Jesus and the Pharisees, how are you challenged to reconsider your own attitude and values?*
> *When has someone's acceptance, encouragement and friendship helped you change your life in a positive way?*
> *Who is waiting for you to take initiative and reach out to them?*
> *How does your faith community experience division because of the judgmental attitudes of some members?*
> *Who are the people who are considered sinners today?*

Jesus then tells the parable of the shepherd who leaves the ninety-nine and goes after the lost sheep. This action would not have made sense to the people of Jesus' time for two reasons. First, it was a disproportionate risk to leave the ninety-nine to fend for themselves without assurance that the lost one would even be found. The action of the shepherd in the parable teaches us that God does not follow human logic when making such decisions. The Lord is not content to play number games when it comes to seeking the conversion of sinners. God desires that every single person participate in the life of grace and so God demonstrates a preferential love and care for those who most need it—the ones who stray from the life of grace. Second, the action of the shepherd would have been perceived as unwarranted and undeserved because it was obviously the fault of the sheep that wandered away. Surely, then it was the responsibility of the sheep to find its way back. The Pharisees and scribes most likely thought the sheep deserved to die because of its actions. Jesus reveals that God values mercy over merit even when can be perceived as risky or unwarranted. We all know someone who is a lost sheep and this parable challenges us to re-examine the excuses we use to exempt ourselves from reaching out to them. The Pharisees and scribes believed that they deserved God's attention and Jesus' friendship because they merited it; Jesus reveals His desire to share His life with those who most need it instead, and sometimes that means those who wander from the Lord and the life of grace. Because Jesus is motivated by mercy rather than merit, our Lord rejoices when His mercy is effective and reconciliation is achieved.

> *When do you find yourself budgeting your mercy based on the probability of success in your efforts?*
> *How can we as a faith community play a number's game when it comes to our efforts to evangelize? That is how can we contend with the ninety-nine in such a way that we dismiss our obligation to go after the lost one?*
> *When do you find yourself thinking that people deserve alienation and suffering because of wayward decisions?*
> *What are the excuses you use to exempt yourself from reaching out to bring back a lost sheep?*
> *When have you been frustrated because you haven't received the attention you think you deserve for living a good and faithful life?*

The next parable is about a woman who lost a drachma. It is important to note that a drachma was of very little value (approximately nineteen cents in contemporary valuation). The parable focuses on her enormous reaction to this lost coin; she lights a lamp, sweeps the house, and carefully searches. No one would do that for nineteen cents. Whether or not others valued the coin as worthy of such a search the point is that she did. Some scripture scholars think that the lost coin may have been part of the woman's dowry (as evidenced that it was one of a set of ten such coins). If this interpretation is correct then the woman would be searching for the lost coin with diligence because it represented a lost relationship.

It does take enormous effort sometimes to help reconcile someone who has lost or strained his or her relationship with God. It can be especially difficult when the person is perceived as unworthy of such effort. This parable teaches us that God highly values every human person no matter what others think of them. It is because of the precious worth of each human being that God will expend great effort in seeing reconciliation where there has been estrangement. This is an important lesson for us as disciples because we are called to be co-workers with the Lord, express that same dedicated effort in finding the lost, and reconcile them to God.

> *Who has expended enormous energy in order to help you in your relationship with God?*
> *Who today is considered unworthy of the effort it would take to reconcile them to God and the community?*
> *This parable teaches us that God values every human person no matter how society values them. Who does our society consider of less value?*
> *How can you help defend the inherent value of every human being?*

These parables invite us to consider what the Church would be like without God's gracious mercy that seeks after us when we stray and searches for us relentlessly. Saint Paul tells us of his personal encounter with God's gracious love in 1 Tim 1:12–17. The experience of Saint Paul has been repeated in the lives of great men and women of faith throughout the ages who, by no merit of their own, were reconciled to God by the Lord's committed and generous mercy. Such great figures include Augustine of Hippo, Francis of Assisi, Ignatius of Loyola, and Dorothy Day.

> *How would Christianity be different if our relationship with God was based on our merit rather than the Lord's mercy?*

History tells us that St. Catherine of Siena, in an act of mercy, stood next to Niccolò di Toldo during his execution, and when he was beheaded, she received his head and prayed for his soul. Also, St. Thérèse of Lisieux prayed for the conversion of the criminal Henri Pranzini, who had refused to go to confession, but before his execution, he asked to kiss the crucifix three times for each one of his victims.

What would the Church be like without the possibility that great sinners can become great saints?
Who do you think is the person who least deserves God's merciful love in our world today?
Can you sincerely pray for that person hoping that the Lord will transform their life and can you honestly look forward to the day when you can be their companion?

Twenty-Fifth Sunday in Ordinary Time

Our scripture passage for this Sunday comes from the Gospel of Luke 16:1–13. This passage is known as either the Parable of the Dishonest Steward or the Wiley Manager. It is probably one of the most difficult parables to understand in the entire New Testament. We see evidence of this interpretation difficulty in the multiple morals presented at the end of the parable. In order to grasp the meaning of the parable and its challenge for our lives as disciples, we should consider a few points.

The manager in the parable was in a moment of crisis and asked himself a very important question; "What shall I do?" The word "crisis" in Greek means "a time of decision". Indeed, the manager reached a time when he had to make a decision because he saw where his life was heading—namely, he was about to be dismissed. The question "What shall I do?" is the necessary response to the message of Jesus in Luke's Gospel (cf. the crowds to John the Baptist in Lk 3:10–14, the Rich Fool with the Harvest in Lk 12:16, the Lawyer asking about eternal life in Lk 10:25, the ruler asking about eternal life in Lk 18:18, and the crowds to Peter in the Acts of the Apostles 2:37). The manager realized that he had to act immediately because of where his life was headed. Something bad was about to happen, and if he didn't do something immediately, a disaster awaited him. And he did act. Jesus was not praising his dishonesty; rather, Jesus is pointing out the importance of the initiative the manager showed by taking charge of his life and doing what was necessary to prepare for his future. It is that kind of responsiveness that Jesus wants to see in disciples when it comes to our spiritual lives. When we realize our need to grow in faith, or to turn away from sin, then we must act on that need and we must do something to avoid a spiritual disaster or to pursue spiritual growth. Disciples don't just pray about what's going on in their lives; they also do something about it.

What was the last "crisis"(financial, physical, relational) you experienced and how did you respond to it?

What is a typical spiritual crisis that people experience
today and what can they do in response to that crisis?
What tempts you to be passive or non-active in your
spiritual life?

One of the reasons Jesus praises the cleverness of the manager is
because of the awkward situation created by his action. When the
manager reduced the debts owed by the various persons, those
persons were both grateful to the manager but they also praised the
Master. The Master received honor because of the actions of the
manager and the Master could not reverse those actions without
losing honor. To lose honor in the ancient world was a terrible thing
and so the Master had no choice but to follow the decision of the
manager. Jesus praised the actions of the manager because he both
brought honor to the Master (through the gratitude of the debtors)
and he ensured his own future by the debtors' indebtedness to him!
At last the manager understood that the purpose of his job was
to honor the master all along through the generous and merciful
administration of his master's possessions. This dimension of the
parable has much to say to us. Jesus wants us to understand that we
are stewards of the Lord's gifts and that God has given us blessings
so that we can do the Lord's will. God's will is always merciful and
generous toward those in need. When we administer the resources
entrusted to us in such a way, we bring honor to the Master and
ensure our own future through faithful discipleship.

When have your actions brought honor to God because of
other people's gratitude?
How can we be tempted to use our possessions as a means
of self-honor?
What can you do today to bring honor to God?

As was mentioned previously, this parable is problematic to interpret. There are several possible morals to the story that are supplied
in the various endings provided in verses 9–13. Let's look at some
of these morals to see what they can teach us.

It is interesting that Jesus uses an image from a secular environment to teach the disciples about how to act in their faith lives.
Jesus says, "For the children of this world are more prudent in dealing with their own generation than are the children of light." Many

preachers over the centuries have interpreted this parable to mean that the Church should learn best practices from secular models so as to be more effective in the mission of the Gospel. Although this interpretation may not be exactly what Jesus intended, it is certainly worth considering as we reflect on this parable. While the Church is not a business, it can benefit much from learning and implementing best practices.

> *What are some of the best practices that you think our faith communities should review and consider for implementation?*
>
> *What other ministries or secular endeavors might have something to teach us so that we can be more shrewd in our efforts to promote the mission of the Gospel?*
>
> *What dangers can exist when the Church adopts secular business models for its ministries and administration?*

Jesus offers an additional teaching at the end of the parable when He says, "Make friends for yourselves with unrighteous mammon so that when it fails you, they will receive you into eternal tents." Jesus is reminding us that all the possessions of our lives will inevitably pass away but that those things are important tools in the present with which we can do good for others. We are not to make friends of mammon itself (money) but rather to make friends with mammon. That is what the manager in the parable did—he made friends through generosity and in doing so prepared for his future. Jesus is not telling us that we can earn eternal life but rather that the awesomeness of the present is that it influences eternity. The message is this; what we do now has eternal consequences.

> *How does this teaching on the right use of material possessions speak to you?*
>
> *How can you "make friends for yourself" through your generosity and charity for others?*
>
> *When has an act of charity been an experience of faith for you?*

An additional moral for this parable is found in the instruction on faithfulness and reliability in verses 10–12. This is a common principle in almost every aspect of our lives—we expect people to demonstrate their trustworthiness in small ways before we entrust them with great responsibility. The same is true for God. This interpretive theme invites us to consider how we have administered what does not belong to us (namely the blessings in our lives that ultimately belong to God) as a measure for how we will administer what does belong to us (namely our own life [v. Lk 12:15] and Baptized identity in Christ). If we have not been faithful in carrying out God's will in how we manage His blessings then we will not be faithful in managing our own life and relationship with the Lord. In order to be faithful to God's will in our administration of physical possessions we have to first know what is God's will. That knowledge comes from the Gospels and the teachings of Jesus. The failure to administer possessions according to the will of God is not so much a claim of personal ownership as it is a rejection of God's ultimate ownership. For that reason, the selfish administration of material possessions can actually be a rejection of God's will and an act of infidelity. That is a very strong statement. The administration of our personal possessions actually becomes a reflection of our interior dispositions.

> *When have you been tested in small ways before being entrusted with greater responsibility?*
> *How have you been tempted to administer your personal possessions without considering God's will?*
> *What is the ultimate gift you hope for from God and how is the Lord inviting you to demonstrate your trustworthiness for that gift by your present actions?*

The final interpretation offered for this parable is the caution against trying to serve two masters. This caution reminds us that there are competing forces for our attention, devotion, and loyalty. We can only serve one Master. When we ultimately commit our lives to anything other than God, then we have become idolatrous. We know that our ultimate commitment is to God when we can freely let go of any other attraction or desire in our lives. If we cannot let go of some other attraction or desire then we are trying to serve two masters. Material possessions are meant to be an instruction for our salvation but when we allow them to dominate our lives then they become our master. Sometimes the only way we know what is really important to us is when we let go of what is not important. In those moments the experience of sacrifice also becomes an experience of clarification and purification.

What are some of the influences or attractions that try to dominate people's lives today?

When has the experience of sacrifice been an opportunity for clarification and purification in your life?

What can we do as a faith community to help people choose God first and foremost as the only master of their lives?

Twenty-Sixth Sunday in Ordinary Time

Our scripture passage for this Sunday comes from the Gospel of Luke 16:19–31. It is the parable of the Rich Man and Lazarus. In this parable, Luke continues his teaching on discipleship and the right use of material possessions. It is a striking message in which Jesus points out the difference between what human beings value and what God values. Note that this parable follows upon two previous passages (the Prodigal Son and the Dishonest Manager) in which they both changed their lives so as to secure a good future for themselves. However, unlike the Prodigal Son and the Dishonest Manager, the Rich Man in this parable does not change his life and as a result does not have a good future. These three parables should be read together.

The first part of the parable introduces the two main figures with a description of each one. It is important to pay attention to these details because they are telling us important information. For example, we are told that the Rich Man is dressed in purple, which is a description of his wealth and prominence as someone associated with the royal or imperial family. This description indicates that he has position, power, and wealth. Also, we are told that he feasts every day.[15] Next, the passage tells us that his home has a gate, which is a sign of his security, privacy, and separation from others. Indeed, he has insulated himself from the suffering of others and in doing so has also isolated himself from God. Finally, we are told that the rich man died and was buried—a sign that he received all the honor and ceremonies associated with expensive and grand funeral events. In contrast to the rich man, we are told that Lazarus was "dumped" outside the man's gate indicating that he was most likely crippled and unable to maneuver on his own. Also, he hungered (like an animal) to eat the remnants of food that were discarded from the Rich Man's table. Next, Lazarus' plight

---

15. The word for "feasts" was used to describe special occasions that might normally take place a couple of times each year but this man eats that way every day.

was worsened by the fact that unclean animals (dogs) touched him and licked him. Finally, we are told that Lazarus simply died—the absence of any burial rite or other indication of remembrance indicates that he was forgotten as a nobody in the eyes of society. These dramatic differences between the two realities of the rich man and Lazarus invite us to reflect on our world today.

> *How do we practically and emotionally insulate ourselves from the suffering of others?*
> *What are the "scraps" that fall from the tables of our Time, Talent, and Treasure for which others are hungering?*
> *Who are the poor at our gate (family, friends, co-workers, community, or larger world) and what are the ways in which we avoid them or keep them at a distance?*
> *When have your eyes been opened so as to see the needs of others as a blessed opportunity for your generous mercy rather than as an unpleasant burden imposed on your life?*

The second part of the parable has to do with the different situations the Rich Man and Lazarus experience in the afterlife. More important insights are offered for our consideration and it is necessary to study this passage carefully so as to not miss the subtle lessons it contains. First, note how the Rich Man is only concerned for himself and his own family. He still considers Lazarus as no more than a servant to bring him water and to be the messenger for his brothers. He also reveals that he knows Lazarus by name yet did not help him as he lay at his gate each day. Thus, the rich man cannot claim ignorance of Lazarus or his need; he had incriminated himself by every statement and attitude revealed in the afterlife. The Rich Man was seeking mercy for himself even after refusing to show mercy to others. The Rich Man also is absorbed in self-concern rather than acknowledging his sin against charity and asking forgiveness. The implication of the parable is this; had the Rich Man shown mercy, then mercy would have been shown to him. In short, the teaching for us is that we should not deny to others what we ourselves are seeking from God. That is a powerful message! The heart that is open to give is also open to receive; the heart that is closed to give has closed itself off from receiving as well.

> *What do you pray for (mercy, forgiveness, love, blessing)?*

What opportunities do you have to give to others what you yourself are asking from God?

The great medieval author Henry Suso asked God, "Gentle Lord, tell me, which suffering do you think is extremely useful and good?"[16] How can we translate the tragedies of this life into blessings?
God wants to bless us all with eternal gifts; by being a blessing to others we open ourselves to receive what God wants to give us. How can this insight affect your life as a disciple?
The rich man reveals his self-centered and unrepentant attitude in the afterlife. What statement of his strikes you as being particularly troubling or challenging for your life?

The third part of the parable is about how the Rich Man finally realizes he had pursued false values in his earthly life. He then wishes that others might be informed of their erroneous values so that they can change their lives—that is repent and act differently in the present in order to be granted a blessed future. The action of repentance involves a change of mind with a corresponding change of action. While the rich man wanted such a change of mind to be brought about through miraculous events (for example, someone rising from the dead), the response of Abraham indicates that God desires our change of mind (repentance) to be accomplished through the ordinary means of studying God's Word (Scripture and Tradition). We need "wake-up" moments to help us realize what is true, good, and how our values are distorted. Sometimes these wake-up calls occur through dramatic life-changing events and sometimes they happen through ordinary daily insights of faith. It is important that we seek ways to acquire these insights so that we can repent in the present before it is too late to positively affect our future.

What are some of the wake-up calls you have experienced that have caused you to change your values and act differently?
What are some of the values you changed because of those wake-up calls?

---

16. See Henry Suso, *Little Book of Eternal Wisdom*, Chap. 13.

How has the study of God's Word in scripture and Tradition provided the insights of faith you needed to change your life?

This parable speaks to us about the need to not be deceived by the glories of this world such as clothing, feasting, and lavish homes. Of interesting historical note, from 1409 until 1963, when a newly-elected pope was led to his throne for the first time, his procession was stopped at three moments and the Master of Ceremonies would kneel before the Holy Father holding a piece of smoldering fabric and shout the phrase *"sic transit Gloria mundi"* which means "Thus passes the glories of this world." This action was meant to keep the pope humble and remind him of the transitory nature of life and earthly glory lest he become caught up in the entrapments of power, prestige, and pride.

What helps you keep the things of this world in proper focus so you do not become caught up in the allurement of earthly glory?

Lastly, it is important to note the terms of relationship used between the Rich Man and Abraham. He repeatedly calls him "Father Abraham" and Abraham even responds by saying, "My son". To be a Son of Abraham meant to be a member of God's faithful people. In the beginning of Luke's Gospel (v. Lk 3:8), John the Baptist warned the crowds that being a "Son of Abraham" required much more than just hereditary lineage or religious identification; rather, to be a "Son of Abraham" required a living faith that led them to act like Sons of Abraham and not just claim the title without living it. Thus, John commanded the crowds to bear witness to their faith through their lived works of charity and justice. In Luke 19:9, Jesus will identify someone who truly is a "Son of Abraham" when He sees Zacchaeus manifest his repentance through acts of generosity and justice.

In what ways can it be easy for us to rely upon our hereditary lineage (charitable family, institution, or profession) or religious identification ("Christian", "Catholic", attending Mass every week, and so forth) as a source of security and presumption of God's favor?

If we were to be in eternity and find ourselves separated from God, what would be the basis of our claim for inclusion among the Lord's Elect?

How can we better live in the present so as to manifest the relationship we claim by title in this life and hope for in eternal life?

Twenty-Seventh Sunday in Ordinary Time

Our scripture passage for this Sunday comes from the Gospel of Luke 17:5–10. It is an odd passage that probably generates a lot of curiosity when we read it. In order to understand the issues Jesus is addressing, it is important to remember that in the four verses that precede this teaching, Jesus has instructed His disciples on the need to avoid giving scandal and to forgive someone who sins against us. Thus, it is a challenge to the entire Christian community to be active agents of faith who live their discipleship and help others do so as well. Following this previous teaching on forgiveness and giving good example, Jesus then offers this Sunday's Gospel passage about faith.

It is interesting that the disciples asked for "more faith". Their request follows our Lord's challenging instruction that disciples be proactive rather than reactive in their interaction with the world. The disciples weren't challenged as long as Jesus was teaching about how the rich should act (v. Parable of the Rich Man and Lazarus) or about how stewards in charge of vast resources should act (v. Parable of the Dishonest Manager). However, the disciples did react when Jesus presented this teaching on ethical behavior and forgiveness that challenged even the poor and the powerless to act in a heroic way. This challenged overwhelmed the disciples and so they ask for more faith in order to fulfill the Lord's expectations. Sometimes it isn't the quantity of our faith that's the problem but rather the quality of our faith that needs to be addressed. When Jesus makes His comment about having "faith the size of a mustard seed", the implication is that the disciples don't have even a small amount the right kind of faith. If they did, then they would be able to live remarkable lives. Up to this point in the Gospel of Luke we have been introduced to several great people whom Jesus identified as examples of faith. These examples include the men who carried their paralytic friend to be healed by the Lord (v. Lk 5:20), the Roman Centurion who expressed utter confidence in the power of Jesus' word (v. Lk 7:9), the Sinful Woman who overcame social barriers and the scorn of others in order to become a disciple of the Lord (v. Lk 7:50), and the woman with the hemorrhage who approached Jesus for healing and was not afraid of rendering Jesus unclean (v. Lk 8:48). Jesus wants disciples who can imitate these great examples of faith and live out His teachings rather than disciples who think that faith will give them miraculous power to do great and impressive works.

> *Who has Jesus placed in your life as an example of great faith for you to imitate?*
> *What are examples of mistaken faith that affect our world today?*
> *For example, how can people actually end up believing incorrectly about God and discipleship?*
> *What do you do to increase your faith?*
> *What teaching of discipleship do you find most difficult to live out in day-to-day life?*

Next, Jesus addressed some false perspectives of faith that can be destructive or distracting for disciples. Specifically, He used the relationship of a Master and a household slave to make His point. This image is used often in the Gospel of Luke and was a familiar topic in the world of Jesus. Servants performed their tasks out of obligation and not for the sake of acknowledgement. Jesus uses this sense of obligation as the basis for His teaching on discipleship. As disciples, the Lord expects us to act according to a higher standard, a holier standard, than the world around us. We have done nothing great when we carry out our Lord's will and fulfill His expectations by living an ethical life and forgiving those who have offended us; rather, we have only fulfilled the minimum requirements for being a disciple. The danger is that sometimes we expect to be praised or rewarded when we do the right thing. When we do not receive praise or reward then we can become resentful, angry, judgmental, and demanding. By using the image of a slave to describe the right faith of disciples, Jesus is reminding us that whatever we do for the His sake, we do because we are only being obedient to the Lord and following His direction in our lives. We have no claim to reward or praise for doing what is our duty. This teaching may have been to counter the attitude and influence of the Pharisees who considered themselves to be the defenders of God's word while they themselves were not fulfilling it (v. Lk 16:14).

> *How do you see the need for reward or praise as something that subverts Christian faith?*
> *When do you find yourself seeking reward or praise for fulfilling your role as a good husband, wife, father, mother, disciple, or Catholic?*
> *How do you respond when you don't receive the reward or praise you want?*
> *When people don't receive what they think they deserve, then they can begin to compensate themselves in unhealthy ways. How can this be true in marriages, professional careers, parenting, and discipleship?*

This Gospel passage reminds us that it is always an honor and privilege to be a Christian disciple who is given a share in the mission of the Gospel. When all is said and done, it is really we who should be thanking God for having allowed us to be His servants and for giving us the strength, skills, and resources with which to do the Lord's will. That attitude of gratitude is the quality of faith Jesus is looking for in a disciple. To have more of that faith is truly a gift from God. Gratitude is a powerful remedy for feelings of resentment, anger, and entitlement. Gratitude also keeps our hearts and minds focused on God rather than on our own problems or others' faults.

> *How do you foster and express gratitude in your relationship with God?*
> *When have you been profoundly grateful to be part of the Lord's work even though that work was exhausting or even thankless?*
> *Why is it easy to lose sight of our blessings and take them for granted and what can a disciple do to foster an attitude of gratitude as part of their prayer each day?*

When it comes to the life of discipleship then all is to be considered a gift. God owes us nothing for living a good Christian life. The Lord's favor and blessing are graces that cannot be earned. While we deserve nothing, in gratitude we can accept everything. In doing so, we become disciples who forgive others even as we are forgiven and who help others take their next step in discipleship even as we take ours.

> *How does this approach to faith and the Christian life help you to identify areas where your faith needs to change in quality?*
>
> *How can you better allow God to increase the quantity of this right faith in your life?*
>
> *Who has been an example to you of what right faith looks like as exemplified by the servant in the parable that works hard all day out of a selfless sense of duty yet never becomes resentful, demanding, frustrated, or self-pitying?*

Twenty-Eighth Sunday in Ordinary Time

Our scripture passage for this Sunday comes from the Gospel of Luke 17:11–19. In this passage we read about Jesus healing ten Lepers. It is significant that Jesus was just teaching his disciples (and us) in the passage that preceded this one about the need to be servants who know we are "unworthy" of God's blessings. These ten Lepers, especially the Samaritan, serve as examples of people who know they are unworthy of God's blessings but who receive them nonetheless. Thus, this healing ministry of Jesus becomes for us a further instruction on how we are to respond as disciples to the many gracious blessings we receive from God.

The first lesson in this passage is the wording that is used when it says, "Ten lepers met him." Some versions say that there were "ten lepers" but that is not an accurate translation. Luke goes out of his way to make the point that they were men who happened to suffer an illness (see similar examples in Lk 5:18 and Lk 8:27). By doing so, Luke is emphasizing the fact that no matter who we are or with what weakness we are afflicted, we are always human beings and our human dignity (identity) is not destroyed by our weakness or sin.

> *What are typical ways in which we categorize people or define people primarily by their sin, crime, weakness, or illness rather than recognizing them as fellow human beings created in the image and likeness of God? Luke wants us to always see other people as human beings and only then to acknowledge the weakness with which they are afflicted. What experiences have helped you to look beyond another person's distress and to see them first and foremost as a human being?*
> *How can you help dignify and defend the humanity of someone in your life, work, family, or friendships today?*

The second lesson presented is when we are told that both Jesus and the Samaritan with Leprosy see the significance of their encounter.

To have sight in the Gospels is more than physically seeing with the eyes; rather, it is to have insight. This insight allows us to perceive opportunities to be merciful to one another and to recognize when God's mercy is acting in one's own life. Both Jesus and the Samaritan with Leprosy see this moment of their encounter with the eyes of faith from two different perspectives. It is only when we are able to see and understand other peoples' sufferings that we can then see our encounter with them as an opportunity for mercy.

> *What experiences in your own life have opened your eyes to see other people's sufferings and your heart to be merciful to them?*
>
> *Who in your life (family, friend, co-worker) is having difficulty at this time and needs to experience mercy from you?*
>
> *Sometimes the only thing we see in other people's suffering is the symptom. What are the symptoms of suffering and how have you learned to look beyond the symptom to see the deeper cause of pain?*
>
> *In order for Jesus to be our Savior, we have to acknowledge our need for a Savior. What is the mercy you most need in your life at this time?*
>
> *What prevents us from being able to clearly see moments when we have experienced God's mercy acting in our lives?*

The third lesson in today's Gospel passage is that Jesus never directly heals the men with leprosy. Rather, He simply instructs them to go and show themselves to the priests. We are told that it is in their going to Jerusalem that they are healed. The Samaritan alone sees that he is healed and responds by praising God with a loud voice (just as they called out for mercy with a "loud voice" so now the Samaritan praises God with a "loud voice"). The others were healed as well but they did not "see" the hand of God at work in their healing (perhaps they thought it was the walk, the fresh air, something they ate, and so forth). For one reason or another they most likely just thought they deserved the healing. Most scripture scholars believe that this is the intended message of the passage for disciples. The disciples need to be aware of God's blessing and give praise for it. The problem is that we are often like the other nine who think the blessings we receive come from our own efforts or accomplishments and so we fail to see the hand of God at action. In those moments of blindness, we also fail to give God praise and thanks. The truth is that everything in our lives, and life itself, is a gift from God. Great disciples can come from all nations and peoples. Sometimes the greatest disciples come from nations that have no rightful claim on God's mercy. Those nations know that anything they receive from God is a pure gift. Those nations, too, can respond with gratitude to God's generous mercy. Nations that believe they are somehow closer or more deserving of God's grace oftentimes fail to see God's work and therefore fail to be thankful.

> *What are some of the most recent blessings you have received in your life?*
> *How and when do you express your praise to God for those blessings?*
> *What are some of the false beliefs that can cause us to be blind to the hand of God at work in our lives?*
> *When the lepers needed mercy they called out with a loud voice but when it was time to thank Jesus only one of them called out with an equally loud voice. How does the intensity of your prayer differ when you need something from God as opposed to when you are thanking God?*

The fourth teaching moment in this passage occurs when the Samaritan with Leprosy gives thanks to Jesus and prostrates himself at the Lord's feet. The word for "thanks" in Greek is *eucharistein*, which is the same as our English word "Eucharist". Thus, when the Samaritan praises God and offers his life at the feet of Jesus, he performs a Eucharistic action. The Samaritan had received his health and he now offers it as a gift to the Lord to be used according to God's will. That moment of giving thanks and praise involved not only words but also the offering of his life.

> *How does this action of the Samaritan affect the way you prepare to come to Mass?*
> *What are some blessings you have received (physical, material, spiritual) and how will you place those blessings "at the feet of the Lord" so they can be faithfully used according to God's will?*

Jesus wonders where are the other nine. Where do you think
they are? What do you think they did with the gift of health
the Lord gave them?
What are gifts in your life that you have not yet placed at
the Lord's feet?

As a closing reflection, we might consider how the experience of
encountering the Lord changed the lives of these ten men. For nine
of them, it was the gift of health, but for one of them it became the
gift of faith and a real relationship with the Lord. Only one leper
was able to be thankful and not only for the gift received but also
for the one who had given that gift. Ultimately, we are called to be
like the Samaritan who is thankful not only for the gift he receives
but above all for the presence of God in his life who generously
bestows such blessings. Our greatest act of thanksgiving (Eucharist)
is for Jesus Himself. We acknowledge that in Jesus the giver and the
gift are one person. We also acknowledge that we do not deserve
so great a gift and have no right to God's grace and favor. Because
of that humble attitude, the Lord invites into that relationship
which is salvation.

How has an experience of God changed your life? What
was it? How did you respond?
How have you come to personally know the Lord through
his saving action?
When have you prayed simply to offer thanks to God for
the Lord's presence in your life?
The most humble lives were the lives most changed. That's
because they knew the healing came from someone other
than themselves or their actions; the healing came from
God. The humble ones could be people of great faith. When
has an outcast person (Samaritan) shocked you by their
deep faith?

Jesus sends the Samaritan on his way by identifying what "saving
faith" looks like. That identification is stated so as to encourage us
to model that same faith in our lives. Saving faith recognizes every
gift as coming from the hand of God, praises God for it, and offers
it to the Lord to be used according to His will. For your spiritual

enrichment, please pray the following prayer from Saint Ignatius of Loyola, which expresses this faith.

> Lord,
> I freely yield all my freedom to you.
> Take my memory, my intellect and my entire will.
> You have given me anything I am or have;
> I give it all back to you
> to stand under your will alone.
> Your love and your grace are enough for me;
> I shall ask for nothing more.

Twenty-Ninth Sunday in Ordinary Time

Our scripture passage for this Sunday comes from the Gospel of Luke 18:1–8.In this passage, we read Jesus' teaching on the need to persevere in prayer. To communicate this message, Jesus uses the image of a widow who pesters an unjust judge. Prayer is an important theme in the Gospel of Luke where we find eight instances of Jesus withdrawing to pray and seven times when our Lord instructs the disciples about prayer. Given the predominance of this theme, we need to study this passage to understand what our Lord wants to teach us as disciples.

Jesus uses the image of a widow intentionally. The teaching on the need for persistent prayer could have communicated effectively with a wide variety of images. Our Lord' choice of a widow to communicate His instruction is a teaching in itself. Widows in the ancient world were particularly powerless and vulnerable. They had little or no influence in society and are mentioned by the Prophets and other Old Testament writings as warranting particular care (cf. Mal 3:5, Is 1:17, Jer 5:28, Ez 22:7, Ps 67:5, Ps 145:9, and Sir 35:14–18). Women in the time of Jesus were dependent upon the men in their lives (sons and husbands). Widows could not even inherit their husband's estate as it was passed on to the deceased man's brothers or sons. However, in the early Church widows occupied a distinct role of honor as is evidenced by Jas 1:27, "Religion that is pure and undefiled before God the Father is to care for orphans and widows in their distress and to keep oneself unstained by the world." Jesus wants us to see the world through the eyes of the powerless and marginalized as well.

Who are the widows in our world who have no recourse for help but God?
When have you been in a situation where prayer was your only recourse?
Who is most vulnerable in our society due to lack of rights in our legal system?

In our contemporary culture we make great efforts to never be powerless. When we have a need we are more inclined to trust in our own strength and resources than we are to turn toward God in prayer. Sometimes, it is only when we are brought to the limits of our own ability that we ever really cry out to God as our only hope. In reality, prayer is often our last recourse rather than our first recourse. That experience of reaching the limits of our human ability can occur through a variety of settings including tragedy, illness, addiction, loss of a loved one, and so forth. Nonetheless, the experience of utter reliance on God's intervention teaches us dependence on the Lord and awakens us to a better understanding of His power in our lives. It is sometimes situations of grave need and even desperation that cause us to realize the futility of trusting in our own strength. Such situations are rarely pleasant; usually they are quite agonizing and even painful. These situations can be an experience of faith when we allow them to focus our attention on the Lord and His power in our lives.

> *When have you had to wait patiently for God's response to*
> *a grave need in your life and what was it like?*
> *What did you learn as an enduring lesson of faith as a*
> *result of that experience?*
> *What efforts do you take to make sure you are always in*
> *control of your life and personal circumstance?*
> *Have you ever experienced a powerlessness that was freeing?*

By identifying with the widow and understanding the experience of being powerless, the Lord intends that our eyes should be opened so that we can see the needs of others and become their source of justice and mercy. In doing so, we can be people who "fear God" and "respect others". It is important to remember that this parable is not just about a widow but it is also about an unjust judge who is moved to do the right thing regardless of his personal character flaws. There are lots of times when we find ourselves in positions like that of the unjust judge. We may not be asked to issue judicial decisions but we do, in fact, make judgments of people's need, trustworthiness, and character. These judgments happen in our families, friendships, and professional lives. If our hearts are compassionate and we are willing to see the suffering and distress that surrounds us then we will also see the possibility of our caring response. Most often, God answers prayers through the lives of faithful disciples; thus, our assistance to another person in need may very well be how God is answering their prayers. This is a clear reflection of the Communion of Saints we confess every Sunday in the Creed and an important teaching for us as disciples because it challenges us to be willing instruments of God's mercy and love for a wounded world.

> *The parable of the widow and the unjust judge shows us that even people of questionable character are capable of doing the right thing. How much more should this statement be true for disciples who have committed their lives to Jesus and the Gospel?*
>
> *Has anyone ever told you that you are an "Answer to their prayers"? As you look at your life now, for what need are you crying out to God?*
>
> *Is it only for your own need or do you cry out for the widows in our time?*
>
> *How have you been a source of justice and mercy for the powerless who you have encountered?*

This parable is one of Jesus' many teachings on prayer in the Gospel of Luke. It is an encouragement to not lose heart in the face of long suffering. We live in a culture of "instant gratification". That means when something is not resolved in a very short amount of time that we tend to either give up or pursue another solution. The culture of instant gratification undermines the virtue of persistence. The widow in this parable didn't give up because her first request was not answered. Rather, we are told that they "kept coming and saying" which implies an ongoing action. Her ongoing action is both a statement of her confidence in the Judge's power as well as her determination and persistence. God's Mercy and Justice are never in question; what is in question is whether or not we will persevere in our prayer because we don't receive immediate gratification for our requests. The New Testament has several passages that stress the importance of perseverance and caution against discouragement (cf. 2 Thes 3:13, Eph 3:13, Gal 6:9, 2 Cor 4:1,16). The presence of such a persistent theme indicates that Christians of the early Church needed encouragement as well.

> *With what effort have you been most persistent in your life?*
> *How do you see the culture of instant gratification as having destructive effects in people's personal, professional and family lives?*
> *How do you think the culture of instant gratification has undermined our faith lives?*

Jesus ends the parable with a simple question: "When the Son of Man comes, will He find faith on the earth?" It's a good question that invites us to consider the basic dynamic of faith and how we pass it on. Faith is a dynamic reality, a trusting life-giving relationship of love and knowledge in Jesus Christ. It must be actively communicated to other people in an intentional way or there is great danger that the gift of faith will not be passed on. For many decades, and even centuries, the Church has relied on cultural settings to pass on the gift of faith. These cultural settings include parish community and cultural events, parochial schools, and even some devotional practices. In studying the challenges of the twentieth century, it is important to note that many of these traditional cultural approaches no longer effectively communicate the faith experience to younger generations. For this reason Saint John Paul II, Pope Benedict XVI, and Pope Francis are all calling for a new evangelization so that the gift of faith can be effectively passed on to future generations with greater certitude and responsibility. In this way, the Son of Man will find faith on earth. While faith is a gift that comes from God, the reality is that the Lord works through the Church and individual disciples to cooperate in the distribution of that gift. We are responsible and accountable for both how we receive that gift and how effectively we pass on that gift.

> *Why do you believe in God and live a faith-based life?*
> *How was the living faith experience communicated to you?*
> *How do you communicate the faith experience to your family and friends?*
> *What are the primary factors that cause people to fall away from a life of faith?*
> *What can you do now to strengthen your faith?*

In what ministries is the living faith experience most intensely communicated in our community?
In what ministries do we need to refocus and strengthen them so they can effectively communicate the gift of faith?

Thirtieth Sunday in Ordinary Time

Our scripture passage for this Sunday comes from the Gospel of Luke 18:9–14. Last week we received Jesus' teaching on the need for perseverance in our prayer; this week we receive a teaching about the equally important nature and quality of our prayer. Each of these two teachings is important for us as disciples lest we end up persevering (last week's scripture teaching) in an erroneous manner (this week scripture's teaching). Let's study this passage and use it as a spiritual self-examination for our prayer.

The scene in this parable is simple and reflects the stark contrast between the prayer attitudes of the Pharisee and the Tax Collector. Let's look at both of these examples to discover what Jesus is trying to teach us through both negative and positive means.

The Prayer of the Pharisee

First, notice that the Pharisee prays to himself. That is an intentional description. It means that his prayer was self-centered and selfish. As such, his prayer actually became idolatrous in that he made himself god. The twentieth century philosopher and theologian Paul Tillich described faith as the ultimate concern that determines our being and guides our actions.[17] While that definition may not cover all aspects of faith, it does articulate the dynamic occurring in the prayer of the Pharisee. The Pharisee reveals that his ultimate concern is himself—his own standing in society, his own holiness, his own security, and his own justification. The only concern the Pharisee shows for others is that he can consider himself better than them. That can happen to us in our prayer as well —whenever we pray only about ourselves and our own concerns; whenever we consider our own point of view as the only one to be considered; or whenever we fail to consider that God's will is more perfect than our own and that God knows what is best for our lives. Basically,

---

17. See Paul Tillich, *The Dynamics of Faith*, p. 5.

anytime prayer becomes a monologue within ourselves then we have left little room for God to speak. Prayer is meant to be a conversation and the word "conversation" comes from the word "conversion". Prayer is meant to be a dialogue that changes us.

> *What are subtle ways in which our prayer can become idolatrous?*
> *When have you experienced that self-centeredness in prayer?*
> *How do you practice prayer as a conversation rather than a repetitious monologue?*
> *When has your prayer been an experience of conversion for you?*
> *What ultimate concern dominates your prayer or guides your actions?*

Second, the Pharisee offered thanks that he is not like the rest of humanity. In doing so the Pharisee revealed that his prayer is one of judgment and condemnation of others while acknowledging no fault within himself (that is, no need for personal conversion). It is significant that he makes his prayer as an action of thanksgiving because in doing so the Pharisee prays the Greek word *Eucharisto*—a clear connection to the Christian Eucharist. What Jesus is trying to tell us by the use of this word is that Christians must be careful lest their prayer become like that of Pharisee when they gather for the Eucharistic celebration. When we take our eyes off of Christ or when we are unaware of our failings, we are danger of giving thanks for the wrong reasons. We can find ourselves gazing around the Church and looking down on others for their failures, weaknesses, or sins. We can have similar judgmental attitudes towards others based on how they attend Mass, dress, behave, and so forth. In doing so, we give in to the temptation of making ourselves look good (in our own eyes) by pointing out the faults of others. We can even end up excusing ourselves from the need for conversion because we think we are already so much better than "the rest". That is self-justification and false self-promotion. It might work in our eyes, but it doesn't work in God's eyes.

> *When do you find yourself tempted to compare yourself with others?*

*Does this attitude ever affect your prayer or participation
in Mass?*

What helps you avoid being judgmental in those moments?

What helps you keep your attention focused on God?

*The celebration of the Eucharist is supposed to be the one
prayer that brings us together in communion as the Body of
Christ. What aspects of the Mass can be a source of division
rather than communion in our worship experience?*

*When have you seen others' sinfulness in visible or public
ways?*

*Have you ever been moved to pray for them as a brother
or sister in Christ?*

Finally, the Pharisee points to his religious practices as the basis of
his righteousness. He asks nothing from God because he doesn't
think he needs anything from God. Fasting twice a week was going
beyond the norm as was paying tithes on everything (tithes were
only required on some things and most people only fasted one day
a week). In his own eyes, the Pharisee is already spiritually rich and
so he is blind to his real spiritual need. The very actions of faith
(fasting and tithes) that were supposed to deepen his love for God
and neighbor ended up separating him from God and neighbor
when those practices became a source of selfish pride and a judgmental attitude toward others. Rather than those actions making
him a better person, they just made him an arrogant person. Such
an attitude can happen in the lives of faithful Christians as well.
We can become so reliant on our religious practices and sacrifices
that we lose sight of our real need for God.

*What religious practices or experiences in your life have
led you into a deeper love of God and Neighbor?*

*What religious practices or experiences have become the
basis of your comparison with others or caused you to have
a judgmental attitude toward others?*

*What is a practical way in which you can remind yourself
daily of your need for God so as to avoid the temptation to
pride and self-righteousness?*

The Prayer of the Tax Collector

The prayer of the Tax Collector is far simpler than that of the Pharisee. The tax collector's prayer is marked by three distinct qualities: humility, simplicity, and honesty. The humility is manifested by the fact that he would not raise his eyes to heaven. His humility is also evidenced by the indication that he beat his breast as a sign of remorse and grief. The simplicity is manifested by the fact that his prayer didn't become wordy. Rather than trying to explain, justify, or defend his sins, the Tax Collector simply states his petition and entrusts himself to the Lord's compassion. The honesty of his prayer is manifested by the fact that he acknowledges who he is (a sinner) and his need for God (mercy). That type of prayer, Jesus says, is what justifies a person in the eyes of God. How one prays reveals the nature of their relationship with God. The Pharisee prayed with self-promotion and self-concern revealing that his relationship was based on his self-absorption. For the Pharisee, praying was about doing God a favor. The Tax Collector prayed with humility and compunction revealing that his relationship was based on his need for the Lord. Thus, for the Tax Collector, prayer was about opening himself to God's healing grace. Of interesting note, the revised English translation of the Missal (used in all English-speaking countries since 2011) reinstated the striking of the breast as part of the prayer known as the *Confiteor*. This prayerful action in the Penitential Rite is meant to connect us with the righteous prayer of the Tax Collector in this Gospel passage.

> *How does this understanding of the passage change the way you pray the Penitential Rite at Mass?*
> *Which aspect of the tax collector's prayer challenges you the most and why?*
> *How do you demonstrate humility in your personal prayer?*
> *What keeps you honest in your prayer?*
> *When does your prayer seem to become complicated?*
> *When do you pray most like the tax collector (that is, in what setting)?*

THIRTY-FIRST SUNDAY IN ORDINARY TIME

Our scripture passage for this Sunday comes from the Gospel of Luke 19:1–10. It is the story of Zacchaeus the tax collector and his response to Jesus as the Lord passes through Jericho. This is more than just a story of someone who meets Jesus. This passage is the climactic episode in Jesus' ten-chapter journey to Jerusalem. In these ten chapters (Luke 9:51–19:10), Jesus has been offering the most important teachings on discipleship. Now, finally, we see an example of what ideal discipleship looks like in the person of Zacchaeus. Thus, this story is given to us so that we might look at our own response of discipleship and see how we need to be more like Zacchaeus and less like the crowds who stand in the way and grumble because Jesus has welcomed a sinner and a tax collector.

The first thing to note is the difficulty that Zacchaeus experienced when he tried to see Jesus. Because he was short of stature, we are told that the crowds blocked him from being able to have sight of Jesus. At various times in the gospels we are similarly informed of crowds that prevent people from being able to approach Jesus. This identification of the crowds who became an obstacle is no accident. Luke is trying to tell us that sometimes Christians (that is, those who surround Jesus) can actually be an obstacle, an impediment, for others who want to meet the Lord. The term "to see" means more than just physical sight; it is really the experience of coming to faith and seeing Jesus with the eyes of a disciple. Zacchaeus wanted to have that faith in Jesus but the crowds stood in the way. These same crowds grumbled later in the story when Jesus accepted Zacchaeus' welcome because he was a notorious sinner and tax collector. There are various ways in which Christians can become obstacles to another person's quest for faith. Sometimes it is the poor witness of Christians that actually turns people off to the message of Jesus. Sometimes it happens when someone steps inside the doors of a church for the first time and feels unwelcomed. It can also happen when someone is looked down on with disapproval because of their attire, appearance, notoriety, and so forth.

> *When have you been offended or scandalized in your faith by the poor example of someone who claimed to be Christian?*
>
> *What actions of Christians today are causing damage to the message of the Gospel and to the Church?*
>
> *How can we as a faith community become better at helping people meet Jesus rather than grumbling and standing in the way?*
>
> *What are actions in your own life that discredit the message of faith you profess?*
>
> *Being short of stature may have been a description of Zacchaeus' character as much as his physical build. What makes people feel short of stature in character today?*

The second thing to note is that Zacchaeus ran and climbed a tree in order to see Jesus. In the time of Jesus, it was considered shameful for a grown man to do either of those actions. Luke tells us these details so we will know that Zacchaeus was willing to be perceived as ridiculous in the eyes of others and even willing to break social norms in order to meet the Lord. He would not allow anything — not even other people's expectations or public embarrassment—to keep him from reaching out and seizing this opportunity of faith. We were told earlier in Luke's Gospel that those who humble themselves will be exalted (v.. Lk 14:11) and Zacchaeus shows us what it looks like to humble oneself in the eyes of God. Jesus does indeed exalt Zacchaeus when our Lord announces that He must stay in the wealthy tax collector's home. To stay in someone's home brought honor to the host. Jesus is honoring the one who humbled himself in the search for faith.

> *When have you had to go against other people's expectations or contradict social norms in order to witness your faith?*
>
> *What are examples of things Christians do today when they "go out on a limb" and take a risk in order to witness their faith?*

Have you ever defended someone who was being ridiculed
by others because of their witness of faith?
What curiosity of faith has led you to undertake extraor-
dinary effort in your desire to see the Lord?
When have your humbling efforts of faith resulted in being
unexpectedly exalted?

The third thing to note is that Zacchaeus accepts Jesus' initiative to
relationship and he welcomes the Lord to his home. Not everyone
is pleased by the fact that Jesus is establishing relationship with a
known sinner. For this reason we are told that the crowd began to
grumble (or murmur). This was a critical moment of decision for
Zacchaeus; he must decide whether he will back away from the relationship offered to him and accept the identity of a sinner (by which
the crowd so identified him) or will he choose the new identity of a
disciple and accept the challenges that come with that new life. It
is at this critical moment when his welcome is challenged that he
gives half of his possessions to the poor and repays anyone whom
he has defrauded. All of these actions are important statements of
what true discipleship looks like.

To have welcomed Jesus means more than just a verbal greeting; it means that Zacchaeus made room for Jesus in his life and
gave the Lord a place in his home. Sometimes we have to clear
out a lot of clutter to make room for the Lord! In giving half of his
possessions to the poor, Zacchaeus is demonstrating his sacrificial
charity for others, which Jesus teaches is an essential part of being
a disciple. This radical sharing of resources was first advocated by
John the Baptist as one the fruits of repentance which would mark
the life of a disciple (v. Jn 3:11). By making restitution for wrongs
committed (repaying those whom he defrauded), Zacchaeus is
showing us that disciples are people who make extra amends when
they have hurt others (Note: The practical standard for restitution
was twofold; by offering fourfold restitution Zacchaeus is demonstrating his willingness to fulfill the highest standards of the Law
as represented in Ex 22:1). Zacchaeus is giving us a great example.
Such actions of generosity and justice are not easily carried out
in our lives. Sometimes it's easier to see ourselves as sinners who
are unworthy of relationship with Jesus than it is to welcome the
Lord and make the necessary changes His presence warrants in

our hearts and homes. When Zacchaeus was faced with the challenge of either remaining a sinner (v. Lk 19:7 the grumbling of the crowd) or taking a stand, he chose to claim the life of discipleship and make the changes it required.

> *Which of those three aspects of Zacchaeus' discipleship do you most respect and admire: welcoming Jesus, sacrificial charity, or restitution for wrongs committed?*
> *Which aspect do you think you most need to work on now in your life as a disciple?*
> *Who in our world today do you admire and respect because they are "taking a stand" for Christian principles?*
> *When have you had to "take a stand" because of another's challenges to your faith?*
> *What are ways in which others have tried to prevent you from changing your life by reminding you of your past sins or wrongdoings?*
> *How can we be like the crowds who can actually discourage others from changing their lives by constantly reminding them of the wrong they have done?*

Finally, Jesus announces: "Today salvation has come to this house because this man too is a descendant of Abraham." Our Lord also proclaims that, "For the Son of Man has come to seek and to save what was lost." With these words, Jesus is affirming that Zacchaeus has become a true disciple and that Jesus welcomes anyone who welcomes Him. No one has been referred to as a "Son of Abraham" until this moment in Luke's Gospel. This is the ultimate title of right faith and discipleship. The fact that Jesus recognizes this exemplary discipleship in Zacchaeus is particularly important because he was not only a tax collector but also a wealthy man. Luke's Gospel relates several instances in which Jesus commented on the difficulty the wealthy would have entering the Kingdom of God (v. Lk 6:24, 12:16, 20, 16:19–31 and 18:23–25). When Zacchaeus gave half his possessions to the poor, he was demonstrating that his true treasure is in heaven and not in material wealth. Our Lord is also stating that this moment of conversion and grace was not so much Zacchaeus' initiative as it was Jesus' initiative. Everything Zacchaeus did, everything he desired, was really God's grace working within him to bring him to this moment. God's grace calls all of us to discipleship and salvation as well. Sometimes God's grace also brings us to a moment of sacrificial decision to place our priorities with the Lord and let go of false senses of security. Sometimes we respond, but so many times we don't. Zacchaeus is an example of responsiveness as he takes advantage of even remote opportunities of faith and lets nothing pass by that might serve as the means of his growth in faith.

> *When have you had a faith-enriching experience? What did you do to make it happen?*
> *Have you ever looked back and realized that it was really God inviting you to that experience?*
> *How does that awareness change your understanding of your relationship with God?*
> *What current faith enrichment opportunities might God be inviting you to undertake at this time?*
> *What is the next step of discipleship for you?*
> *How does the statement "Jesus welcomes anyone who welcomes Him" give you hope in your discipleship?*

Zacchaeus is given to us as a perfect example of discipleship. In this very brief passage we have so many themes of Luke's Gospel come together to show us what saving discipleship looks like. These themes include joy (Lk 1:14, 2:10, 6:23, 8:13, 10:17, 20) and especially that joy associated with repentance (Lk 15:5, 7, 10, 32); salvation (Lk 1:69, 77 and Lk 2:11, 30) Son of Abraham (Lk 3:8): almsgiving as sign of righteousness (Lk 6:30–31, 38, 11:41, 12:33, 16:9, 18:22, 29); and the Son of Man seeking and saving what was lost (Lk 5:32, 7:34, 9:56, 12:49, 18:8). There is not another story in the Gospel of Luke that contains such a concentration of central themes. It is most appropriate that the conversion of Zacchaeus takes place in Jericho because it is a city rich in biblical symbolism. It was in Jericho that Joshua first broke down the walls showing God's victory over resistance. Now in the example of Zacchaeus we have a human soul breaking down the walls of isolation and division that would keep a potential disciple from the Lord.

> *What are some of the walls of division and isolation that God wants to overcome in your life?*

What can your community do to encourage you to respond like Zacchaeus?

What will be the lasting challenge for you as you reflect on his example?

Zaccaheus shows us that the ministry of Jesus is for everyone whether they be man or woman, rich or poor, sinner or saint; sometimes all it takes is a simple invitation to come and see the Lord. Whom can you invite to meet this Lord?

THIRTY-SECOND SUNDAY IN ORDINARY TIME

Our scripture passage for this Sunday comes from the Gospel of Luke 20:27–38. In this text we read about Jesus' dialogue with the Sadducees and the controversy over the resurrection of the dead. It is more than just a controversy over resurrection, however. It is really on the necessity of being open to the fullness of truth that God reveals and never limiting the Lord by our own understanding of reality. The Sadducees were one of the primary religious and political groups during the time of Jesus (the Pharisees, the Scribes, and the Essenes were the others). They were closely associated with the Temple in Jerusalem and the ruling aristocracy. Because of their inherent connection to the Temple, the Sadducees ceased to exist after the destruction of Jerusalem in AD 70. The dialogue between Jesus and the Sadducees offers some points for our reflection as well.

The Sadducees did not believe in either the resurrection of the dead or the existence of angels. This lack of belief forms the basis of their hypothetical question to Jesus. Their lack of belief came from the fact that they only accepted the first five books of the Old Testament —those books believed to have been written by Moses as true scripture. They did not accept anything as true that was not found in the first five books of the Bible (also known as the "Pentateuch" or "Torah" or "The Law"). In many ways, they were the biblical fundamentalists of the ancient world. They believed that revelation stopped with Moses and so they would not accept any teachings from later writings (Note: Belief in the resurrection of the dead and angels both come from later writings in what Christians believe to be the Old Testament). Thus, the Sadducees believed that God had to conform to their limited understanding of revelation and, as a result, they refused to accept the insights being taught by Jesus.

What challenges do we face today because of biblical fundamentalism?

What teachings of the Catholic Church do people have dif-
ficulty with because they have limited their understanding
of God's revelation in a narrow way?
Jesus is called the "Word" of God in John's Gospel because
He is the fullness of the revelation of God. How has Jesus
continued to reveal God's will to us throughout history?
When you have a question of faith, where do you go to find
the answer?
What is the basis for our trust that the teachings of the
Church are true?

The Sadducees also revealed a mistaken and incomplete faith
because they believed the reality of this world is more real than
the reality of heaven. They took the principles and institutions of
this world as the guiding principles and institutions of eternal life
as well. Jesus showed them that their understanding was incorrect
and that they needed to reverse their thinking. The truest reality
is that of heaven; what we experience on earth should conform
to eternity and not the other way around. The Sadducees were
concerned about providing children for the widow because they
believed in the necessity of children for the perpetuation of life
(of the deceased husband) and for the inheritance of property.
Jesus explains that in the eternal life of heaven, where mortality is
no longer a factor, some of our earthly institutions are no longer
necessary and so concerns about inheritance and descendants no
longer apply. We can sometimes be mistaken in our understanding
of reality as well and sometimes we can fall into the trap of believing
that the concerns of this world are ends in themselves rather than
seeing the situations of this world as the means to heaven. When
we make an absolute out of this present world then we try to seek
immortality through our accomplishments, children, or reputation.
In losing sight of the resurrection, we seek to fulfill our hopes and
find all our meaning in the present.

What are temporal concerns that dominate people's lives
today in such a way that those concerns make it difficult
for them to follow the teachings of Jesus?
What do you spend time on now that will not matter in
eternity?

What don't you spend time on now that is important in eternity?

How does belief in the resurrection and eternal life change the way you handle the situations of your life on a daily basis?

What are the three most important things in your life right now? What do you think God considers to be the three most important things in your life right now?

What will you take with you into eternal life?

Jesus is able to show the Sadducees an inherent belief in the resurrection of the dead by pointing out an obscure passage of scripture that they had not previously interpreted in that way. If they were open to Jesus' interpretation of the scriptures then they would have been able to have a correct understanding of God's revelation. That means it is always necessary for us to read the scriptures through the lens of the person of Jesus and His teachings.

What are some teachings of the Bible that people can take out of context and read in such a way that they become "un-Christian" in their meaning?

When was the last time you allowed your opinions to be changed because of a teaching of Jesus?

What do you think the Sadducees did after Jesus offered them a new insight into heavenly truths?

Our Church year ends in a few weeks with the celebration of the Solemnity of Christ the King. As we approach the end of the year, the readings increasingly speak to us about the future reality of heaven and the Second Coming of Jesus. Through these readings, the Church turns our hearts and minds to the future so as to help guide us in the present. Every time we approach the end of a cycle, our human nature becomes aware of the constant tension between eternity and time in which we live as humans. In the fourth century St. Augustine said, "You hear people complaining about this present day and age because things were so much better in former times. I wonder what would happen if they could be taken back to the days of their ancestors."[18]

---

18. St. Augustine, *Sermo Caillau-Saint Yves* 2, 92: *PLS* 2, 441-552.

To what future are you leading your family by your decisions and actions?

To what future are you leading your marriage?

To what future are you leading your friends and business associates by your word and example?

Do you believe that the invitation to eternal life requires only a personal response or do you believe that, as a disciple, you also have a responsibility to lead others to heaven? Jesus teaches us about the future reality of heaven so that we will know how to act in the present. What situations have you faced recently that you would have handled differently had you been focused on eternity rather than caught up in the present?

THIRTY-THIRD SUNDAY IN ORDINARY TIME

O
ur scripture passage for this Sunday comes from the Gospel of Luke 21:5–19. In this passage, Jesus prepares His disciples for the future by giving them a set of cautions so that they will not be surprised when certain necessary events come to pass. People oftentimes interpret this passage as a reference to the "End Times". However, in Luke's Gospel it relates more to particular events in the life of the early Church during the First Century AD. Even though we live in the midst of very different historical circumstances, this passage offers important guidance for us as well.

Jesus offers His teaching in response to the crowds who were marveling at the beauty of the Temple. For them, a building had become the focus of their faith. Jesus cautions them to base their faith upon what is eternal than the temporal beauty of a physical structure; their faith should be rooted in a deep commitment to Him and the Gospel. It is possible for Christians to focus their faith on temporal or ornamental things as well. "Religious things" don't make us "faithful Christians"! Sometimes religious buildings can actually become a distraction of faith when we, too, marvel at the beauty but fail to grow more deeply in committed discipleship or when a faith community spends more resources on maintenance than on mission. The greatest and most inspiring "monuments" in Christianity are the lives of holy men and women rather than buildings or art. The distracted faith of the crowds reminds us that there are a variety of ways in which we can place our faith in the wrong things. It is important to periodically reflect on the frequency with which we allow our attention to be dominated by institutions, achievements, health, beauty, pleasure, relationships, bank accounts, and so forth. All these things have the potential to become false gods in our lives when we give them greater attention than we give to our relationship with God. All these things, like the Temple building in Jerusalem, are temporal and do not last. Eventually they fail us and disappoint our hope in their lasting value and enduring importance. This disillusionment is actually a healthy process of recognizing ways in which we have misplaced our faith so that we can reaffirm the importance of our relationship with God and directs our energy and attention into that enduring reality.

> *In what ways can religious things actually distract us from the person of Jesus and the message of the Gospel today?*
> *How can religious things help facilitate your relationship with Christ?*
> *How do you know when your attachment to a religious thing has become spiritually unhealthy?*
> *What can we do to ensure that our service to the Gospel is about mission and not just maintenance?*
> *What are some of the other false gods in which people mistakenly place their trust?*
> *How have you experienced the purifying effect of disillusionment and disappointment?*

The next teaching Jesus offers the disciples is a set of cautions. The first caution is to not be deceived. He assures us that there will be those who make two fundamental claims: "I am He" and "The Time is Near". Both of these claims are significant. When someone makes the claim "I am He", then they are seeking to become the false god of our lives.[19] When someone claims that "The Time is Near", then they are wanting to interpret our life experience for us in a way contrary to the Gospel. No matter what age we live in, there are always people who try to take the place of God. God alone is the one who can give us our true identity (Baptized in Christ Jesus), our inherent value, and has the plan for our lives that will lead us to eternal happiness and peace. There are lots of other people and agencies that try to tell us who we are and what should be our values and priorities. Certainly those same agencies seek to tell us what will make us happy. The caution of Jesus that we should not be deceived by those who try to make themselves the god of our lives is as important today as it was two thousand years ago. So, too, there are always people who are eager to interpret our experience

---

19. To communicate the pretender's claim "I am He", Luke uses the Greek phrase eigo emi which is also the divine name of God most properly translated as "I AM".

for us so as to motivate our response in the direction they desire rather than the direction God wills. The forces of a secular society try to interpret our experience in the absence of faith that leads to despair, hedonism, fear, and relativism. Disciples are called to interpret the experience of their lives in the light of faith that trusts in God's love, mercy, and providence. Without this faith-filled interpretation of our everyday situations, we can become misled and can act in faithless ways. In these moments, too, Jesus cautions us; Do not be deceived! The second caution Jesus gives is that we should not be afraid. The events Jesus has described (wars, earthquakes, uprisings and so forth) can be terrifying for those without faith. Disciples are called to trust in God as the Lord of History and to have confidence that whatever takes place, even calamities, are part of God's will. The proper response for a disciple is not fear but rather faithful action. Because these events are permitted by God, they are meant to be the means of our salvation. When there is persecution, suffering, and violence, then disciples are called to witness perseverance, compassion, and forgiveness. Disciples who witness in this way will have ever-greater hope for the coming of the Kingdom of God and welcome our Lord's return, not fear it.

> *How do "false prophets" in our world today try to take the place of God by telling us who we are, what gives us worth, or what is the meaning for our lives?*
>
> *What is their message? How do you see others responding to the message of false prophets and what is the effect in their lives?*
>
> *What are some of the situations families face today that are being interpreted in ways contrary to Christian teaching? What does it feel like to stand up against the false prophets of our time and reject their misinterpretation of our professional and personal challenges?*
>
> *When are you afraid because of the news you receive in the media?*
>
> *How can faith change the way you receive bad news so that it becomes an opportunity for discipleship and witness?*

The final teaching of Jesus concerns the inevitability of Christian suffering. The disciples asked for signs so that they could have advanced warning of coming difficulties in order to avoid them. Jesus doesn't grant their request for information about signs because discipleship is not about saving one's life (that is, avoiding the sufferings and persecutions of being a Christian). Rather, discipleship calls us to faithful and patient endurance in the face of challenges. That faithful and patient endurance is what saves us! Salvation for a disciple means being so committed to Jesus that we would be willing to accept even death in witness to Him. The encouragement for patience and endurance in suffering was important for Christians of the first century who were facing the first persecutions. Other instances of this encouragement for the Christian community can be found in Rom 5:3–4, Rom 8:25, 2 Cor 1:7, Col 1:11, 1 Thes 1:3, 2 Thes 1:4, Heb 10:36, Heb 12:1, Jas 1:3–4 and Rev. 13:10. For disciples, moments of persecution are seen as opportunities for witness. We see the early Church responding to persecution in this way in the Acts of the Apostles (Acts 3:15, 4:33, 5:32, 20:26, and 26:22).

> *Who are examples of faithful perseverance that inspire you?*
> *When has your faith or discipleship been challenged and were you prepared for it?*
> *Do you pray more to avoid challenges or to persevere faithfully through challenges?*
> *What current moments of challenge can be opportunities for your witness?*

Lastly, Jesus offers the disciples all these teachings so that they will know what's coming and be prepared for it. He wants them, and us, to "prepare now" so we can faithfully endure the future. By doing so, we will bear witness to the power and presence of Jesus in our lives. That's discipleship! All we have to do is look around to see what kinds of challenges people face in their lives. Although the situations may differ from person to the next, the basic challenges remain the same for everyone. By knowing what challenges are taking place in other people's professional, familial, marital, and personal lives, we can better prepare ourselves to face those challenges in our own lives. The time to prepare is now. If we are not preparing now then we will not be prepared when the time comes.

> *What are the challenges people face in their marriages?*

What are the challenges people face in their families and raising their children?

What are the challenges people face in their personal lives?

What are the challenges people face in their professional lives?

How can you prepare now to remain faithful through each one of those challenges in your own life?

What are the temptations that cause so many people to act in an unfaithful way when faced with these challenges?

What can we do as a parish to help prepare people to be Christian men and women who faithfully respond to these challenges?

SOLEMNITY OF CHRIST THE KING

Our scripture passage for this Sunday comes from the Gospel of Luke 23:35–43. It is the scene commonly known as the "Good Thief". As we celebrate the Solemnity of Christ the King, this passage offers us some particular points for reflection.

This passage clearly states that Jesus is tempted three times to save Himself by coming down from the cross. The phrasing and frequency of these temptations are intentional. He was tempted three times in the desert as well and at the end of those desert temptations Luke told us, "Satan departed until an opportune time" (Lk 4:13). Now we see that opportune time occurring when Jesus was mocked and challenged to prove Himself as the Christ (Messiah), Chosen One, and King of the Jews. The power of evil may not be very creative yet oftentimes remains effective! We all have fundamental temptations that keep coming back to us at opportune times in our lives as well. Like Jesus, those temptations challenge us to either be faithful to the identity God gives us in Christ through our baptism or to prove ourselves by acting in a way contrary to the will of God. Jesus remained faithful in the desert and He remained faithful on the cross. He could do so only because He was secure in His relationship with the Father.

> *What are three of the fundamental temptations that look for opportune times in people's lives today?*
>
> *How can a disciple foster a deeper security and trust with the Father so as to not be deceived by those temptations?*
>
> *When are you tempted to prove yourself so as to fulfill the false expectations of others?*
>
> *Satan no longer tempts Jesus directly as he did in the desert. Rather, he now tempts Jesus through other people—leaders, soldiers, and those closest to him.*
>
> *How has temptation occurred in unexpected ways for you?*
>
> *When are you most susceptible to temptation?*

It is interesting to read how often royal references are made to the kingship of Jesus in this passage (cf. the jeering of the soldiers in Lk 23.37, the inscription over Him in Lk 23:38, and the appeal of the Good Thief in Lk 23:42). The high concentration of kingship language tells us that this passage is identifying the nature and ministry of Jesus as King. Throughout the Gospels, Jesus always avoided the title "King" but in this passage He allows it to be given to Him. It is only through our Lord's suffering and death that He established the Kingdom of God by obedience to the Father's will. That kingdom is not a temporal one of power and opulence but an eternal one of truth, life, holiness, grace, justice, love and peace. Although the crowds cannot see it, Jesus is manifesting His royal identity by embracing His suffering rather than by avoiding it. How different His kingship is from that of other royals of His time! Other kings tried to distance themselves from the suffering of their people while Jesus embraces it and enters into the depths of our human condition. Other kings sought titles of honor to promote their status while Jesus dies as an outcast with criminals. Other kings sat on large thrones while Jesus ascents the throne of the cross. Other kings surrounded themselves with the best and most luxurious things the world could offer while Jesus feels the pain of the nails and is offered vinegar to drink. Other kings wear fine robes and a crown of gold while Jesus is stripped naked and wears a crown of thorns. Jesus is a king who knows our human experience better than we do! There is no darkness we will ever face that He has not already overcome. The challenge for us is to accept the Kingship (Lordship) of Jesus in every moment of our lives —especially our moments of suffering, weakness, and darkness.

> *How does the suffering of Jesus encourage you in your faith life?*
>
> *When do you feel most distant from the Lord?*
>
> *What would it be like to invite Jesus into your dark moments and ask Him to be the Lord of your life then as well?*
>
> *What are the primary "titles" of your life ("Father/Mother", "Husband/Wife", "Disciple", and so forth) and when do you most authentically live out those roles?*
>
> *When do you fail to live out those roles?*
>
> *If you were to be put to death for your faithfulness as a disciple today, what is the "charge" that would be inscribed on your cross?*

*Who for you most witnesses the qualities of the Kingdom
of God today?*
*Jesus is a king who establishes His throne on Calvary. What
happens when we try to make Jesus a king without the cross?*

It is important to note the two-fold response offered to Jesus by
the criminals who are crucified with Him. For one of the criminals
the experience of suffering led to anger, bitterness, and rejection
of Jesus. For the other criminal, the experience of suffering led to
deeper trust, a profession of faith, and an appeal for mercy from
Jesus. These two responses are instructive and insightful for us
as disciples. The way a person responds to suffering says much
about their faith. It is very understandable, and quite human, to
experience questions when we face a situation of serious trial.
Without realizing it, we can fall into the false presumption that
suffering means the absence of God. However, the cross teaches
us that God is with us in our suffering even as Jesus was with the
criminals. Sometimes those who suffer need a faithful witness to
help them understand their trial in a faithful way and to give them
encouragement to persevere. That faithful witness comes from the
lives of faithful disciples as Jesus speaks through us to bring His
word of hope and inspiration to those in distress. For this reason,
it is important that faith communities stand in solidarity with, and
demonstrate Christian charity for, those who suffer in our world.

*What are some of the false presumptions that can lead
people away from God in moments of suffering?*
*What helps us to remember the presence of God with us in
moments of suffering so as to remain faithful?*
*The name "Jesus" means "God Saves"—from what situation
do you most ask Jesus to save you?*
*The Good Thief asked only to be remembered but Jesus
promised him paradise. When have you been overwhelmed
by God's generous mercy in your life?*
*How can a faith community encourage its members to
respond faithfully to situations of suffering in their own
lives and in other people's lives?*

Next, we should note how willing Jesus is to reach out to those in
need and minister to them even as He is in the midst of distress.

We see this ministry to others occurring throughout the Passion of Jesus in Luke's Gospel (Jesus healed the severed ear of the High Priest's slave in Lk 22:51, He reconciled Pilate and Herod in Lk 23:12, and He instructed the sorrowful women in Lk 23:28). It is easy to help others when we are rested, have spare time, and are focused on doing good but it can be difficult to make time for others when we are tired, preoccupied with our own needs, and stressed. Jesus always had time to reach out to others—even to the Good Thief on the cross. He manifested this compassionate ministry even as He was suffering.

> *When do you find it easy to reach out to others?*
> *When do you find it difficult?*
> *What practices or efforts can help you to be more respon-*
> *sive to those who will ask for your help today when you are*
> *stressed, preoccupied, and tired?*

Finally, this passage invites us to reflect on two lasting lessons that Jesus gives from the Cross of Calvary. The first lesson is this: it is never too late to ask for God's mercy. The Good Thief turned to Jesus in his last moments of life and Jesus accepted his act of faith. Regardless of what the Good Thief had done, it is this final act of faithful petition and acknowledgement of his need for God's mercy that our Lord hears and to which our Lord responds. It would have been easy for the Good Thief to give into despair or desperation in his final moments. It would also have been easy for the Good Thief to believe that his sin was beyond forgiveness and his life beyond redemption but he didn't do that. Instead, the Good Thief made an act of faith and hope in God's mercy at the last minute and Jesus granted that mercy. This scene teaches us that it's never too late for us to seek God's mercy either and that there is no reason to ever despair or think that we are beyond redemption. Jesus is a king who wants every possible subject to be with Him in paradise forever and He simply waits for us to ask for that privileged sharing in eternal life. The Good Thief knew that he did not deserve such mercy and so he could receive it as a pure gift from God. That is an example for us to imitate and celebrate when it is occurs. The second lesson is this: love never dies. Because God is love, any action done with love is done with God and is eternal. The love of Jesus manifested for us on the cross is an eternal witness of God's love for His people. That witness never dies and has inspired generation after generation of heroic saints and martyrs to imitate the love of Jesus on the cross. That love inspires men and women to lay down their lives day after day in faithful service to others. Any truly loving action reflects this love of God and partakes in the love of Jesus manifested on the cross. The love of Jesus conquered sin, death, and hatred. The love of Jesus forgave, reconciled, and redeemed. The mission of the Church is to live in the shadow of the cross and to make this divine love known to all humanity throughout history. The Church, then, is commissioned to love as loved.

> *How can we be tempted to think that people earn God's forgiveness and mercy?*
> *How does the example of the Good Thief inspire you to seek God's mercy now?*
> *What situations can lead people to think that they are beyond redemption or reconciliation?*
> *How does despair manifest itself in our contemporary culture?*
> *How do you see the love of Jesus on Calvary being manifested today?*
> *When has your own decision of sacrificial love led you to identify with the love of Jesus on the cross?*
> *Why do you think Jesus wanted the reconciliation with the Good Thief to be the last ministry He accomplished on earth?*
> *In what ministry experience have you experienced the living love of Christ most clearly and effectively?*

The crowds who heard the conversation between Jesus and the Good Thief must have been shocked that our Lord reconciled so readily and generously a criminal whose crimes warranted the agonizing punishment of crucifixion.

> *Whose wrongdoing is so great that you do not pray for their conversion and eternal salvation?*
> *How does this passage challenge you to be a faithful subject of Christ the King who exemplifies such mercy and generous love?*

With this Sunday's Solemnity of Christ the King, we bring to a close the Church's liturgical year. This is our last reflection from the Gospel of Luke. Next Sunday we begin to read from the Gospel of Matthew. It is worth reflecting back on the many passages we have studied this past year and to consider which of those passages has affected you most.

What will be the long-term effect of that passage in your life?

BIBLIOGRAPHY

Barron, R. WordonFire.org. Retrieved December 2014-August 2015 from WordonFire.org Website: http://www.wordonfire.org/resources/homily/.

Brown, R. *The Gospel According to John I-XII* Anchor Bible Volume 29. New York: Doubleday, 1966.

Brown, R. *The Gospel According to John XIII-XXI* Anchor Bible Volume 29. New York: Doubleday, 1970.

Catechism of the Catholic Church. New York: Image, Doubleday, 1995.

Desmond, E. W. 'Interview with Mother Teresa: A Pencil in the Hand of God'. In: *Time Magazine* (4 December 1989).

Didymus the Blind. *Treatise on the Trinity.* Paris: J. P. Migne Imprimerie Catholique, 1857-1866.

Fitzmyer, J. *The Gospel According to Luke I-IX* Anchor Bible Volume 28. New York: Doubleday, 1981.

Fitzmyer, J. *The Gospel According to Luke X-XXIV* Anchor Bible Volume 28A. New York: Doubleday, 1985.

Harrington, D. *The Gospel of Matthew* Sacra Pagina Series Volume 1. "A Michael Glazier Book." Collegeville: The Liturgical Press, 1991.

Johnson, T. *The Gospel of Luke* Sacra Pagina Series Volume 3, "A Michael Glazier Book." Collegeville: The Liturgical Press, 1991.

Kierkegaard, S. *Attack Upon Christendom 1854-1855,* Translated by Walter Lowrie, Princeton: Princeton University Press, 1946.

Kowalska, M. *Diary of Saint Maria Faustina Kowalska: Divine Mercy in My Soul.* Stockbridge: Marian Press, 2005.

Maloney, F. *The Gospel of John* Sacra Pagina Series Volume 4. "A Michael Glazier Book." Collegeville: The Liturgical Press, 1998.

The New Interpreter's Bible Volume VIII. Nashville: Abingdon Press, 1995.

The New Interpreter's Bible Volume IX. Nashville: Abingdon Press, 1995.

The New American Bible Revised Edition. Wichita: Fireside Catholic Publishing, 2010.

St. Catherine of Siena, *Dialogos*. Madrid: Biblioteca de Autores Cristianos, 2011.

Saint Augustine, S. *Aurelii Augustini Operum Supplementum* I, 2,92 (Paris: A.B. Caillau and B. St. Yves, 1836) reprinted in *Patrologiae Latinae Supplementum* 2, Turnhout: Brepols, 1960.

Lightning Source UK Ltd.
Milton Keynes UK
UKOW02f0434031115

261980UK00001B/6/P